D1156851

Casino Capitalism

Casino Capitalism

Susan Strange

Basil Blackwell

© Susan Strange 1986

First published 1986

Basil Blackwell Ltd
108 Cowley Road, Oxford OX4 1JF, UK

Basil Blackwell Inc.
432 Park Avenue South, Suite 1503,
New York, NY 10016, USA

British Library Cataloguing in Publication Data
Strange, Susan
  Casino capitalism.
  1. Finance
  I. Title
  332   HG173

  ISBN 0–631–15026–9
  ISBN 0–631–15027–7 Pbk

Library of Congress Cataloging in Publication Data
Strange, Susan.
  Casino capitalism.

  Bibliography: p.
  Includes index.
  1. Speculation. 2. Stocks. I. Title.
HG6041.S82 1986   332.64′5   85-28696
ISBN 0–631–15026–9
ISBN 0–631–15027–7 (pbk.)

Typeset by System 4 Associates, Gerrards Cross, Buckinghamshire
Printed in Great Britain

Contents

Acknowledgements   vi

1   Casino Capitalism   1

2   Key Decisions and their Consequences   25

3   Some Other Interpretations   60

4   Betting in the Dark   103

5   The Guessing Game   121

6   Some Prescriptions   146

7   Cooling the Casino   170

Bibliography   194

Index   201

Acknowledgements

I owe a great many debts to people who have helped me write this book. Acknowledgement in a preface does not discharge them and is but a poor way even of recognizing them. My debts are of two kinds – to people who found me funds and/or an academic home-from-home where I could get on with writing more or less undisturbed; and to friends and colleagues who have been kind enough to read and comment helpfully on some bits of the book.

John Steinbrunner offered me the splendid facilities of the Brookings Institution for part of a summer term in Washington, with funding provided by the British Economic and Social Research Council. Werner Maihofer and Marcello de Cecco combined to get me two months at the European University Institute in San Domenico di Fiesole. Harlan Cleveland and Bob Kudrle were instrumental in getting me to the Hubert Humphrey Institute at the University of Minnesota in April/May 1983, where I had a little teaching and time and facilities to make some progress. And finally in 1984 Bruce Miller arranged for me to take a similar break from administration and daily distractions at the Australian National University in Canberra.

As for comments, I sought particular help – and never was refused – with the survey of other interpretations of the decade 1974–84, which appears here in chapter 3. A longer and earlier version was published as my main contribution to the joint LSE/Chatham House project, 'International Monetary Relations in the 1970s' funded by the British Economic and Social Research Council. The project was actively directed from Chatham House by Professor Tsoukalis, who edited a collection of essays, *The Politics of International Monetary Relations: towards a new international economic order* (Sage, 1985). Helpful suggestions came from Loukas Tsoukalis, David Calleo, Jerry Davis, Ladd Hollist, Bob Cox, Bob Keohane, Gautam Sen, Jeff Frieden, John Barrett and Wolfgang Deckers.

For the rest of the book, I am deeply in debt to three tough editorial critics: my husband, Clifford Selly; my friend, Frances Pinter and my publisher, René Olivieri. The errors that remain after that are all my own. Finally, the customary acknowledgment for research assistance and secretarial help does less than justice to the diligence of Nilesh Dattani, Art Kilgore, Hilary Parker and Pam Hodges, assisted by Anna Morgan and Liz Leslie.

CHAPTER 1

Casino Capitalism

The Western financial system is rapidly coming to resemble nothing as much as a vast casino. Every day games are played in this casino that involve sums of money so large that they cannot be imagined. At night the games go on at the other side of the world. In the towering office blocks that dominate all the great cities of the world, rooms are full of chain-smoking young men all playing these games. Their eyes are fixed on computer screens flickering with changing prices. They play by intercontinental telephone or by tapping electronic machines. They are just like the gamblers in casinos watching the clicking spin of a silver ball on a roulette wheel and putting their chips on red or black, odd numbers or even ones.

As in a casino, the world of high finance today offers the players a choice of games. Instead of roulette, blackjack, or poker, there is dealing to be done – the foreign exchange market and all its variations; or in bonds, government securities or shares. In all these markets you may place bets on the future by dealing forward and by buying or selling options and all sorts of other recondite financial inventions. Some of the players – banks especially – play with very large stakes. These are also many quite small operators. There are tipsters, too, selling advice, and peddlers of systems to the gullible. And the croupiers in this global financial casino are the big bankers and brokers. They play, as it were, 'for the house'. It is they, in the long run, who make the best living.

These bankers and dealers seem to be a very different kind of men working in a very different kind of world from the world of finance and the typical bankers that older people remember. Bankers used to be thought of as staid and sober men, grave-faced and dressed in conservative black pinstripe suits, jealous of their reputation for caution and for the careful guardianship of their customers' money. Something rather radical and serious has happened to the international financial system to make it so much like a gambling hall. What that change has been, and how it has come about, are not clear.

What is certain is that it has affected everyone. For the great difference between an ordinary casino which you can go into or stay away from, and the global casino of high finance, is that in the latter all of us are involuntarily engaged in the day's play. A currency change can halve the value of a farmer's crop before he harvests it, or drive an exporter out of business. A rise in interest rates can fatally inflate the cost of holding stocks for the shop-keeper. A takeover dictated by financial considerations can rob the factory worker of his job. From school-leavers to pensioners, what goes on in the casino in the office blocks of the big financial centres is apt to have sudden, unpredictable and unavoidable consequences for individual lives. The financial casino has everyone playing the game of Snakes and Ladders. Whether the fall of the dice lands you on the bottom of a ladder, whisking you up to fortune, or on the head of a snake, precipitating you to misfortune, is a matter of luck.

This cannot help but have grave consequences. For when sheer luck begins to take over and to determine more and more of what happens to people, and skill, effort, initiative, determination and hard work count for less and less, then inevitably faith and confidence in the social and political system quickly fades. Respect for ethical values – on which in the end a free democratic society relies – suffers a dangerous decline. It is when bad luck can strike a person not only from directions where luck has always ruled: health, love, natural catastrophes or genetic chance, but from new and unexpected directions as well, that a psychological change takes place. Luck, now, as well as idleness or inadequacy, can lose you a job. Luck can wipe out a lifetime's savings, can double or halve the cost of a holiday abroad, can bankrupt a business because of some unpredictable change in interest rates or commodity prices or some other factor that used to be regarded as more or less stable and reliable. There seems less and less point in trying to make the right decision, when it is so difficult to know how the wheel of chance will turn and where it will come to rest. Betting on red and on black has equally uncertain results. That is why I think the increase in uncertainty has made inveterate, and largely involuntary, gamblers of us all.

Moreover, the vulnerability to bad luck in a system which is already somewhat inequitable is itself far from equal. Some can find ways to cushion or protect themselves, while others cannot. And inequities that were originally due to a variety of factors become suddenly much more acutely felt and more bitterly resented. Frustration and anger become sharper and are apt to be more violently expressed when the realm of luck becomes too large and when the arbitrariness of the system seems to operate so very unequally.

If this is true for individuals, it is also true for large enterprises and for the governments of countries. Political leaders, and their opponents, like to pretend that they are still in control of their national economies, that their policies have the power to relieve unemployment, revive economic growth, restore prosperity and encourage investment in the future. But recent years have shown again and again how the politicians' plans have been upset by changes that they could not have foreseen in the world outside the state. The dollar has weakened – or become too strong. Interest rates have made the burden of servicing a foreign debt too heavy to sustain. The banks have suddenly decided to lend the country no more money. Oil prices have suddenly risen – or fallen. Other commodity prices, on which export earnings may depend, fall, because the major economies of major consuming countries are going through a recession. The uncertainty that rules in the financial world spills over not only into individual lives but into the fortunes of governments and of countries – and sooner or later into the relations between states. That spillover happened 50 odd years ago, after the Great Crash of 1929, and whether this time the uncertainty leads to a dramatic crisis or – as seems far more likely – to a stubbornly continuing malaise in the world market economy, this must be of general concern not just to economists.

The mess in perspective

If we stand back from the headlines and concerns of the immediate present we might observe two things. One is that the changes leading to the present mess have happened very fast, in the short space of about 15 years. The other is that in that space of time, change has affected coincidentally some of the key prices which order the functioning of the world economy. They have all become increasingly unstable in the same period – the price of currencies in the foreign exchange market which connects all the national economic systems with each other; the rising price of goods in general in terms of money, otherwise known as the inflation rate; the price of credit, otherwise called the rate of interest, which is a major factor in the production of all goods and services; and the price of oil, which is the other major input on which all mechanical production and the transport of goods depend. Uncertainty in each has fed the uncertainty and the volatility of the others. And the common factor linking them all to each other has been the international financial system. That is the rootstock, from whose disorders stem the various problems which afflict the international political economy, just as blight, disease or mildew attack the different branches of a plant.

Everyone is familiar with these problems, thanks to newspapers, television and a spate of books and pamphlets. Best known and understood is the debt problem of the developing countries: the fact that too many were lent too much on terms which laid them open to the risk that if the loans ever stopped, they would be in trouble with the creditors. That is related to the second problem, which is the slow growth of the whole world economy in the late 1970s and the recession of the 1980s. The instability of the banking system is the third problem. But it is not limited to the debtor countries; the extent of corporate debt to the banks is equally great and, if slow growth continues, could be equally menacing, in the absence of a credible lender of last resort. Fourth might be added the uncertainty over oil prices, of consequence to producers and to consumers and, thus, a decisive factor in many countries' balance of payments not least of the major producers in the Middle East, an area doubly afflicted by economic and political instability, both domestic in some cases and international. All these problems are recognizably mainly economic in character. But as big as any is the fifth problem: the precariousness of the international political situation – notably the unstable Soviet–American balance and the uneasy American– European alliance. Even these have some roots in the financial disorder and uncertainty. Both are affected by – as they in turn affect – the strength or weakness of the dollar on those flickering computer screens in the foreign exchange rooms of banks around the world.

If, as I shall argue, all these problems are interconnected, and in all of them there is the common factor of financial uncertainty and therefore vulnerability to the play at the tables of the great financial casino, then it must follow that some attention to the common denominator would certainly make the solution of any one of them much easier. It might not be a sufficient condition, but almost certainly it is a necessary one. Any help that restoring financial certainty and stability would give to each one of the problems would also make the solutions of the others a less formidable task.

Before we consider solutions, though, we must ask when and how the rot in the old system set in. When did this rapid change with its many political and economic repercussions really begin? How did it start? It is only by looking back and reviewing how the multiple mess developed that we shall ever be able to work out a solution to it.

How did it start?

The year of 1973 stands out as a benchmark, a turning point when the snowball of change from the leisurely 1960s to the hectic yo-yo years of the 1970s and 1980s began to gather momentum. It stands out as a year when several big changes coincided – an effective devaluation of the dollar and the accompanying decision to leave the determination of exchange rates to the markets. This is known as the move to floating rates – not a very apt description because some sink while others rise. It was also the year of the first major rise in oil prices, to be followed by much increased dependence on the banking system to find the finance for the current consumption bills and the economic development of the poorer countries (and some developed ones). Each of these changes was to add in a different way to the uncertainty of the system.

It may help to recall a little of the history of international monetary relations to see how this came about. It will also explain why the choice of 1973, or any other precise date, is bound to be somewhat arbitrary. All that can be said is that it seemed to mark a sort of change of gear, as the system moved from a more stable period into a much more unstable one.

Cracks and weak spots in the system had been detected a full 15 years before, when it became clear that the monetary rules and arrangements agreed by the United States and other countries at Bretton Woods during the war were not working out quite as planned. Instead of an even-handed system in which the same rules applied to all, a highly asymmetric one had developed in which continuing deficits on the US balance of payments were matched by increasing dollar holdings by America's trading partners. These dollar reserves allayed other countries' anxieties that they might run out of money to import – as Britain had in 1945. Trade revived, but the accumulated dollars, though they also helped to finance investment, especially in Europe, were sooner or later going to exceed even the very large gold reserves of the United States. For it was an essential part of the system that the dollars were held as IOUs by the Europeans and others, partly because the United States offered to exchange them for gold at a fixed pre-war price. The inherent dangers of this 'dollar overhang' were pointed out as early as 1958 by Professor Robert Triffin (Triffin, 1958) in America and by Professor Jacques Rueff in France (Rueff, 1971). This analysis was taken up by the French and other European governments who (somewhat ambivalently) wished to enjoy both growing prosperity and the right to complain about the injustice of a system which allowed the Americans (and to some extent the British) to enjoy the special privileges that came from other countries holding their currency as a reserve of IOUs. This was what General de Gaulle called 'the exorbitant privilege', meaning that the Americans could pay their bills – for defence spending among other things – with IOUs instead of exports of goods and services.

As the 1960s progressed, the cracks widened and the system began to creak under the combined pressure of growing international financial and capital markets, moving more and more money across the exchanges, and of political disagreement among governments about what was wrong with the system. The cracks were patched with such palliative measures as the Gold Pool, and the General Arrangements to Borrow augmenting the resources of the International Monetary Fund set up at Bretton Woods to lend its member countries foreign currency in an emergency. To prevent their payments deficits from being made worse by foreign borrowers coming to New York for loans, the Americans taxed such loans – but in doing so forced their own banks abroad, fostering the nascent London market for the Eurodollar credits. The disagreements continued but some compromises were reached – as for example the agreement at Stockholm in 1968 to allow the IMF to issue Special Drawing Rights (SDRs) which would supplement, but not supplant the dollar as an asset which governments could hold in their reserves.

The strains in the system, even late in the 1960s, seemed to afflict mainly the strong European currencies, like the German mark (revalued in 1969), and the weak European currencies like sterling (devalued in 1967) and the French franc (devalued in 1969). Eventually, however, they also affected the US economy. Holding the dollar's exchange rate, while spending heavily on the Vietnam War, had led President Johnson to resort to a deflationary tight money policy at home and to high interest rates which helped somewhat to mitigate the worsening trade balance.

But while Johnson saw the foreign exchange markets as enemies putting the dollar under speculative pressure, Nixon, Kissinger and Connally were well advised and saw that the markets could also be used as allies, helping the United States to engineer a devaluation of the dollar which other countries could neither resist nor match. The unilateral abrogation by Nixon of the Bretton Woods system in August 1971 closed the gold window (i.e. he refused to exchange any more dollar IOUs for US gold reserves) and allowed the dollar to come down off its fixed exchange rate with other countries.

That was the first step towards the decision in 1973 to abandon fixed exchange rates for good. In the interval there had been the Smithsonian Agreement of December 1971, a negotiated realignment of dollar rates with the Japanese yen and the German mark. But continued inflation, and a commodity boom, partly set off by uncertainty about the future of the dollar, first took the pound sterling out of the fixed rate arrangements and then tore apart the Europeans' 'snake in the tunnel', their first attempt to hold their currency rates steady with each other. Turbulence in the currency markets finally led the United States to take the plunge and let the markets, not governments, decide how many pounds, yen or marks should be exchanged for a dollar.

The effects of floating rates

The record, however abbreviated, of the events leading up to this point is chiefly important because of the yawning discrepancy between the promise and the performance of floating exchange rates. The great majority of economists, led by the Americans, had promised that the change would bring the alarming and disturbing currency crises of the previous five years to an end: 'The strain,' they assured us, 'can be taken on the rate instead of the reserves – so governments will not need to worry. The markets will only reflect step by step the proper relation of costs and prices (and inflation rates) in each country with those of its trading partners. There need be no more violent shifts in exchange rates.'

That was the theory and the promise. But practice proved very different. Instead of reducing the volatility of the markets, floating rates – or to put it another way, the abstinence of governments from intervening in the markets – seemed to increase the volatility.

After only five years' trial, it was already clear that both the surpluses and the deficits on the major countries' balance of payments were getting larger, not smaller. The invisible hand of a free currency market somehow was not working. In 1978, the countries that had had the largest surpluses under fixed rates – Japan, West Germany, Switzerland, the Netherlands and Belgium – now had surpluses twice as large, a combined total of $9 billion on average in 1972–3 and of $18 billion in 1977. The deficit countries – the United States, Britain, France, Italy and Canada – had deficits more than three times as large as before, even though the market had devalued their currencies (Triffin, 1979). Thus, instead of needing smaller reserves under a floating rate system, everyone needed still larger reserves in order to cope with the possibility of larger deficits.

This, of course, did not apply to the United States. As the chief reserve currency country in what was now, in effect, a paper-dollar system instead of the gold-dollar system that functioned in the 1960s, its reserves of dollars were unlimited. Its economy was also far less vulnerable to exchange rate changes than those of the Europeans. Not only did the Europeans trade much more than the Americans, much of their trade was with their fellow Europeans. They found that the floating rates tended to push their currencies to extremes, polarizing them into the weak and the strong. Especially as the dollar weakened after 1976, footloose funds fled into D-marks or Swiss francs, pulling those currencies further than ever from those of the deficit countries, Britain, France and Italy (Fabra, 1978). In year-to-year exchange rates, changes were almost twice as large in the 1970s as in the 1960s (Vaubel, 1980).

Moreover, while the need to hold reserves increased because of the added uncertainty of future rates, there remained the question of what to hold in the reserves – dollars, gold, D-marks, or some other asset. To defend the dollar, the Americans had conducted an anti-gold campaign in the mid-1970s, holding its price for official sales or purchases by central banks first to the original $35 and then to $42 an ounce, until as late as 1979, when, in response to dollar weakness, the private gold price took off, and some governments decided to revalue their gold holdings.[1] The campaign had meant that the chances of acquiring larger gold reserves were limited. The bulk of the increased reserves therefore – all but $29 billion out of over $250 billion added by 1978 to the level of reserves 20 years before – were in foreign exchange. And the possibility that governments, as well as the private operators, might change their preferences only added to the instability of the foreign exchange markets.

Nor, it must be added, was the increased movement of financial managers, public and private, in and out of currencies on the foreign exchange markets a once-for-all phenomenon marking the change to floating rates. It was cumulative. The more players joined the game, the greater the volatility of the markets; and the greater the volatility, the more new players were drawn into it and the harder it was for

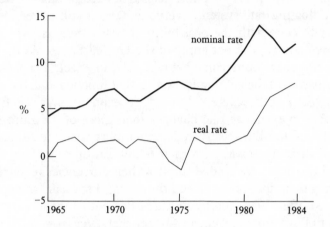

Figure 1.1 Long-term interest rates in the United States, 1965–84.
(*Source*: *World Development Report*, 1985, p. 5.) All data are averages of quarterly data.

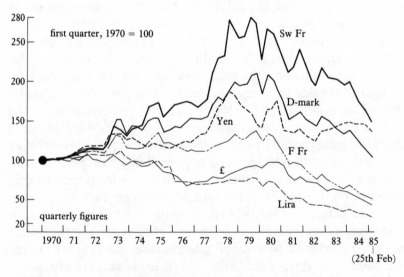

Figure 1.2 Exchange rates against the dollar 1970–85.
(*Source*: *The Economist*, 16 March 1985; from IMF/OECD data.)

anyone affected by variations in exchange rates to stay out of it. By 1977, the Federal Reserve Bank of New York estimated the *daily* turnover on the New York foreign exchange market alone at somewhere between $10 billion and $12 billion. Three years later, their estimate was somewhere around $25 billion, nine-tenths of the dealing being done by banks. Over the same period, 1977–80, forward exchange trading in New York rose from a daily $3.5 billion to a daily $10.8 billion (Blin, 1981). Some estimates by the Group of Thirty suggest that the figure for daily turnover in the foreign exchange market in London in 1980 may have been twice as much and by 1985 had doubled to an estimated $45 billion. Worldwide, the Group of Thirty thought that *daily* foreign exchange transactions in 1985 amounted to some $150 billion.

The reasons for this truly revolutionary expansion in daily dealing in foreign exchange – an expansion far, far greater than could possibly be accounted for by the expansion in international trade – are clear enough. They can explain the hyperactivity of the chain-smoking young men in the city-centre tower blocks.

Under the fixed exchange rate system, corporation finance managers would use the forward market in foreign exchange to protect themselves against possible changes in the interest rate differential between financial assets or commitments incurred in different currencies. Occasionally, when a change was anticipated in any particular exchange rate there was some incentive for companies to join the speculators by buying or selling it according to the direction of the expected change (or more commonly, to indulge in 'leads and lags' in payments across the exchanges). But for the most part the acknowledged responsibility of the central banks for holding the rates fixed relieved corporate finance managers of the need to worry about day-to-day changes.

Under the floating or flexible exchange rate system, however, the company had to cope with the day-to-day shifts in the dollar's rate of exchange with other currencies. It is arguable that the costs to the central banks of intervening with their reserves to check exchange rate changes would have been in total far less than the costs of currency hedging now borne by corporations in the private sector. This increased the profits of the banks and caused attention to the financial side of businesses to grow in importance compared to attention to the directly productive side.

What was certain was that the cost had shifted, from the public sector to the private and then, in the end, to the consumers. For under flexible rates, because of the inevitable mismatch of money in different currencies coming in and going out of corporate bank accounts, the finance manager, in order to budget ahead, had either to cover or to safeguard his accounts against the expected receipts being less than they would be at today's exchange rate, and the anticipated payments being more for the same reason. He could do this by buying a currency forward and investing the equivalent in the short-term money market, or by investing in the Eurocurrency market. Every such order given to the corporation's bank would be offset by another contrary transaction because the banks were usually unwilling to have 'open' – that is, unbalanced – positions in currencies overnight. The need to swap deposits in different currencies in order to match corporate hedging transactions and to square the books is largely responsible for the growth and size of the interbank market referred to above. And the consequent price of the forward cover (i.e. the premium or discount on a currency's spot value) has tended to be set by these interbank market operations according to the differences between interest rates offered for Eurocurrency deposits in different currencies. This is the link that connects the foreign exchange market with the short-term credit market, exchange rates with interest rates. And because of the greater volatility of exchange rates, the Eurocurrency markets became a channel by which any event which affected an exchange rate, whether that was a change in the trade account or some political event regarded in the market as a plus or a minus for a particular currency, was immediately transmitted to the credit markets. The necessary conditions for this transmission were the unwillingness of the banks – in the light of their own and others' past experience – to take risks in foreign exchange, and the need of international business and exporters and importers to protect themselves against such risks (cf. Moffitt, 1982; Mendelson, 1980; Lever and Huhne, 1985; Sampson, 1981; Versluysen, 1980 and many others).

That need arose from the growth in international trade and from the internationalization of production by so-called 'multinational' or, more accurately, transnational corporations. But there is a circularity here too. For, as companies have discovered, forward markets gave them only limited protection. Corporations suffer variations in their cash-flow positions, in profits and losses, investments and sales in different countries and currencies. Yet a company's stock exchange rating and the composite company balance sheet at the end of its financial year has to be calculated in one currency. There is therefore a long-term incentive to the finance managers to find additional ways of dealing with this other kind of risk and of protecting themselves against criticism if the balance sheet should show a 'loss' which was not a 'real' loss but due entirely to the valuations of certain operations in another currency. Managers have therefore tended first to diversify the company's capital assets and liabilities as much as possible – financing locally or borrowing from local banks or better still, financing in convertible Eurobonds, for instance, and they have often sought to acquire local shareholders who will assume some of the risks. Indeed, geographical diversification of the firm's operations would be a rational long-run hedging strategy. In short, floating and volatile exchange rates, by increasing risks for multinationals, have made them still more 'multinational' in response. But this resulting long-run strategy will tend, in turn, to increase their short-term needs for hedging against exchange rate risks, thus adding still further to the volume of transactions in the financial casino.

It goes almost without saying that the volatility of exchange rates especially between the dollar and other leading currencies has also increased risks for developing countries even more than for the mobile transnational companies. The latter at least have a variety of products, a variety of countries to operate in and an army of highly-paid and well-equipped tax-advisers and financial managers to work on the problem. The developing countries are not so well served. In addition to all their other problems, since 1971 they have had to choose between a number of exchange rate strategies for their currencies. They could decide, like Mexico, to peg to the dollar, or like Senegal to the franc, or to the SDR or some other basket of currencies; or they could leave it to the market to decide.[2] But as rates between the pegs changed, some who had pegged had clearly chosen wrongly. Furthermore, the value of their export earnings from primary products was apt to be substantially affected by changes in the dollar, or sometimes even by the sterling rate (Stewart, 1981). For example, one developing country's financial fortunes might be magically enhanced in a year when the dollar appreciates and the D-mark weakens if its currency is pegged to the dollar and its exports are primary products quoted in dollars, while its imports come from Germany, its debts are mostly to German banks and it is able to borrow in D-marks. But equally, opposite changes in exchange rates could have precisely the opposite effects.

The volatility of interest rates

From the mid-1970s onwards, the instability of the currency markets was compounded by a marked increase in the volatility of the price of borrowing money.

From the 1930s until the mid-1960s, the level of interest rates in industrialized countries remained remarkably low, considering that in that time there was a world war, rapidly succeeded by a long cold war. Defence budgets were heavy, even for neutral states like Sweden, and when superimposed (as in Europe) on social welfare programmes, they caused the share of national income taken by government to rise. The first breach in the dyke is conventionally blamed on President Johnson and the Vietnam War. His administration was reluctant to finance both the war and social reforms by taxation and so resorted to increased government borrowing to meet the increased federal budget. But as Calleo has pointed out, this version is too simple (Calleo, 1982). The increase in US defence costs was not enough to account for so pronounced a worldwide phenomenon as took place in the period 1971–84. In 1963 commercial bills in New York were still paying less than 4 per cent, US Treasury Bills just over 3 per cent. By 1966 the commercial bill rate was over 6 per cent and the rate in the Eurocurrency market, known as LIBOR, or London Inter Bank Offer Rate, was over 7 per cent. By 1969 the respective rates were up to 8 and near 11 per cent. Thereafter both show a marked increased in the yo-yo tendency, with the New York rate always moving in less extreme fashion.

The Eurocurrency market, undoubtedly contributed substantially first to the rise and then to the volatility of interest rates. Mainly located in London, the market's growth owed a great deal not only to the permissiveness of the British authorities but also to their active participation. Through the 1960s, Britain not only had a comparatively large national debt – other countries, having been defeated in the war, were fortunate enough to have been allowed by that fact to default on their creditors both at home and abroad – but suffered a persistent loss of market confidence in sterling. Successive governments responded (in effect) by bribing holders of sterling reserves not to run away. They were offered high interest rates on British Government Treasury bills and gilts (gilt-edged government stock), and by the late 1960s, both high rates and a dollar guarantee. As the Eurocurrency business grew, it first of all allowed people to arbitrage between currencies, so that funds could be attracted on a covered basis into weak currencies by relatively high interest rates while strong currencies could keep interest rates low and still attract foreign funds. Secondly, it allowed funds to move and people to arbitrage between the domestic market and the Eurocurrency ones.[3]

But the choice was inevitably affected by two politically determined factors: the extra risk involved in dealing in a 'foreign' currency and the regulations imposed domestically on almost all national bank operations compared with the freedom from control of similar operations conducted in the Euromarkets. The point of this is that the Eurocurrency markets allowed the US banks (who dominated the market) to offer higher deposit rates because the former were free of the reserve requirements asked of banks in the Federal Reserve system. So, as the growth of the Euromarkets exceeded the growth of the domestic credit markets, so their competition tended to push interest rates upwards, though never in a steady or regular fashion. Yet another unpredictable factor was then added to compounded uncertainty.

From the late 1960s onwards, as markets became increasingly aware not only of accelerating inflation, especially in the United States, but also of the anticipated inflation differentials, divergence naturally widened between the nominal interest rate and the real interest rate. In other words the anticipation of the inflation component in interest rates on bank loans became more important as compared with the 'price of money' component. It probably cannot be proven, but it seems likely that the nominal interest rates of those economies that were largest and whose banking and credit system was most developed and extensive have had a greater influence than others on

16   Casino capitalism

Table 1.1 LIBOR and LDC debt at floating rates 1973–83[a]

	1973 %	1975 %	1977 %	1979 %	1980 %	1981 %	1982 %	1983 %
Proportion of developing countries' debt at floating rates	6.4	9.4	11.8	15.5	17.3	19.0	20.2	21.6
LIBOR[b]	9.2	11.0	5.6	8.7	14.4	16.5	13.1	9.6

[a] The overall figures conceal wide differences between countries. In 1983, for instance, Argentina, Mexico and Brazil had more than 75 per cent of their debt at floating rates, compared with 25 per cent for Turkey and 9 per cent for Kenya.
[b] London Inter Bank Offer Rate, the base for bank loan interest rates.
Source: World Development Report, 1985, p. 79.

the Euromarket rates of interest. By the same two-way transmission system they will also have had a stronger influence on the domestic markets of others than will the policy decisions taken within the smaller national credit systems. Big markets always do sway little ones and there seems no reason to suppose that this does not happen with the market for credit once an easy, cheap and efficient transmission system like the Eurocurrency market is placed between them. At any rate, the observable and observed fact is that during the 1970s, interest rates generally tended to follow (at different distances given inflation differentials), the lead of the US market.

This phenomenon was apparent even before the major turning point in US domestic monetary management strategy took place in 1979. And of course the US influence on others became far more pronounced when, having arrested the slide in the value of the dollar by the Carter measures of October 1978, the Reagan Administration appeared to go into reverse gear with the adoption of so-called monetarist methods.

The adjective 'so-called' is necessary because of the inability of the Reagan Administration (like others before it) to keep the Government's budget deficit under control. This inability was largely due to the escalating cost of defence. It is fair comment, therefore,

Table 1.2 Real long-term interest rates (9)[a]

	United States	Japan	Britain	W. Germany	Switzerland
1965–9	1.8	2.1	3.1	4.7	1.0
1970–4	0.7	−3.4	1.0	3.2	−1.3
1975–9	0.3	0.5	−2.2	3.0	1.6
1980–4	4.9	4.1	2.9	4.2	0.3
1983	8.1	5.6	6.2	4.6	1.2
1984	8.2	4.5	5.8	5.4	1.6

[a] The real interest rate is the amount charged to borrowers taking account of the rate of inflation. A minus sign therefore denotes that borrowers are lent money at a price less than the rate of inflation.
Source: Bank for International Settlements.

that in such circumstances *monetary theory* which implies a real control of the money supply could not possibly work. It has therefore never been properly tried out in practice. For even if the monetary authority both restricts and closely monitors the monetary base for credit but at the same time pre-empts a rather large share of that credit for itself, the natural result will be a restriction of supply of credit and consequently an increase in the price, that is, the rate of interest.

It was not surprising, therefore, that some of the volatility that has been so marked in the foreign exchange market for dollars shifted in the late 1970s and early 1980s to the market for borrowing dollars. Of course there were other factors too – not least the Soviet invasion of Afghanistan[4] – that at least for a time stabilized the dollar exchange rate. Through the mechanism explained earlier, this gave the European Monetary System an easier birth and infancy than recent historical experience might have led anyone to expect. The price of that easier birth, though, was a new vulnerability to any event or decision that altered the level of US interest rates.

The oil price

Compounding the volatility of currency and interest rates have been the fluctuations in real oil prices throughout the 1970s and 1980s.

When the era of accelerating change began, in 1973, the general expectation was that, once the price had been raised by the combination of OPEC solidarity, booming demand and panic buying as a result of the October War between Israel and her neighbours, the oil price would stay up. It could hardly have been predicted that it would jump again, in 1979 by over 50 per cent or that in real terms it would fall twice in the decade, in 1977 by nearly 9 per cent (following an increase in 1976 of 20 per cent) and again in 1983–4 by an average of over 30 per cent.

The first oil price rise not only produced the $80 billion surpluses of 'petrodollars' for the banks to recycle, thus swelling the importance of the financial markets and the institutions operating in them, but it also introduced a new, sometimes decisive and usually quite unpredictable factor affecting the balance of payments positions of both the consumer, and eventually the producing, countries.

In Germany's case, for example, a high dependence on imports and the first oil price rise brought the D-mark down on a trade-weighted currency-basket basis from 121 in mid-1973 to 116 at the end of 1975. But Germany reacted with tough enough financial policies to bring the rate back up again – only to suffer another check in 1981 after the second oil price rise. Japanese susceptibility, and responses, especially in exporting more to pay for costlier oil, were even more pronounced. Between 1972 and 1981 the yen yo-yoed from three 'highs' in July 1973, October 1978 and September 1981, to two lows (following oil price rises) in 1974 and 1980. At these points, both the dollar and sterling had exactly opposite reactions from the foreign exchange markets.

The differential effect of oil price changes on the OECD countries individually was important for the general stability of the world economy mainly because it was they who traded most heavily with each other. They account for most world trade. It is they, too, who invest most heavily in each other's economies and who account for most international capital flows. It is also they who therefore provide most business to the international markets for foreign exchange and for credit. In the face of the historical record it is hard to disagree with the conclusions (1) that the oil price has contributed to instability in exchange rates; and (2) that these rates cannot easily be stable until oil prices are steadier or until oil becomes less important in world trade and payments. This could happen by states either becoming more self-sufficient in oil or developing alternative energy resources that have less impact on their balance of payments and the external value of their currencies.

Although it may be true that it is the disparities between OECD exchange rates that caused most disruption to the international monetary system, it seems that the consequences of this uneven pattern of oil prices were most sharply felt by the oil-importing developing countries. Although other LDC commodity prices were ahead of oil on a 1972 base in 1973, none of them ever again caught up; and by 1981, food prices, agricultural raw materials and mineral prices in more or less real terms were all less than a sixth of the price of oil. The oil price index, in short, had outdistanced all the other price indices – for food, agricultural raw materials and minerals – by a factor of six or more. Though the recycling of the OPEC surpluses in the mid-1970s allowed the non-oil producing developing countries, or NOPECs, to borrow enough to pay for dearer oil, their development strategies immediately became vulnerable to further rises, *or* to increases in interest rates, *or* to periods of dollar strength, *or* to any combination of these factors. For a country such as Brazil, for example, the country's balance of payments may benefit to the tune of millions of dollars from a 1 per cent fall in the price of oil – but equally would lose as much as $1 billion from a 1 per cent increase in bank lending rates. While for Mexico, another debtor in trouble but an exporter of oil, both changes would be disastrous.

Like many other countries and corporations, the NOPECs suddenly found themselves playing Snakes and Ladders. And for them, while some of the ladders became longer, the snakes became more numerous and some also became longer. Decision-making on long-term choices – in energy or food production particularly – became an elaborate gamble. A case in point was Brazil's vast hydroelectric project, in which Paraguay is a minor partner, at Itaipu on the Parana River. In the long run, the turbines on this dam will produce 12.6 billion Kw, more than any hydroelectric project anywhere in the world. But the calculations on the economics of its construction were made in the early 1970s. They have looked better, then worse, then better and worse again as time has passed.

In the long run, an independent supply of cheap electricity must be the right policy for Brazil in terms of cost as well as for the economic security of the state. But meanwhile, the price of credit to finance the construction of this and other expensive projects brought Brazil reluctantly to seek help from the IMF and the banks – a humiliating experience for a country which, only a few months earlier, had been proud of having so far avoided involvement with the Fund.

As with interest rates, the problem with oil prices is not so much that they have been high, but rather that they have also been so unpredictable and so unstable. Again the instability has engendered a new game in the great financial casino – oil futures. This evolved in the following way. In the 1980s as OPEC's command over the oil market weakened, with some producers desperate for foreign exchange ready to undercut the agreed price with secret, under-the-counter deals, more and more oil cargoes came to be traded on what is rather misleadingly called the Rotterdam spot market. But this is not a market in the ordinary sense in which buyers and sellers are identifiable and prices known to everyone. It is just a network of about a hundred oil traders and brokers, connected with each other by long distance intercontinental telephone and telex. Like other brokers in grain or porkbellies or frozen orange-juice, they are often tempted to increase their profits by talking the market price up or down. As late as 1978, the spot market deals still accounted for only 5 per cent of all trade in oil. They now account for 40 per cent or more. Inevitably, because of the close connection between oil prices, generally denominated in dollars, and the price of the dollar in foreign exchange markets, there has grown up in London and New York a futures market in 'paper barrels' to match the forward and futures markets in dollars and dollar assets. These 'paper barrel' contracts can change hands as many as 50 times, and do not need to be based on barrels of real oil. Futures contracts on the British Brent blend of North Sea oil are thought to add up to as much as eight times the total annual output of the Brent field (Hooper, 1985).

In short, while there is little doubt that the instability of exchange rates has helped to destabilize the oil market, the oil market is now adding its own gambling game to all the others.

Stronger markets or weaker states?

The picture so far is one of an international financial system in which the gamblers in the casino have got out of hand, almost beyond, it sometimes seems, the control of governments. The question has occurred already to a good many people whether it is the governments that have got weaker over the past 15 years, or whether it is a fortuitous coincidence of economic forces that have combined to make the markets more powerful. It is an important question, for the answer will dictate what has to be done to control, to moderate, or to close down the great financial gambling game.

That question is linked with a second one: have all states weakened in relation to markets, or only one, or perhaps just a few of the more important governments? Those who think that all governments have weakened tend to find rather broad general explanations of how this has come about. If they offer solutions they are apt to be of the most vague and general kind. In contrast, those who think the explanation lies with the few, or even just with the USA as the dominant power in the international financial system – as all the figures show it to be – tend to be much more specific both in the explanations they put forward and in the solutions they suggest.

Curiously, these explanations come from both the political Left and the Right, each having grasped a part of the answer. From the Left, there has come the appreciation of the part played by the USA ever since the Second World War in bringing about a more 'open' world economy: open, that is to investment and international production as well as to international trade (Block 1977; Wallerstein, 1979; Magdoff and Sweezy, 1969; Parboni, 1980). Instead of competing for territory and command over people and resources, they say, the advanced industrial states have begun increasingly to compete on behalf of their producers for shares of the world market.

It is a perception which accords with some analyses of state policies coming from academic writers on the American Right (Gilpin, Krasner, Katzenstein and others). The state in an open, interconnected world economy needs not only a military strategy, but also a scientific and industrial strategy, if it is to hold its own in economic growth and market shares. Japan has seemed more successful than the United States at this new game; and the United States, this argument goes, has been undermining its own power and wealth by following the British example and letting its financial institutions build up the wealth and power of others, especially through investment.

Through the 1970s, this notion of the self-defeating behaviour of a hegemonic power in the world economy took such a hold that whole journals and research projects in the United States have been devoted to what became known as 'hegemonic stability theory'. This was the idea that the stability of the world economy had to be sustained by a dominant state or hegemon. But it followed that there was a 'hegemon's dilemma' which was that in sustaining the world economy, the hegemonic power (i.e. the United States) destroyed itself. Therefore, if the world economy appeared less stable than it used to, this must be because the United States had lost power, partly because it had borne the burden of acting as hegemon (Krasner, 1983; Keohane, 1984).

To most people outside the United States, this argument sounded very much like an elaborate but unconvincing excuse. It seemed hard to reconcile this whining complaint with the magnitude of American military power and, so far as the financial system was concerned, with the size and influence of the American banks (Sampson 1981). It was inconsistent with the universal use and acceptability of the US dollar which, as explained earlier, had made the United States less vulnerable than others to the volatility of exchange rates and other prices than the other advanced industrial countries. Many Americans were not as acutely aware as other people that when US domestic monetary policy changed direction, and when interest rates in the United States responded to changes of policy, other states had no choice but to adjust their own interest rates and their domestic policies to such changes, whereas it never happened the other way around.

Far more convincing was the observation, sometimes made by the same writers, that the United States was, and for a long time had been, a 'weak state' in the rather special sense that its government was permeated by pressure groups and pushed around by special interests each possessing a 'black ball' to veto positive policies so that there was no strong or consistent pursuit of the general national interest. This situation was contrasted with that of post-revolutionary China or the Soviet Union which looked like 'strong states'. The reason for the weakness of the American state could be ascribed partly to its constitution, and the principle of the separation of powers between the executive, legislature and judiciary which it contained; and partly to the liberal ideology of market-oriented economy in which the freedom of economic enterprise to function free of government interference was enshrined as a political principle.

What was less often mentioned, either because it was less evident to people living in such a large continental country or because it implied an unwelcome acknowledgement of American responsibility for the growing instability of the whole international financial system on which the market or capitalist system depended, was that American banks had taken very large profits from that financial system but had been saved from the consequences of very risky operations by the financial power of the US government. There was, and still is, a conflict of interest within American society between the banks and large corporations on the one side, who can profit by and survive – for the most part – in this unstable, uncertain environment, and the farmers, workers and small businesses who find it far more difficult. So long as life in the United States can, by various short-term measures, be made to look better than life in other parts of the world, there are not many politicians who find that it pays to draw attention to the asymmetry of the system, both outside and inside the United States.

Political horizons are notoriously limited, in the United States as elsewhere. But the limited perceptions and foreshortened political horizons of American politicians matter far more to the system than do those of other countries. The record of the last 15 years suggests that in making certain key decisions affecting the international financial system, successive US governments have been far more swayed by short-term domestic considerations than by any awareness of the long-term national interest in building a healthy, well-ordered and stable financial system capable of sustaining a healthy, stable and prosperous world economy.

Notes

1   The market price – overshooting as usual – rose to around $800 an ounce, before eventually falling back below $400.

2   A few countries in 1971 chose to peg to sterling but have since thought better of it. Three peg to the South African rand and one to the Spanish peseta (see Strange 1972, 1976, ch. 11). Forty-two countries, mainly in Latin American and the Middle East, peg to the dollar. The risks of pegging to one particular currency can be somewhat modified by pegging to a collection or 'basket' of major currencies weighted according to their importance. The SDR (see above, p. 7) is one such basket. The European Currency Unit (ECU) is another which does not include the US dollar.

3   To 'arbitrage' means to shift money (assets or liabilities) from one market to another so as to make a profit, or avoid a loss.

4   The Soviet invasion increased fears of an escalation of the cold war between Russia and America. Many people then calculated that if this happened their money would be safer in America than in Europe or the Middle East.

CHAPTER 2
Key Decisions and their Consequences

We are looking for the key decisions which have altered the course of world economic history in recent times, and which have shaped the development of the world economy and determined shifts in the costs and benefits, the profits and losses, the risks and opportunities amongst nations, classes and other social groups. But it is important at the start to be clear as to what we mean by a key decision and what we should be prepared to look for and include.

In the first place we are analysing the monetary system. Decisions here are not quite the same as in the study of international diplomatic relations, for instance. There, states decide to make war or to make peace, to make alliances and to intervene in the affairs of others. The action is between foreign ministers and diplomats and the key decisions are up to them. Monetary systems are different. In the real world – though not always in the fairyland of economic theory – a monetary system must have both political authority and a market. The market is essential whenever economic exchange between buyers and sellers is not all done by command of a third party. If buyers and sellers are free to exercise some degree of choice, however limited, and if their transaction is not conducted through barter, there must be money. But a monetary system cannot work efficiently unless there is political authority to say what money must be used or may be used; to enforce the execution of agreed monetary transactions; and to license, and if necessary support, major operators in the system.

It follows that, in the context of a monetary system, the origins of a key decision may be found both on the side of the market and on the side of political authority. A change in the size or character of the market – perhaps even the relations of supply and demand within it – will face authority with a decision either to respond or not to respond. A change in the locus of authority over the market, or perhaps in the objectives and priorities of that authority, can also bring about a key decision. But whatever the origin, whether the change originates with the market or with the authority, the decision will be made by a political authority. It may be a positive decision – for example, to intervene with rules or with resources to influence or restrain the market. Or it may be a negative decision (i.e. a non-decision) to leave the market alone and to allow it more freedom, not less. In this monetary context, therefore, key decisions relate more to the balance of power between market and state (or other political authority) than to the balance of power between state and state.

On the whole, it is probable that non-decisions will be more common than positive decisions. There are two reasons for this. One is the globalization of markets. The other is the acceleration of technical change. As to the first, so long as markets – particularly financial markets – are predominantly national, then national authorities can control them and decide how much or how little they shall be regulated. But when they become closely integrated and interdependent – in short, global – then authority can often be exercised only by the collective agreement of all the states concerned, or sometimes by one dominant state. There will be a non-decision if the dominant state does not want to act, or if one influential state refuses to cooperate, even if others are agreed. An example of this would be the US decision not to go ahead and ratify the negotiated text hammered out after so many years' patient diplomacy at the UN Law of the Sea Conferences. Another would be the negotiations over SDRs, held up first by the United States, then by disagreement among the Europeans. As for the technological reason, the ingenuity of inventors and promoters often leaves governments lagging behind. This has happened with some pesticides, with short-wave broadcasting and with many synthetic materials. It can also happen with financial innovations.

Even the simple and ubiquitous telex, when used to transmit politically sensitive news or ideas as well as everyday business messages, has been able to steal a march on the ability of governments to monitor and censor the flow of information across state borders. When we come to the financial field, the outdistancing of regulatory authority by advancing technology has been particularly marked, and it has not only been mechanical technology to do with means of communication and data collection and retrieval, but also financial technology that 'invents' totally new credit instruments or forms of financial transaction that the regulatory authorities never even dreamed of.

The point made earlier, that passive decision-making in the form of non-decisions can be just as important as positive decision-making, effecting shifts in structural power between states and markets, can be illustrated by random examples of a non-monetary kind. In the 1960s the United States reversed its policy of holding substantial grain stocks. The then Secretary of Agriculture, Earl Butz, took the decision for domestic policy reasons: the cost of holding these stocks was considered too high. The US Department of Agriculture therefore began to unload them on the market with the result that by 1970, little was left of them. During the 1950s and early 1960s, world grain prices had remained remarkably steady, and most experts seem to agree that this stability was due more to the existence of North American stockpiles than it was to the rather precarious International Wheat Agreements (Morgan, 1979; Hopkins and Puchala, 1979; Davies, 1984). So long as the stocks were there, it was dangerous to speculate on a meteoric rise in the price of grain, however bad the world harvests, because it would always be open to the US and Canadian governments to relieve the shortage from their stockpiles. Once these were exhausted, however, no such sword of Damocles hung over the speculators and it was entirely possible, as the well-known story of the Soviet grain buying of 1972 showed only too clearly, for the grain price to rocket upwards – and in due course, to crash downwards. In both the boom and the crash, the balance of bargaining power between buyers and sellers – and between both and the grain brokers – was changed, the balance of payments of exporting and importing countries substantially affected, and a further important element of uncertainty and instability added to the world economy as a system. Yet the key decision had been made not as a matter of international negotiation, but in the course of domestic policy-making toward American farmers.

In the same area of policy, one could point to Reagan's 1983 Payment in Kind (PIK) policy to relieve the distress of those same farmers, more deeply in debt even than in the interwar depression and often unable to earn enough, as a result of poor grain prices, to service their debts to the banks. Once more, government stocks, now somewhat rebuilt, came into play; the farmers were given grain to sell in lieu of the crops they agreed not to grow. The farmers gained – briefly, as it turned out – from the improvement in prices that followed, but the manufacturers of fertilizers, pesticides and other supplies, whose sales slumped, complained bitterly. Thus, intervention in one market is often apt to have repercussions on the balance of bargaining power in a related market.

The Law of the Sea imbroglio, just mentioned, had similar repercussions. The origin of the need to renegotiate some sort of agreed set of rules regarding the extent of state authority beyond the shoreline lay in a disagreement between the federal government and the state of Texas about their respective rights to license oil exploration in the Gulf of Mexico. International customary law since the eighteenth century had accepted the Grotian principle of a three-mile limit to state sovereignty over coastal waters. President Truman reasserted the authority of the federal over state government by enunciating in 1948 a new doctrine regarding the rights of states over the continental shelf, to an offshore distance of 200 miles. The governments of other countries were not slow to copy and even extend the American example. The consequences for fishermen (not to mention fish), for oil companies, for new oil-producer states like Britain or Norway, and for remote communities like the Shetland Islands have been immense. Even international relations were affected as first Britain and Iceland tangled over the unsettled question of offshore fishing rights in the 'cod wars', and later Britain and Denmark, both members of the European Community, wrangled bitterly over Danish fishing rights in 'British' waters.

In each of these specific instances, and in many others, most people would not quarrel with the idea that any of these unsettling departures from previous practice or convention was indeed a key decision as

I have defined it. But not everyone accepts the wider implications for any general discussion of the nature and locus of power in the international economy. Two American professors, Bob Keohane and Joe Nye, for instance, who began and led a great deal of work on the question, made a useful distinction some years ago between the 'vulnerability' and the 'susceptibility' of states to the consequences of 'interdependence': that is, trade, investment, sourcing of production, banking, insurance, and other services sold worldwide (Keohane and Nye 1977). States, they said, were unequally susceptible to change resulting from this interdependence. But some who were susceptible had greater capacity than others for averting or offsetting the unwanted effects of this interdependence. Thus there was greater asymmetry in vulnerability than there was in susceptibility. But in further discussion of the distribution of power and the reasons for what they called 'regime change' in the international political economy, they appeared to assume that the asymmetry of vulnerability was either the result of unequal power in the political structure – weak states having less power than strong ones to defend themselves economically as well as militarily – or the result of blind economic forces. Regime change, they suggested, could be attributed either to changes in relative political power, or to economic process (or, they added, to internal changes within international organizations responsible for the 'regime'). This framework for asking the question, 'Who has power to effect change?' therefore did not go far enough. It did not admit the importance of economic structure as the complement – indeed an inseparable part – of the political structure. Nor did it recognize the unequal power of states in their domestic decision-making to modify, alter and shape the economic structure. Whereas this is precisely the sort of 'structural' power to which attention to key decisions inevitably and naturally draws attention. Hence the question, 'What were the key decisions?'

When it comes to the world's monetary and financial structure, people are often tempted to write about economic trends – the ups and downs of commodity markets, for example – and to changes in the financial charts and indexes – as if indeed they were blind economic forces. It is very easily forgotten that markets exist under the authority and by permission of the state, and are conducted on whatever terms the state may choose to dictate, or allow. Only a few 'black' markets exist outside the law of the land and are conducted despite all the efforts of governments to close, tax or control them – for example, drugs in most states, arms and abortions in some, stolen or smuggled goods, labour for cash – a relatively short list, considering the enormous extent of open markets. It is therefore all the more important to trace back to their origins the details of particular authority–market relationships, to see when and why, as well as who, took the key decisions in defining that relationship.

It is also important to recognize that the roots of most of those relationships which are relevant to the current state of the world's money system are often long ones. We must sometimes search quite far back in history to find the points at which policy-making decisions on particular issues were first taken, even though today these 'decisions' have become 'facts'. In the same way, if today I am offered a cigarette, I may reply 'Thanks, but I don't smoke.' That looks like a statement of fact. But the origin of the fact that I don't smoke lies in a decision I took years ago to stop smoking. It is the same with decisions of state: their consequences soon become so taken for granted that they become unquestioned 'facts of life'.

Secondly, I would hold that in this international monetary structure, no change in collective management takes place – whether for better or worse – that is not initiated by the United States (Strange, 1976). From time to time, it is true, the United States has had to be nudged and diplomatically shoved by its affluent allies to take a decision which others agree is necessary or desirable. (The setting up of the Gold Pool under pressure from the Bank of England in 1960–1 was such a moment.) But the shovers and pushers cannot act on their own; no one else shares this over-riding power to block change or to initiate change. Thirdly – and this follows directly from the examples of key decisions of a non-monetary nature given earlier – the search for key decisions cannot stop short at multilateral agreements and decisions reached in international organizations, but must encompass domestic policies towards the private operators in a number of important financial markets.

Five distant 'non-decisions'

Let me briefly review some of the evidence for each of these contentions in turn. For the notion that the policy-making roots of present troubles lie deep in the past, there are at least five distant decisions – or, for the most part, non-decisions – that come to mind, and it would not be hard to make a much longer list.

One such non-decision was the failure of the European members of the North Atlantic Treaty Organization (NATO) in the early 1950s to respond to American appeals for some financial burden-sharing of the costs of European defence. At the time, it seemed to the Europeans that only rather small contributions were required of them. The Americans had the atomic bomb and the development costs of that had already been paid for. The Russians did not have it, but the United States needed bases for its forces in Europe, who were there as much to convince the Russians and reassure the Europeans that the Americans meant what they said about holding the line at the Iron Curtain, as they were to take part in a conventional war if that should be started, whether on purpose or accidentally. Secure under the American nuclear umbrella, the Europeans – even those in the European movement – could afford to forget their dreams of an European army; once the French National Assembly turned down the idea of a European Defence Community in 1954, nothing more was heard of it. That non-decision nurtured the habit of dependence on security provided by the United States – a habit which persisted even when circumstances changed and the Soviet Union acquired both a bomb and the means to deliver it, and as the costs to both sides of a nuclear missile arms race escalated to the point where the United States found itself saddled with a perpetual budget deficit and a recurrent deficit on its balance of payments. The story is familiar enough. The point about the European non-decision of the early 1950s is only that, had they not taken that particular turning (and found it hard to reverse it later when times changed) at least some of the troubles afflicting the world's monetary system might have been avoided.

A number of other important non-decisions of the same decade, the 1950s, had to do with the failure to arrive at any agreed system or process for the provision of credit and the management of debt. There were three separate questions here, on each of which the leading members of the post-war international economic organizations failed to reach decisions that would have saved a lot of subsequent trouble. Perhaps the most fundamental one was the rejection of the early proposal, in 1957, for a Special United Nations Fund for Economic Development. I believe the reasons given at the time for turning the idea down have been proved by subsequent experience to have been groundless. In view of the credit later found, first on a public bilateral basis and second from the private sector in direct investment and in Eurocurrency bank loans, it was not true that the rich countries could not afford SUNFED or that they would have impoverished their own economies if they had taken the plunge and set up such a Fund, or that large-scale aid would have been dangerously inflationary. (Instead, it will be recalled, they stalled with the pathetically small Special Fund and a whole series of lesser and later palliatives like quota increases for the World Bank and the International Monetary Fund, the UN Development Decade and so forth.) Of course, such a development fund would not have solved all the problems and would have created a lot of new ones. More difficult decisions and hard choices would have ensued and new risks would have been incurred – for instance, of setting up what critics of the Brandt Report later caricatured as the 'poverty industry', and of opening the door to waste, corruption and boondoggles of all kinds. But a UN development fund would at least have set important precedents for a process of using multilateral resource transfers to developing countries as a stabilizer that *could* have made the system more stable and less politically capricious and could have directed investment more purposefully into long-term productive projects than the more capricious financial flows which did subsequently take place and were recorded by the OECD's Development Assistance Committee (DAC).

A second failure with far-reaching consequences was the collective refusal to devise any standard process for the handling of bad international debts. The problem after all was not new even in the 1950s; governments and their nationals had been failing to pay interest and repay capital on money borrowed from foreign creditors for over a hundred years. It was more than likely that others would continue to do so, and that confidence in the system would be less apt to be shaken by shocks and jolts and the threat of possible default if, instead of *ad hoc* measures being taken in each case, some standard procedures and elementary rules could be agreed beforehand that would correspond to the treatment of bankrupts in national systems. But by the end of the 1950s, by which time the first few debt problems of the many to follow had appeared, it was abundantly clear that the chief creditor countries valued their freedom of action in foreign policy far above any possible benefit that a more orderly procedure might bring to the world's monetary system (Strange, 1976). In each case, creditors' clubs were set up on an entirely *ad hoc* basis. Each time, negotiations among the creditors were started from scratch as to who was to be paid back what percentage of old debt, and who was to provide how much of the necessary new financing. Each time, the debtor state, whether under old or (preferably) new management, had to bargain with the creditors on the terms for its recovery of normal creditworthiness. It is not hard to see why. The consequent uncertainty was a useful bargaining weapon in the hands of the creditors, and one which could be used with restraint or with ruthlessness according to the strategic importance of the country and the domestic character and prospects of its government. But the failure to set any clear rules also meant that as the financial system became more fragile and precarious in the 1970s and 1980s, the uncertainty over Mexican rescheduling, for instance, was apt to spill over on Brazil and its capacity to roll over its foreign debts, just as the uncertainty over Poland's rescheduling spilled over on to Hungary.

Closely related to the creditors' club question was the management of competition among industrial exporting countries in the tying of aid and the subsidization of credit and insurance for export contracts. The two policies were close substitutes for each other. If a government provided tied aid, it was offering vouchers redeemable only with its own exports. If it subsidized an agency that gave export credit insurance on easy terms to its national exporters it was offering a discount to the importer on deals done with them as opposed to deals done with others. The fact that the United States and the Europeans, and later Japan, given this wide choice of methods, adopted somewhat different ways of accomplishing the same purpose, helps to account for the recurrent breakdown of a series of 'gentlemen's agreements'

made first through an obscure body called the Basle Union of Credit
Insurers and later through the OECD. In these agreements the major
industrialized countries promised not to undercut one another on
the terms offered to debtor countries for export credit. But because
of their endemic competition for world markets, the promises were
always being broken so that it was extremely difficult to be sure,
at any given moment, precisely how much short-term export credit
was being offered to specific countries by all those competing in the
game. For, whenever an indebted country appeared to be heading
for trouble, it found itself able to replace old debt falling due for
repayment only with much shorter-term loans. And of all the short-
term credit to be had, export credit was often the most readily
available. But the collection of data on the volume and *terms* on which
it was given was apt to be both slow and often incomplete.[1]

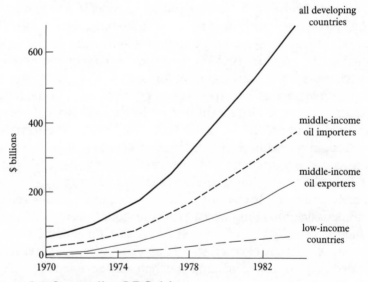

Figure 2.1 Outstanding LDC debt.
(*Source*: OECD Development Co-operation.)

This failure to agree and to act at a far earlier stage, in the mid-1950s
when the problems first appeared as an issue, is open to another
interpretation. Whereas I would say that the creditor governments
concerned failed then to take a hard decision, others would say this

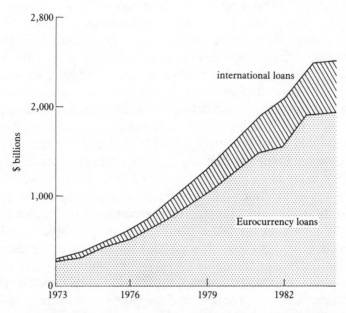

Figure 2.2 Stock of international and Eurocurrency loans, 1973–84.
(*Source*: BIS *Quarterly Report* 1974–85.) Data indicate stock at the end of the last
quarter of each year, except for 1984 data which are as of the end of the third quarter.

was an inevitable consequence of the international system. In this
view, the changing structures of world production and trade have
so altered the rules of the game in the political system of international
relations that states are no longer seriously competing with one another
for territory or for population. Instead, they are driven by economic
and technological change to compete for technological pre-eminence
and for larger shares of a world market. They need these in order
to acquire both more power and greater wealth, so it is naive to
criticize them for doing what came naturally. My view is that though
this is true about the competition of states in the modern world, it
is not the whole truth. If it were, why should they make *any* effort
to moderate their competition? The very attempt to reach some
gentlemen's agreement on the rules of the export credit game – the
most recent was 1982 – surely suggests that each also shared some
concern to keep an open, liberal, competitive world economy. At

any moment and on all sorts of international issues there is always an indeterminate trade-off between the two imperatives – between the need to compete and the need to moderate competition for the sake of order. Thus, there was a certain measure of free will in choosing what the agreed rules of the export credit game were going to be. After all, much the same choice of trade-offs faces governments as they struggle to decide what rules should govern the conduct of war on land and at sea, or the degree of immunity granted to diplomats in time of peace. And it is an easy and unfortunately common error to assume that there is anything completely inevitable about either the behaviour of states in their international relations or the behaviour of corporations and states in a market economy. As Ralph Nader, the champion of American consumers, once recalled, there was nothing inevitable about the wholesale departure in the United States around the turn of the last century from the principle of federal chartering of corporations (Nader, 1976). This led to the dilution of shareholders' powers and to a situation in which majority shareholders, and later managers, were free to expand, merge and otherwise conduct the affairs of large corporations more or less as they pleased. On those political decisions was based the strong trend toward economic concentration in all industrial countries, but especially in the United States, which was so well described by Berle and Means in their classic study, *The Modern Corporation and Private Property*. This study, written in 1932, provided the foundation for much of the better known work of J. K. Galbraith. It produced incontrovertible empirical evidence that the modern economy was split into a part in which market forces still operated to determine price, and another in which concentrations of economic power allowed powerful corporations to 'administer' prices. It also anticipated much of the early work of Raymond Vernon, Charles Kindleberger and others, on the so-called multinational corporation. The concluding paragraph by Berle and Means is particularly relevant:

> The rise of the modern corporation has brought a concentration of economic power which can compete on equal terms with the modern state – economic power versus political power, each strong in its own field. The state seeks in some aspects to regulate the corporation, while the corporation, steadily becoming more powerful makes every effort

to avoid such regulation. Where its own interests are concerned, it even attempts to dominate the state. The future may see the economic organism, now typified by the corporation, not only on an equal plane with the state but possibly even superseding it as the dominant form of social organization. The law of corporations, accordingly, might well be considered as a potential constitutional law for the new economic state, while business practice is increasingly assuming the aspect of economic statesmanship.

Before we leave our list of distant decisions (or non-decisions) which have helped to shape the international monetary system we have today, there is one specifically British decision in the post-war period that might be noted as one of the distant roots of later difficulties and dilemmas. It was the decision by Harold Wilson in 1951 – he was then President of the Board of Trade – to allow the reopening of the London commodity markets for international trading. By doing so, he gave the blessing of a Labour government to the revival of the City of London as a financial marketplace more open than any other to bankers and to all sorts of financial operators from all over the world. Yet at the time, it would have been quite consistent with a lot of socialist thinking – and even with Keynes' scornful opinion of capitalists – to have gone beyond the nationalization of the Bank of England. That somewhat symbolic step might have been followed up with policies that would have inhibited the resurrection of an institution that had been regarded by many of Wilson's older colleagues in the Labour Party as a bastion of privilege, a power base for the ruling class, and a fatal magnet drawing talent and resources away from the modernization of British industry and the improvement in the living standards of the British workers. I have argued elsewhere that the reopening of this financial marketplace, and the primarily political refusal to give up the use of sterling as an international currency, made the pound far more vulnerable to speculation set off by balance of payments deficits than any other European currency (Strange, 1971). Throughout the 1950s and 1960s it was this vulnerability which led to the adoption by Britain of stop–go policies toward credit and industry that had the worst possible influence on British industrial management, on industrial relations and trade union bargaining strategies and on the investment decisions of banks and other influential financial institutions (Hu, 1984).

Keeping the City permanently closed, as it was during the war, so that it would not again become an open market to the world might not have avoided all these ills. Admittedly, there would have been costs as well as benefits, risks as well as new opportunities, to such a decision. But the net result for British society and for the British economy would, I still believe, have been better than the consequences of Harold Wilson's first unthinking (and typically shortsighted) steps to hasten its rebirth. And for the world economy, who can say that the internationalization of American banking would have taken place so fast and furiously if London had not been there, ready and waiting with 'Welcome' on the mat? The open door and the welcoming mat were still there when Harold Wilson returned to power as Prime Minister in 1964. By then, the big American banks were already arriving in London to do profitable business in Eurodollars. It was astonishing that a socialist politician who prided himself on his grasp of economics should have been so indifferent to the long-term consequences of allowing a totally unregulated financial market to grow up on his doorstep.

So much for the long roots of the monetary problems – and hence of economic difficulties – in the 1980s. The other proposition I put forward was that no change in the collective management of the world's monetary and financial system – whether it was a reform or the reverse – took place in the 1970s that was not initiated and supported by the United States. Again, from a much longer list that could be made, I shall select five of the key non-decisions in the field of collective management that were made from 1971 to the present that seem to me to support this contention.

Leaving the markets alone, 1972

The first non-decision to do with *not* exercising some authority over the foreign exchange markets came in the wake of the Smithsonian Agreement of 1971. This agreement to allow a devaluation of the US dollar, as Nixon and Connally had intended, was supposed to restore an international monetary system based on fixed exchange rates. Yet the United States refused to back the declared aim with action to check foreign exchange markets. This was the direct result of Washington (more particularly the US Treasury) over-ruling the better judgement of the Federal Reserve Bank of New York when it came to checking and flattening short-term ups and downs in the dollar's exchange rate in that market. As Charles Coombs, who from 1961 to 1975 was in charge of all US Treasury and Federal Reserve operations in it, wrote:

> By its very nature, the foreign exchange market is a nervous, high risk, ultra-sensitive mechanism primarily geared to short-term developments. Of the tens of billions of dollars in daily transactions cleared through the market only a fraction is derived from such fundamental factors as foreign trade and longterm investment. On a day-to-day basis the market is instead dominated by short-term capital movements *in search of quick profits or a hedge against exchange rate risks* (Coombs, 1976, my italics).

Long experience had led Coombs to the same opinion as that held by central bankers in Europe: that a build-up of speculative pressures on an exchange rate in this volatile market could often be checked (and at modest cost) by firm and well-timed official interventions – buying or selling currencies to check the speculation. It was his view that the 'fatal weakness' of the Smithsonian Agreement of December 1971 on new parities for the major currencies was 'the total absence of any commitment by the United States to help defend the new structure of parities' (Coombs, 1976, p. 225). In his book he gave an account of his own repeated (and mostly unsuccessful) efforts to persuade the Treasury to let him demonstrate in the market American determination to back the fragile Smithsonian structure. For instance, in May 1972, he and Arthur Burns (Chairman of the Federal Reserve Board) were publicly contradicted and over-ruled by a Treasury official when they put the case. But the 1972 sterling crisis won them a brief conversion, allowing Coombs to resume operations in the market and to reactivate the swap network. But Burns' announcement that the US would play its part in restoring order to the foreign exchange markets (as, under Coombs, it had already begun to do), and that it would continue to do so on whatever scale and whenever transactions seemed advisable, was almost at once counter-manded from Washington, with a peremptory telephone message to pull back. Although the success of even this brief and limited intervention was vindicated by the results, Washington remained adamant. Even in May 1973, when a much more serious cascading of dollar rates swept through the market, so that by July German marks were up 30 per cent over the February rate, and trading brought almost to a standstill, the Treasury once again stepped in to limit intervention to 'defensive operations'. This, in Coombs' opinion, cost far more than a forceful approach would have done, because it fatally conveyed to the market an impression of timidity and lack of confidence in the future of the dollar. This American non-decision, moreover, went clean against a joint decision by the central bankers, taken at Basle the previous weekend, that they would act in concert to maintain the rates. Thereafter, for two years, the absence of a firm official hand in the New York market produced what Coombs called 'absurd and damaging gyrations' of the dollar against the continental European currencies, usually in response to some relatively trivial and short-term disturbances or shortlived fears and anxieties. Only for six months, from the time of the Heathrow airport meeting of the four major central bankers – Burns, Leutwiler, Klasen and Emminger – in February 1975 to the following mid-summer, was some moderate degree of order restored.

During this crucial time, neither Coombs nor any other central bankers would have claimed that intervention by monetary authorities in the market could prevent periodic exchange rate adjustments when inflation rates diverged widely and currencies were clearly grossly undervalued or overvalued. The argument was rather that unnecessary and exaggerated movements in the foreign exchange market could have been prevented, and at no great cost to the monetary authorities. Left to themselves, the central banks have usually managed to come out nearly even over a period of time even if their disciplinary operations seem expensive on a single day or in any given week or month. The significance of the failure of Washington to listen to the Federal Reserve Bank and the Europeans in these years is that it vastly encouraged the speculative fever of the times, not only in the foreign exchange market but in other markets as well. As Coombs remarked, writing of the summer of 1973 (i.e. before the oil price rise):

Nor was the damage confined to the exchange markets. Worldwide inflation had gathered momentum as the successive devaluations and depreciations of the dollar set off speculative buying in the world commodity markets and particularly intensified inflationary pressures in the United States and other countries whose currencies had moved downward with the dollar.

The no-rules regime, 1972

Perhaps the second important non-decision, which was a step away from the collective management and multilateral negotiation concerning the international monetary system, and a step toward greater anarchy and unilateralism, was not at first perceived as being a decision. It was the decision *not* to go back, once the Nixon–Connally dollar devaluation had been successfully managed in 1971, to some modified form of the gold-exchange standard – the 'Bretton Woods system' as it is often loosely called – and *not* to have a clear set of rules regarding the issues of adjustment, reserve-holding and exchange rate management which that system had tried to settle. It took the deceptive form of a decision in the IMF in the summer of 1972 to set up, by postal ballot of the members, a Committee of Twenty to carry on the discussion, already well advanced within the Fund secretariat, of international monetary reform. In fact, those discussions had already been overtaken by events – notably the dollar devaluation – just as the Special Drawing Rights issue in 1970 had quickly been swamped by the expansion of Eurocurrency lending from the private sector.

Yet many of the experts closely involved with these matters were unable to see the political wood for the technical trees. They still fondly believed that economic rationality and international goodwill would triumph over all the difficulties and would lead onward and upward to a better and more orderly world (e.g. Shonfield, 1976; Williamson, 1977). The truth was that the United States, having devalued the dollar, and slammed and closed the gold window in August 1971, was no longer bound even by the tenuous restraints of the gold-exchange standard. But though what Triffin called 'the paper-dollar standard' which replaced the gold-exchange standard gave even greater freedom to American policy-makers, the United States still needed the IMF, if only as watchdog and sheepdog to keep the lesser fry in order. Helped by the British, Washington had got rid of Pierre-Paul Schweizer as the IMF's Managing Director. But the new freedom would sooner or later have to be made legitimate by amendment of the Articles of Agreement, and there might be other tasks best done under a multilateral cloak through the Fund than by the United States on its own. There was also a need, perceived ever since the Azores rapprochement between Nixon and Pompidou in early December 1971, to mend transatlantic (and trans-Pacific) relations badly damaged the previous August. But the Americans thought it best not to do so in the Group of Ten where the United States was now totally isolated (Williamson, 1977, p. 61). As on many previous occasions – San Francisco was the first – the United States saw the advantages in dealing with its European allies of inviting others to join in what might otherwise be an embarrassingly contentious discussion. In a larger forum, the Europeans could often be outflanked and outvoted.

Thus was begun the totally cynical pantomime of discussing in the Committee of Twenty a report on the reform of the international monetary system written by the Fund officials and laying out at length the options 'available' – by which they meant options suggested by monetary reformers – for re-establishing order in the system. The report was published the month before the 1972 Fund annual meeting, and welcomed as a working agenda by all except the United States. Mr Connally's successor at the Treasury, George Shultz, produced his own counter-proposal suggesting a new rule of the game to replace the old ones. This was that countries should either adopt adjustment policies or change their exchange rates up or down in accordance with gains or losses in their reserves. In return the US would restore gold-dollar convertibility *once the US liquidity position permitted*. This blithe promise to abjure sin and live by the good book when the Greek Kalends dawned clearly indicated the contempt in which Washington held the whole exercise.

John Williamson's narrative of the negotiations makes this clear. His subsequent search for an explanation of why the Committee of Twenty was so ill-fated – the state of the wicked world, the conflicts of national interest, the negotiating process, the failures of intellectual understanding – was conscientious but quite unnecessary. The plain fact – as he himself says more than once – was that there was no reason of perceived incentive or of countervailing coercive power to make the United States give up the super-exorbitant privileges which it had won in 1971. All the reform pantomime did accomplish was to gain time in which a revision of the Articles of Agreement of the Fund could be worked out, so that each Fund member, including the United States, was legally free to choose its exchange rate policy without resigning from or disrupting a useful piece of multilateral machinery.

Not negotiating with OPEC, 1973

The third non-decision of collective management needs only a brief discussion, since it is well known to all. It concerns the American reaction to the OPEC oil-price rise of October 1973, and the sub-sequent rejection at the Washington Conference the following February of British and French proposals that in view of the massive deficits which oil-importing developing countries – the so-called NOPECS – were bound to incur, the resources of the World Bank and Fund should be quickly and substantially increased. That was a far less radical or emotionally unpalatable solution than the alternative, which was to work out a negotiating process with OPEC to accept the oil price increase with a good grace, make it proof against dollar depreciation by indexing – but in return to seek measures that would achieve greater stability in oil prices in the future. To most Americans, that seemed far too pro-Arab, too much like knuckling under to impudent newcomers. Yet the increase in Fund quotas then, rather than later, would have made it unnecessary to depend so heavily on the banking system to cope with the 'recycling of petrodollars' in the 1970s. This dependence was tolerable so long as there were large OPEC surpluses to recycle, and confidence in the prospects for economic growth. But later, after the second oil price rise in 1978–9, it left governments wondering how to persuade the banks not to cut off too abruptly the supplies of credit to developing countries.

In that emotional American reaction to OPEC in 1973–4, there were thus two related non-decisions, each with far-reaching consequences.

One was the confrontational posture adopted towards the oil-producing states; the other was the indifferent posture adopted towards the NOPECs, the oil-consuming developing countries. In retrospect, both were fatally shortsighted. The confrontation with OPEC did not go as far as some Washington hawks might have liked, but it did lead Henry Kissinger to propose the setting up of a consumers' alliance in the shape of the International Energy Agency (IEA) which accomplished relatively little in the way of improved security of supply, but which convinced the Arab states (not counting Egypt) that the United States was far from non-partisan in the matter of Arab–Israeli conflicts, and that their oil revenues were far safer in Euromarket deposits than in US government securities, or even US corporation shares.

This mutual distrust continued to poison relations for a decade, despite the obvious fact that oil prices without OPEC would have been still more chaotic, and the economic repercussions far worse. As Edith Penrose rightly remarked at the time: 'If OPEC did not exist, it would be in the interest of the industrial world to promote its creation in some form (Penrose, 1971; Mikdashi, 1985; Rustow and Mugno, 1976; Rustow, 1983). Reviewing subsequent US policies towards the oil-producers, Professor Zuhayr Mikdashi has noted a series of gratuitously offensive (my description, not his) American decisions hardly conducive to the calm reconciliation of producer-consumer national interests. The series began by revoking the most-favoured-nation clause in respect of OPEC member states, quite contrary to the GATT agreement. It excluded them from such benefits as were conferred by the General Specialized Preference scheme in favour of imports of manufactures from LDCs. And by a Congressional amendment to the 1974 Trade Act, it was stipulated that OPEC members were ineligible for any further concessions negotiated in the Tokyo Round. Instead of offering these insulting pinpricks, the Unites States might have offered to negotiate an exchange of guarantees by both sides. Had it done so, there can be little doubt that subsequent oil shocks (price falls as well as rises) would have been less extreme and their destabilizing effects on the international monetary system would have been substantially moderated.

American indifference to the plight of oil-importing developing countries was made abundantly clear when, under pressure from France and the Washington Conference of February 1974, the United States reluctantly agreed to take part in a Conference on International Economic Co-operation (CIEC) in Paris in 1976. CIEC's four commissions (on energy, finance, trade and commodities) ended in stalemate, boredom, and bitterness. The efforts of Witteveen as head of the IMF to set up a special Oil Facility from OPEC loans, and the agreement to direct some of the proceeds of IMF gold sales to a Trust Fund, barely scratched the surface of the problem. Once again, without the sort of American lead which President Truman had given in his inauguration address in 1949, nothing much of consequence happened. Even the rather novel proposal from Iraq in 1979 to set up a joint OPEC–OECD long-term fund for compensating developing countries for imported inflation on the one hand and any increase in crude oil prices on the other, fell on deaf American ears.

No lender of last resort

Last of the five wrong turnings in the decade I would put the reaction – primarily American, but also shared by the other major monetary authorities – to the bank failures of 1974. The collapse within a short time of Bankhaus Herstatt, Franklin National, First National of San Diego, and others, drew attention to the weaknesses of a system in which many bank transactions in the Euromarkets lay beyond the reach of national regulations and supervision. Even more important was the fact that these Euromarket transactions could be conducted in currencies other than that of their own home base. The reaction, through the meetings of central bankers at the Bank for International Settlements, came in the Basle Concordat of 1975 – the agreement whereby each agreed to increase surveillance over and to assume responsibility for supporting (if necessary) its own commercial banks. The Cooke Committee on the regulation of international banking was set up, and as no domino-effects followed the first bad run of failures, policy-makers (with a few notable exceptions) heaved sighs of relief and dismissed the whole issue from their minds for another seven or eight years, until the Continental Illinois scare in 1984. Among the notable exceptions, I would mention particularly the staff of the

BIS itself, Henry Wallich of the Federal Reserve Board; Emile van Lennep at the OECD, and a team of former central bankers organized as the Group of Thirty and including, among others, Jeremy Morse, Otmar Emminger and Johannes Witteveen. The secretariat of this Group proceeded to conduct a series of useful studies on the subject of security in international banking. But the disuse since 1974 of the Group of Ten arrangement for meetings of finance ministers and deputies (an American decision, see above) meant that such fears hardly registered at the various summit meetings of the heads of state held in the late 1970s and early 1980s. The consequence was, as many others have noted, that the system continued to suffer from the lack of a lender of last resort (Kaletsky, 1985; Lever and Huhne, 1985; Lipton and Griffith-Jones, 1984).

This was an institution which every government had found it necessary to provide in any country where credit markets had developed and on which economic confidence and growth depended. It is of the essence of such an authority that it is able not only to impose penalties on banks that overlend when the condition of the market dictates greater prudence in the interests of the whole system, but also that it should be able effectively to encourage them to lend more freely when banks are smitten with an attack of nervous paralysis. Such an authority the Basle Concordat did not provide. And the results were to be seen in the Mexican case in 1982, when action could only be taken with the United States, Britain and the IMF in the lead, *after* President Portillo had at last retired leaving his successor, President de la Madrid, the unpleasant task of declaring his country's inability (in the wake of falling oil prices and fast-vanishing bank confidence) to service its past debts. The collection of data from the banks about their loan portfolios and maturities is not a sufficient substitute for this delicate balance of brakes and accelerator, of rein and heels, that a central bank in charge of financial markets just as highly strung as any thoroughbred horse must exercise. For a lender of last resort must not only be able to remedy disaster when it has happened (as in the Mexican and other cases), but it must also be able to avert disaster *before* it happens. What alternatives might be considered to remedy this very important lack in the world's monetary system is a question I consider in the final chapter of this book.

Domestic decisions

Lastly, we come to the third of my propositions about key decisions. This was that, because of the accelerated integration of the world's financial markets, some of the domestic decisions of the United States with regard to its own banks, to the financial markets within the country and with regard to the management of its own domestic economy must be included as key decisions for the world system, simply because of their far-reaching repercussions beyond the territorial limits of the United States. Many years ago, in the 1960s, Dr Otmar Emminger once remarked on this point that it was very uncomfortable sometimes being in bed with an elephant. The simile was particularly apt because in such a situation the elephant itself is unlikely to be even aware of the existence let alone the discomfort of the smaller creatures in its bed. And so, for the most part, it has been with the United States in its domestic decision-making with regard to Eurocurrency operations, to US banks' foreign lending, to new financial markets, and to new technological developments in banking and finance and, perhaps most important of all, to the wider repercussions of its domestic monetary management.

With regard to Eurocurrency operations, the British reopening of the City of London as a financial market-place for the world has already been mentioned as one of the necessary conditions for the subsequent rapid growth of the Eurodollar market in the early 1960s. The others have been described in innumerable accounts of that market's growth and development so that there is no need to repeat the details here (Strange, 1976; Solomon, 1978; Versluysen, 1981; Moffitt, 1984). Among them, let me recall the Bank of England's agreement to allow British banks to take deposits and make loans in dollars (but not in sterling) when the European currencies went convertible in 1958. This was matched by the United States' permissiveness towards the London subsidiaries of American banks who were allowed to follow suit, and indeed were given strong incentives to do so by the restrictive effects of Regulation Q and other New Deal controls on short-term deposit-taking by their head-offices at home. The added incentive, given by the Interest Equalization Tax (IET) from 1964 on, to the banks to compete *outside* the United

States both for deposits and for would-be borrowers of dollars is also well-known; and so is the effect of the IET in penalizing such borrowers if they tried to raise money in New York.

I would only add to this the subsequent failure of US monetary authorities even in 1974 to give any serious consideration at all to the broader consequences of banks' overseas operations in the Eurocurrency markets. This, as it was subsequently realized, had important consequences for LDC debtors and for the stability of the whole system of global short-term credit. One such aspect was the transfer of risk from the ultimate lender to the ultimate borrower, effected by the adoption of LIBOR as the moveable base on which interest payments on Eurocurrency loans would be made. This meant that if the Eurocurrency interest rate moved up or down, as it habitually did in response not only to supply and demand in the money markets but especially to the movement of the US domestic interest rate, it was the borrower who was taking the risk that LIBOR would increase (or decrease) his debt service liability. By contrast, in the nineteenth and early twentieth century, when most international lending had been done by the issue of bonds, the allocation of risk had been very different. Then it was the bondholder who took the risk both of a fall in the value of foreign bonds – as a result of war, revolution, poor economic prospects or the competition of more attractive bond issues – and of a change in the prevailing interest rates for new bonds. If that interest rate were to rise, and new bonds to be issued at 1 or 2 per cent more than the rate payable on his or her bond, the market value of old bonds would fall, so that it would only be possible to earn the new rate of interest by selling the bond at a loss. Under that system, in the short run at least, the bondholder gained on the yield swings what he or she lost on the market-value roundabouts, even though it was the bondholders who carried the longer-term risk of lending to foreign borrowers beyond the control of their own governments. Millions of French, German and British bondholders (and in later decades Americans too) consequently found themselves holding Turkish, Chinese, Tsarist Russian and other foreign bonds, which for a long time were so much worthless paper – until some of them acquired another kind of scarcity value as collectors' items. They hastened to organize for themselves Councils of Foreign Bondholders, but these seldom achieved much.

The floating interest rate system adopted in Eurocurrency lending meant that it was the borrowers' liability which immediately increased if there was a tightening of credit in world capital markets, so that the burden of servicing became heavier just as new borrowing became more difficult and more expensive. (Under both systems, the bigger banks, whether as bond issuers or as lead banks for syndicated loans, tried hard and mostly succeeded in passing the risk to others. And under both systems, any major build-up of bad debts was apt to induce so much cautiousness that it reduced the opportunities of all three parties – the ultimate investors, the banks and the ultimate borrowers.) From a systemic point of view, the effect of this shift to a number of borrowers whose economic (and political) prospects were bound to be somewhat uncertain inevitably increased the fragility of the system – unless, of course, other compensatory steps were taken to regulate and stabilize it.

The other aspect of Euroloans was the tendency to syndication. At an earlier stage some of the bigger international banks had sought to minimize the risks inherently involved in foreign lending by going into partnership with banks from the other major creditor countries. They set up what were known as consortia banks, usually with an American, a British, a German, Japanese, and a French or Dutch partner in a collectively owned subsidiary. But the difficulties of coordinating lending policies as each partner's national credit policies changed, not all in the same direction at once, and as the parent banks' perceptions of risk and profit opportunities differed, proved larger than expected. Though some were successful, consortium banking went out of favour. But syndication was different. Here the lead bank, who took the responsibility towards the would-be borrower of putting together a large Eurocurrency loan and persuading lesser banks to take a share in the loan, would so write the terms of the deal that it earned a management fee or took a proportionately larger share of the interest payments. Some would call it share-pushing. But whatever the label, the effect was to give a big incentive to the bigger banks to involve more and more smaller ones in this foreign lending. The fact that for US banks the comparative absence of regulation over the Euromarkets compared with stricter regulation of domestic operations meant that, for many of them, this was the only available means of showing profits on their annual turnover and thus persuading shareholders (and depositors) that the bank was a viable enterprise. Although the syndication arrangements were not the primary reason why most US banks made most of their profits in the 1970s from foreign operations – in some cases, 60 per cent or more – they did undoubtedly account for the breadth of involvement of the US banks in foreign lending.

A third feature of regulation of US banking practice came later in the decade, with the International Banking Act of 1980. Although widely welcomed in the United States as a long overdue measure to restore equity between US banks and their foreign competitors, it did amount in many respects to a measure of de-regulation in step with the general trend of American economic policies, not only under President Reagan but also under his predecessor, Jimmy Carter. For it permitted US banks for the first time to operate as freely as the American subsidiaries of their foreign rivals, and to conduct operations in New York that hitherto they had conducted only through their foreign branches in London, Frankfurt, Hong Kong, Tokyo or in tax havens such as the Cayman Islands or Nassau in the Bahamas. The legal change allowing International Banking Facilities (IBF) in New York itself brought about a substantial reduction of US banking business conducted through these Caribbean retreats.

That they should have grown up in the first place was, however, only a reflection of the general American indifference to, and official disinterest in, any activity conducted outside the territory of the United States. There had never been anything to stop the US Congress at any time declaring that banks with headquarters in the United States must conduct their operations in accord with certain regulations, whether those operations were conducted at home or abroad. Reserve requirements were finally imposed on Eurodollar deposits with American banks by Volcker in October 1979 as part of the new tough monetary policy. But they only required US banks to deposit with the Federal Reserve System 8 per cent of funds lent to corporations in the USA – not a very severe restriction.

Similarly, the growth of tax havens and bank-regulation havens could easily have been checked at any early stage. The home governments of the banks, corporations and insurance companies which took advantage of them could at any time have put them out of bounds. That the US Congress did not do so was no doubt partly in accord with the American concept of the role of government and the prime importance given to behaviour within the United States or behaviour directly and visibly affecting the economy or society of the United States. It may also have been encouraged by the peculiarly dispersed nature of monetary authority in that country. While most other countries divided the making and execution of monetary policies between two power centres, the finance ministry and the central bank, the United States had made for itself a veritable cat's cradle of crisscrossing responsibilities shared among a truly bewildering variety of official agencies. Besides the US Treasury, there was the Federal Reserve Board and within that the Office of the Comptroller of the Currency (OCC). The external monetary relations of the United States, however, were (and are) conducted by the Federal Reserve Bank in New York, a *primus inter pares* in the Federal Reserve System, while special regulatory powers with regard to financial and share markets had been allocated ever since 1934 to the Securities and Exchange Commission (SEC). On top of that, the separation of powers gave Congress (through the House Committee on Banking and Finance and the Senate Banking Committee) the power to amend the statutory powers of any of these bodies, while the federal nature of the government meant that in practice the banking business was governed by state as well as federal regulatory bodies – the New York State banking authority being particularly important.

Under the pressure of events and anxiety for the system, there had been a move, after the Herstatt collapse and in accordance with the BIS declaration in 1974 and the formal Basle Concordat of 1975, to tighten up the supervision of the banking system and to allow the OCC much wider powers to collect much more information from the banks about their foreign as well as domestic activities. But the powers were too little and the information too late. For instance, from 1974 on, the OCC began running checks on the lending of individual banks country-by-country. These checks did not stop the big American banks becoming greatly over-extended to the leading Latin American debtors, Mexico, Brazil and Argentina; and owing to the extent of inter-bank borrowing the checks could not tell the whole story, any more than the rule that no US bank should lend more than 10 per cent of its outstanding loan portfolio to any one borrower was sufficient to limit its commitments, through subsidiaries or other banks, to one sovereign debtor. From the end of 1982, all banks had to report to the OCC on overdue loans – but the same *post hoc* defect applies.

Nor has it simply been the unconcern of the United States authorities about the extra-territorial activities of American banks that has led the international financial system as a whole away from better surveillance and regulation just at a time when the integration of financial markets actually called for a move in the opposite direction if the balance of market and authority was to be kept more or less the same. The dominant trend in US domestic policy-making through the past decade under Presidents Ford and Carter, as well as President Reagan, has been toward deregulation. Although far from consistently executed, deregulation was applied to airlines, telephone and financial services. Cloaked (as policy often is) in the fine-sounding rhetoric of liberal ideology, it was actually driven in the latter case by the very strong material interests of some of the biggest and most successful American corporations and their banks, supported by their lobbyists in Washington and promulgated by influential writers, journals and newspapers.

In the course of the decade, each of the three major ways in which the creation of credit had formerly been regulated for the greater security of the financial system and the economy had been eroded. Deposit-rate regulation had been designed to reduce the mobility of short-term funds. But ceilings on deposits left for less than six months were lifted in 1970; and ceilings on demand deposits were lifted in November 1978. In 1980, the process of deregulation was greatly speeded up by the Depository Institutions Deregulation and Monetary Control Act which will result in the total elimination of all controls by 1986. As one OCC official commented in 1981: 'Rate deregulation of course became imperative when inflation-induced high interest rates led to outflows of deposits into unregulated market-rate instruments and created concern about providing small savers with the opportunity to realize market rates.'[2]

From an earlier period, and under the Glass–Steagall and McFadden Acts, US banking law had sought to limit the chances of banking collapse through a domino-process, by restricting the activities of banks both geographically and by function. But the ban on inter-state banking was undermined, when in 1974 the OCC ruled that customer-bank communication terminals allowing the mechanical transfer of funds were *not* against the laws prohibiting inter-state banking. This opened the door to inter-state banking on a wide scale. And it was opened still further when, in the early 1980s, savings and loans agencies (S&Ls, or 'thrifts') were allowed to establish branches on a state-wide basis, and in some cases across state lines. And meanwhile the prohibition on diversification of services was further relaxed. It had already caused trouble in 1974 when the real estate investment trusts (REITs) owned by banks got into difficulties. Subsequently, in the search for profitable business, US banking went far towards seeking freedom of operation for a universal bank – whose difficulties in one area could spread quickly to the parent and to others. Under the Carter Administration, this deregulation was justified on the grounds of equity ('If X does it, why can't Y'). Under the Reagan Administration, virtue was made of necessity. 'We must begin', said Comptroller Conover, 'to work towards a world where government supervision is less important and market discipline more important in guaranteeing a safe and sound banking system.'[3] And while existing restraints on some credit instruments were dismantled, there was a concurrent and equally significant tendency to allow the unregulated growth (or sometimes the relatively unregulated growth) of new forms of trading in commodities and commodity futures, in new financial credit instruments and in new devices such as money market mutual funds, repurchase agreements, and zero coupon bonds. The American Stock Exchange in recent years has seen a boom in new markets in options – a form of financial dealing very little removed from gambling on a horse race or the turn of a pack of cards, the roll of dice, or the rattle of a roulette wheel. It is now possible to place a bet – in effect – on whether the price of gold (or of most other commodities down to pork bellies and concentrated orange juice) will go up or down and by how much within a given time in the future. In 1975, it became possible to trade in 'Ginny May' futures contracts.[4] Now it is possible in Chicago to bet on whether the stock exchange index of 100 large stocks will go up or down or by how much, how fast or slow. And Amex in 1983 introduced a Major Index option based on the Dow-Jones 30 blue-chip (i.e. favourite) stocks plus five others. For each of these options and futures markets there are certain rules about how they are conducted and who may trade in them on a wholesale basis (i.e. on behalf of retail customers). But there is no overall control at the federal level of how many such speculative markets there may be or of the volume of gambling that shall go on in them collectively or even individually.

And just as the ingenuity of the dealers in devising new gambling games has evidently got ahead of the regulatory authorities, so has the technology of banking and finance. It has done so in two ways. Mechanically, it has speeded up the process of making a financial transaction to the point where it will soon be necessary to calculate payments of interest not per year, month or day but to the nearest second. Recent developments in automatic money transfer systems (AMTS) made possible – and, of course, actively encouraged – by the whole computer and electronic industry have implications for such traditional concepts as the velocity of money and for the monitoring of trans-border monetary movements. These implications have still not been fully appreciated, or even worked out. Already in just a few years the banks discovered that they could defeat Federal Reserve requirements by running what were called daylight overdrafts; provided they could use the available technology to restore their reserve position by the end of the US financial day, they were free to evade it for the rest of the 24 hours (Mayer, 1982).

The other way in which technology has got ahead of regulation is in the development of banking by non-banks. Sears Roebuck, originally a national mail-order business in the United States, is now cashing more cheques than any single American bank (Naisbitt, 1984). Though the banks invented 'plastic money' in the shape of the ubiquitous credit card, non-banks quickly copied the idea so that petrol, clothes, food, travel fares and household goods of all kinds are now increasingly bought and sold by these means. No one, so far as I know, has counted the full extent to which personal credit has been, and is still being, extended in this way. But whereas the creation of credit by banks was subject to regulatory limits set by monetary authority, there is no corresponding system for moderating the creation of credit by non-banks, nor of monitoring the activities of financial institutions which behave like banks but are not counted as such. Merrill Lynch is the best known example of an international brokerage business, which acts in international markets to all intents and purposes like a bank. In two years it was reported to have acquired $2 billion more in deposits than Citibank, yet its operations were beyond the reach of banking regulations (Naisbitt, 1981).

In the old days, American permissiveness towards non-banks, towards new technological changes, and towards new financial markets, and an American shift in policy-making towards deregulation instead of regulation would no doubt have set an example which others might have followed. But the imperative need to follow the US example would have been much less than it is now; the choice for other countries would have been far more open that it has been in recent years. Again and again, it is possible to trace the imitation of the deregulation trend by those who have far less to gain from it in invisible exports of service industries than the Americans. Nor has it been only Britain (the dismantling of exchange controls in 1979, the subsequent transfer of Bulldog bonds by non-sterling borrowers, the extension of Bank of England discount facilities and export credit guarantees to foreign banks) which has followed the American lead. More than ideology is at work. In pure self-defence, other financial centres are put under pressure to offer similar facilities, equal freedom to the private banking and dealing operators. Even Japan, the least susceptible to foreign penetration in any shape or form, has been obliged to imitate the American practice of dealing in certificates of deposit, in inter-bank trading and in the extension of other forms of financial activity associated with the internalization of banking in a relatively unregulated system (Kaufman, 1981).

I have already mentioned some of the US domestic policies that have had wider repercussions throughout the world's monetary and financial system: the permissiveness towards Eurodollar lending, towards the proliferation of speculative financial markets, towards its own banks, and toward non-banks behaving like banks. There remains the most important domestic decision of all – the adoption in October 1979 of a so-called 'monetarist' system of managing the US national economy and the consequent imposition on other countries and on the world economy of interest rates that were both high and volatile, and which set off, as Milton Gilbert observed, 'a deflation out of all proportion to the need for corrective action' (Gilbert, 1980). The ill effects of US monetarism have been criticized

– not only by the heads of foreign states affected by it, but also by a large number of Americans and of former international officials who were broadly sympathetic to the proclaimed goals of American foreign economic policy. The literature on the subject is vast and it seems hardly necesssary to rehash all the details of the policy decision, of its consequences within the United States and of its further repercussions in the world at large. It will be enough for present purposes to recall briefly some of the main points of these criticisms.

Perhaps most fundamental was that this was not really a monetarist policy at all so long as the US government was undoing with one hand – through the demand for financing for an ever-increasing budget deficit of government spending over tax revenues – what it was trying by control of the money supply to do with the other. Hence the description of the policy as 'so-called monetarism'. A true monetarist policy, consistent with the underlying theory, would have had government financing playing so small a part in the classic $M/V = P/T$ equation that it had no effect on the price of money (i.e. interest rates). In the United States the government spent 35.4 per cent of the GNP in 1983 compared with 27.4 per cent in 1973. Moreover, its demand for money is so exigent that price does not matter. The government's spending *must* be financed – even if, as in 1982, Congressional rules have to be bent in the process. No matter how high the interest rate, therefore, it has no capacity to influence the level of government spending nor the credit-creating policies of federal credit agencies.

The second major point of criticism has been that the manner in which monetary policy has been conducted was unnecessarily variable and frenetic, actually increasing the volatility and nervousness of financial markets already quite highly strung. Monetary targetting was effected by a weekly announcement of the seasonally adjusted money supply (M) at which Fed policy was aiming. Market reaction to this hypothetical figure was immediate and exaggerated. Often it turned out that these first estimates were, by the Fed's own admission, substantially wrong, and had to be revised. For instance the estimated monthly growth rates for 1983 were later raised by an average of 3.2 percentage points, and later still, in a second version by nearly 5 percentage points (Wenninger, 1985; Heter and Kamilow, 1979).

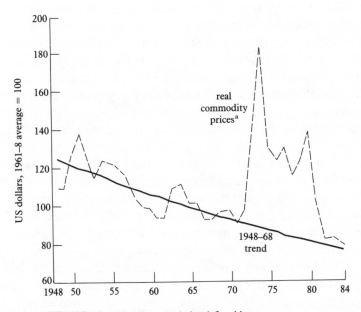

[a]World Bank commodity price index deflated by
United States Producer Price Index.

Figure 2.3 Trends in real commodity prices.
(*Sources*: International Bank for Reconstruction and Development and US Department of Labor, Bureau of Labor Statistics.)

It was also working all the time partly in the dark. The large numbers
put down as 'errors and omissions' in the balance of payments figures
on the flow of funds in and out of the United States introduced a
new and incalculable variable into their sums. Moreover, as Henry
Kaufman, top economist at Salomon Brothers, whose own comments
have also moved markets from time to time, observed, the Fed was
apt to change its definition of money and thus its calculation of the
target. It did so no less than four times between November 1978 and
April 1982 (Kaufman, 1982). The authorities, Kaufman said, were
always playing 'catch-up' in taking financial innovation into account
in the creation of credit, and in estimating the relation between
the monetary base and the overall money supply into account. The

volatility in interest rates is thus exacerbated as the locus of the target is changed. And so is the general move away from long-term and towards short-term (and highly liquid) monetary assets. On top of that, the instability of the system is increased as banks and other institutions move (and are allowed to move) away from fixed-rates contracts toward contracts which vary with prevailing base rates of interest. 'Spread banking', in which banks take care to match the maturities of assets and liabilities, becomes general and the effect is to shift to depositors and to borrowers the interest rate risk which banks themselves have to bear in more stable monetary and credit systems.

A further result was that some of the banks' corporate customers, already far more deeply in debt and more dependent than ever before on bank loans rather than on equity financing, were made more vulnerable still by this shift in risk-bearing, and thus more vulnerable either to bankruptcy or to merger unless supported by overt or covert state intervention. The end result of 'monetarist' policy may easily turn out to be the exact opposite of its ideological intentions. Instead of freeing the private sector and the market economy from the toils of state intervention, it may actually end – as in Mussolini's Italy – in involving the state more extensively and more permanently in industry and business than it had ever been before.

This particular instance of the perversity of policy thus arises from a combination of some economic consequences of the integration of international financial markets, both across frontiers and between markets, with the political response to these developments and the attempt to reassert the autonomy of national policy. But instead of the medicine restoring the patient to health and sanity, as its publicists claimed, it can be argued that it has actually made the patient more vulnerable than ever and less able to resist the very disease – subservience to the state – against which it was prescribed.

Notes

1 See chapter 5, pp. 137–42.
2 Cantwell Muckenfuss III, in hearings before the House Committee

on Banking, Finance and Urban Affairs, US Congress, 22 September 1981.
3 Conover speech, reported in the OCC's *Quarterly Journal*, Oct. 1982.
4 From GNMA, standing for Government National Mortgage Agency.

CHAPTER 3
Some Other Interpretations

In the last chapter, I suggested that the roots of the world's economic disorder are monetary and financial; that the disorder has not come about by accident, but has in fact been nurtured and encouraged by a series of government decisions. This view is shared by a few, but not by all, whether they write for the press, the academic journals or in books. If we look beyond the literature that deals specifically with money and finance, we find a much wider range of interpretations of the causes of our present troubles. To underline the point that decisions in international money and finance have generally been accorded too limited a place in our understanding, it may be useful to attempt a sort of plain person's guide to the full range of contending interpretations of the events of recent years. This is the more necessary because many people deeply concerned with our predicament have neither the time nor the patience to go through them all at length, and also because people tend to read the literature of their own profession or field of interest and that of their own political persuasion. A guide that takes in as wide range of prejudices and perceptions as possible may therefore be useful.

The interpretations that tend to dismiss the monetary and financial aspects of world economic disorder as unimportant seem to fall into two groups: those that put the main stress and blame for disorder on weaknesses in trade policies, and those which avoid putting the blame anywhere in particular by offering one or other form of determinist versions of recent economic history.

Part of the reason for this disregard of monetary explanations lies in the trend towards over-specialization in the study of economics. Trade and money, like investment and employment, have been progressively dealt with inside different theoretical boxes. Each has too often been treated as part of the data of the other, and the connections between them have been consistently overlooked or discounted. Thus, when it comes to contemporary interpretations of the recent past, a split or schism appears between the two. And it is the opinions of the economists concerned with trade relations between states, rather than those concerned with monetary relations, that have predominated and have most influenced informed opinion – at least in the industrialized countries. Any review of the Western press at the time of the meeting of trade ministers in Geneva in November 1982, for instance, or at the economic summit of heads of state in 1983 or 1984, would show that protectionism was widely identified as the greatest danger to the world's future prosperity, not monetary mismanagement.[1]

Yet while the professional schism explains – at least in part – why there has been this broad division of opinion, it does not explain why the trade interpretation has been so predominant over the monetary one.

The puzzle remains why – despite the testimony of many historians – the trade-based interpretation of world economic depression should predominate so strongly over the financially based interpretation (Davis, 1975; Lewis, 1939). The reasons could be professional, historical, or political – or a mixture of all three. Professionally, it is much easier for teachers to explain and for students to understand the depressive effects of trade barriers than the more complex processes of credit shrinkage and monetary uncertainty. Historically, it must be remembered that a major foreign policy objective of the Roosevelt and Truman administrations was to fashion a postwar world economy as wide open as possible to American commercial and financial domination (Block, 1977). To this end, the belief that protectionism and discrimination must at all costs be avoided in the general interest, as well in the national interest of the United States, had to be confidently and repeatedly driven home, even though this was inconsistent with the conclusions reached by most historians of the time that protectionism was a symptom, not a cause, of depression.

Finally, there is a political explanation. Putting the main accent on protectionism serves to share the blame fairly equally among all concerned. The Europeans and the Japanese are as guilty – in some respects, more guilty – of this particular sin as the Americans. Even developing countries indulge in protectionism, so it is not only the rich who are at fault. Power over money and finance, however, is much more asymmetrically distributed among governments, the United States standing clear above all others. It would be hard enough for the Americans to accept such responsibility for the economic ills of other countries if there were more certainty and agreement about what ought to be done and more confidence in how, politically, to get it done. Lacking both, the hot seat is all the more uncomfortable and the monetary interpretation consequently all the more unpopular.

The technical version of determinism

Even more popular than putting the emphasis on trade is to find some reason why whatever happened was bound to happen. The determinist interpretations of current economic troubles go furthest in absolving any government or any class from blame or even responsibility. These interpretations are of two kinds: political and technical.

While the political-determinist explanation excuses policy-makers – in the United States specifically, but in other countries as well – by saying that they could not do otherwise than they did because they had suffered a loss of power, the technical-determinist explanation suggests that the policy-makers have been overwhelmed by the inexplorable forces of economic history, against which no political system ever invented could prevail. The first assumes the loss of American power in the international political system, not so much to the Soviet Union as to Japan, Germany and the other members of the European Community, to OPEC and even to some developing countries. Beyond the American experience it also refers to the loss by all states of the power to manage national economies in so closely knit and integrated a world market economy as we now have.

The other – the technical-historical form of determinist thought – assumes the relative impotence of political organization in the face of economic change, and perhaps more importantly, of rapid technological change. This rests on some empirical statistical work first done by a Dutch marxist, van Gelderen, in 1913, and followed up in the 1920s by the Soviet economic historian, Nikolai Kondratiev. In analysing data on economic growth, and on the relation of prices and wages, Kondratiev believed there was a discernable pattern of long waves of faster and slower expansion, as well as shorter and less powerful trade cycles, and that this pattern had been fairly consistent since the early nineteenth century, with peaks in the 1850s and the 1900s, and troughs in the 1820s, the 1870s and again in the 1920s. Though Kondratiev merely recorded the pattern and did not attempt to explain it, the very idea that the capitalist system had ups as well as downs, and that it was not doomed, as Marx had proclaimed, to an inexplorable decline as a consequence of its own internal contradictions, was heresy. So, Kondratiev ended up, according to Solzhenitsyn, in one of the millions of unmarked graves in Stalin's labour camps.

Since his time, economic and social historians have been coming forward with a variety of explanations of the Kondratiev long waves. The first was Schumpeter in 1939 who connected the first rising wave early in the nineteenth century with the introduction of steam engines in British manufacturing industry, the second with the spread of railways, the third with the technical revolutions in chemicals, electricity, and the internal combustion engine. In each, labour was absorbed in the growth industries faster than it was being shed in older agricultural and industrial occupations. In the downturns, the process was reversed and new industries could not absorb labour as fast as the old industries cut back. Modern exponents of the long waves interpretation of economic history thought they saw a fourth Kondratiev upswing in the 1950s, led by the United States; at the end of the 1960s the crest of the last long wave was beginning to break, ushering in the long downturn in the 1970s. All the consumer durables and office machinery developed in the 1930s and marketed in the 1950s contributed to the last phase of expansion, but it was not clear where the next technological advance would come which would sustain the next upturn around the turn of the century.

One problem with this interpretation is that economic historians cannot entirely agree as to when or why the long swings up and down begin or end. Nor are they agreed on whether technical innovation acts as a starter of growth or whether conditions ripe for growth generate technical change. Is demand or supply the deciding factor? Economists are consequently divided over how the downswings can be shortened and moderated or the upswings extended and reinforced (Schumpeter, 1939; Maddison, 1982; Freeman, 1982, 1984; van Duijn, 1984).

Some 20 years ago, Kuhn in the *Structure of Scientific Revolutions* suggested that a time-lag could be discerned between a scientific discovery or invention and its commercial exploitation, when it acted like a booster rocket accelerating the rate of economic growth (Kuhn, 1962). The inventions, he suggested, came at the bottom of the troughs when the profitability of old technologies was becoming exhausted; the exploitations came on the upswing when investment resulted in mass production. But one trouble with applying these theories to the present times is that scientific and technological advance has become much more unremittingly constant and rather less cyclical. It is true that in some fields (pharmaceutical chemicals, for example), there are signs of diminishing returns setting in; but equally there are others (electronics, bio-genetics) where scientific advance has not stopped over the last decade or more. Moreover, the extensive involvement of states, especially those with large defence establishments, in scientific research rather removes the implicit connection suggested by Kuhn between the exploitation of inventions and the state of the market.

An alternative and non-technical explanation came much later still, in the 1970s, from the American economist, Walt Rostow. In *The World Economy: history and prospect* (1978), and other works (Rostow 1976; 1978; 1980), he argued that the source of the long waves lay in the tendency of market economies led by the newest industrial sectors in any period first to over-invest in the production of primary products and then to under-invest. This produced a contrapuntal relation between commodity prices and the industrial sectors which has continued into the post-war period. Paradoxically, Rostow sees the era of post-war prosperity from 1951 to 1972 as, on the contrary, a Kondratiev downswing in which commodity prices were weak, as in the 1920s. But this time the effects on industrial economies were offset by strong internal consumer demand and by Keynesian policies of full employment. The recession of the 1970s was perversely due to an upswing in commodity prices which struck directly at the leading sectors of industry: cars, consumer durables, plastics and synthetics. The remedy, as he sees it, lies in more state intervention to boost investment in energy, agriculture and other raw materials.

But Rostow's rather individual interpretation has not been widely accepted. And indeed the popularity of the technical determinist explanations of the recession for the most part have little to do with the cogency of rational argument. If there are weaknesses in the logic, or yawning gaps in the empirical evidence, that is not so important as the seductive fact that such ideas absolve everyone from responsibility for the parlous state of the world.[2] If past mistakes and errors of judgement are significant before these historical trends, then there is no point in recalling them, for they did not much matter. There is no point in the Europeans or the Japanese blaming the Americans, nor in the Latin Americans blaming the industrialized countries. Nor is there much point in people blaming their governments or their official bureaucracies. All the establishments around the world can heave comfortable sighs of relief and sleep with untroubled minds. So may corporate managers who can excuse themselves to the shareholders and to the redundant workers for the lamentable annual balance sheet by blaming it all – as they do – on the state of the world economy. 'When things look up and business recovers', they smugly can report, 'the company will be able once again to offer jobs and dividends. We are doing our best. Please be patient.'

Meanwhile, the technologists and the scientific researchers can be consoled by the promise which long waves hold for the future. Blessed are those, it says, who can discover a new technology, conceive a new product for which there would be a mass market or design new processes that will be irresistible the moment the outlook brightens.

Even the changing nature of international politics favours this technical determinism. States are no longer seriously engaged in a competition over territory. It is not just that most frontiers have long been settled and that people have come to accept them for all their anomalies. They are also less important as factors determining relative power of states in international relations. The sort of case between Portugal and the Netherlands which came before an international court before the First World War over the division of the somewhat unproductive and unexplored island of Timor is not really conceivable today. A few quarrels over territory remained – the Beagle Channel for Argentina and Chile, the Falklands for Britain and Argentina – but the issue is primarily prestige and status, or the clash of principles of colonialism with those of self-determination, not the control of square miles. Where states can and must compete is over shares of the world markets, and markets not only of today but tomorrow. The state which can design its own educational system, find and run its own research centres and use its own procurement policies will be the one that stays ahead in the scientific race. A technical-determinist interpretation of recent world economic history gives an added incentive to governments, in alliance with scientists, to be first in catching the next long upswing. They will have an edge on others not only in economic growth but also in relative national power and influence. (Indeed, so hot has this kind of scientific competition become that the head of Control Data in Minneapolis early in the 1980s advocated the exclusion of Japanese students from American universities in order to make sure the United States maintained its lead in certain fields of communications technology!)

Political determinism

The other form of determinism which seeks to offer an explanation of the mounting disorder and uncertainty for the future is more prevalent in the United States than elsewhere. It attributes the disorder to the loss of American authority in the management of the world's monetary and trade relations, and this loss in turn to a redistribution of power in the international political system among a wider circle of states. In this circle, West Germany and Japan figure especially large, but it also includes on its fringes the Newly Indust-rializing Countries (NICs), such as South Korea, Mexico, Brazil, Taiwan, and the larger oil-producing states, notably Saudi Arabia. This view adduces as evidence such facts as their faster rates of economic growth, increase in wages and GNP, in market shares and monetary reserves. It refers to some of the setbacks to US foreign policy, such as the retreat from Vietnam, the OPEC price rise, the fall of the Shah of Iran, the stalemate in the Arab-Israeli conflict, the uncontested Soviet invasion of Afghanistan – and sometimes to domestic political events like the Watergate scandal or to developments like the increase in Congressional intervention in foreign policy-making.

But it rests on a rather narrow (and old-fashioned) understanding of power in world politics – an understanding which is totally blind to the idea of structural power (i.e. power to shape and mould the structures of production, knowledge, security and credit within which others have no choice but to live if they are to participate in the world market economy). It takes power to be based on 'tangible resources that can be employed to affect the behaviour of others in desired directions'.[3] In this 'basic force model' the political analyst can see if outcomes correspond to the relative endowment of actors (states) with tangible and known capabilities. According to Keohane, it follows that power is the obverse of dependence and can be discerned in international monetary matters by the ability of a government to influence the behaviour of others relative to its own dependence on the financial actions of others. Phrased thus, it could be interpreted as embracing structural power (e.g. the power to raise interest rates worldwide). But in fact, Keohane attributes the so-called 'breakdown of Bretton Woods' in 1971 to the decline of American power from the high point attained towards the end of the Second World War (Keohane, 1984).

'The decline of American power', he argued 'is a necessary condition for the collapse of the regime, since had the United States remained as dominant as it was in the late 1940s it could have forced its partners to revalue periodically while keeping gold at $35 an ounce.' (Keohane, 1982, p. 16). Keohane has argued that the United States in 1971 (and later) was therefore in a weak bargaining position and was no longer able to use its power to sustain the Bretton Woods system. But this interpretation totally misunderstands the meaning of power, and gravely misrepresents the reasons why the Bretton Woods system had become unsustainable. It was true that power to maintain order had been lost, but not to other states so much as to market forces liberated by the conscious decisions of the United States aided by Britain. And it had been lost because the United States had used its exorbitant privilege as the centre country of a gold-exchange system to run a perpetual balance of payments deficit and to finance a distant and expensive war in Vietnam by inflationary credit creation rather than by a transfer of resources from the civilians to the military by means of taxation.

Keohane wrote:

> Other countries held large quantities of dollars which the United States was required to redeem for gold at the fixed price of $35 an ounce. *In order to preserve the regime the United States would have had to follow policies that would convince the holders of those dollars* (and after the change in the rules in 1968, the central banks holding dollars) *not to present them for redemption into gold.* This meant that United States macroeconomic policies would have been dependent on the financial decisions of foreign central banks (Keohane, 1982, p. 15, my italics).

But the 'fixed price' of gold had been fixed by the United States and could at any time have been refixed at a higher price. Moreover, it was the United States which made the decisions which weakened the regime. It was the United States which chose not to follow policies sufficient to persuade the dollar-holders to be content *not* to ask for gold in exchange. And it was the United States which took the decision in August 1971 to bring about the system's collapse by suspending convertibility of dollars into gold, imposing an import surcharge and leaving it to the markets to determine exchange rates. Instead of attempting a negotiated realignment in the summer of 1971, Nixon and Connally used their power and that of the markets to bring about a forcible revaluation of the yen and the D-mark and a devaluation of the dollar.

Some while before Keohane wrote the above, however, the hegemonic interpretation of world monetary history had been popularized by others – notably Charles Kindleberger and Robert Gilpin. Kindleberger had written an interesting and scholarly study of the interwar depression, in which he had concluded in his final chapter that the underlying explanation of why the world economy had fallen so deeply into depression in the 1930s, and had taken so long to recover, was that it coincided with a kind of interregnum in hegemonic economic power. Britain in the interwar period, Kindleberger argued (Kindleberger, 1973), had no longer been able to fulfil the role of hegemon, while the United States had been unwilling to do so. The argument was explicitly based on the premise that the world required a top-currency country, or hegemon, which was able to provide the other countries in the system with a stable, usable currency, and with an ever-open door to their exports even when these were unwanted elsewhere. The hegemon, moreover, had to be prepared to provide credit as a lender of last resort when it was necessary to maintain confidence, to prevent panic in times of crisis in financial markets, and to sustain growth throughout the system by an unstinted outflow of capital for investment. Keohane implicitly accepted this premise and proceeded to argue that the costs and difficulties of acting as hegemon had become too burdensome because other countries had become unbiddable. 'Only by breaking the rules could the United States regain the freedom it demanded' (p. 15). What he does not ask himself is why the United States should demand the freedom to break the rules if it was no longer willing to accept the responsibilities incumbent on the hegemon. Or, whether, indeed, the system could be made to work in any other way than with such a hegemon.

Gilpin's views, based on the same premise, were clearer and less confused. Comparing the position of the United States in the post-1945 period with that of Britain in the pre-1914 period, he thought the British experience showed the costs to the hegemon's own economy to have been far too heavy. Capital went abroad instead of to domestic industry. Military and other burdens were accepted beyond the capacity of the economy to sustain. The system therefore contained the seeds of its own destruction. The United States would be well advised to divest itself of the role before, like Britain, it too damaged its economy beyond repair. Gilpin was not interested and did not consider what consequences followed for the rest of the participants in the system (Gilpin, 1975).

All these writers have had great influence on American thinking throughout the past decade. More recently, an economist, Mancur Olson, has produced yet more supporting ammunition for the political-determinist view of trends in the world economy – and specifically for the alleged decline in the power of the United States. Olson already had a wide reputation in American political science as well as economics for his earlier book, *The Logic of Collective Goods* (Olson, 1965), in which he developed an economic theory which accounted for the greater burdens which the United States was obliged to assume for military security and world economic development and the opportunities given to others to be 'free riders' enjoying the benefits without sharing the costs. In 1982, he produced a work of historical interpretation, *The Rise and Decline of Nations* (Olson, 1982), which (perhaps significantly) won immediate attention in American academic journals, but was less enthusiastically acclaimed elsewhere.[4]

Olson's explanation for the rapid rise of Germany and Japan and for the decline of Britain in the post-war period rested on the proposition that the power of states in a world market economy depended on the speed with which new technologies were developed and adopted, and the degrees of freedom allowed to new competitors to challenge established enterprises. Wars and foreign invasions, he argued, broke up the political, social and industrial coalitions of status quo preserving interests and allowed the energy and enterprise of newcomers to accelerated investment, growth and the national dominance of foreign markets. According to this theory, the failure of the United States to maintain the dominant position it had had in the 1950s, therefore, was attributable to the comparative strength of change-resisting coalitions in American society and economy and their comparative weakness in the two most successful industrialized countries, Germany and Japan. Once again, the choices made and the decisions taken in US foreign economic policy were downplayed and depreciated as factors significantly contributing to the economic depression and disorders of the 1980s. The Washington bureaucracy and the politicians on Capitol Hill were not to blame because they had been betrayed by the loss of *élan* and adaptability, the progressive arthritis of American society. As a historical interpretation, Olson's exculpating version has something in common with the Nazis' interpretation of the end of the First World War – it was 'betrayal from within', not military defeat, that accounted for Germany's humiliation at Versailles.

In both cases, however, the facts suggest a somewhat different story. In the mid-1970s the United States was able to recover faster than others from the post-OPEC recession. And in all countries – Germany and Japan included – cartels and mergers have multiplied in recent hard times just as much as in the United States.[5] Facts, in short, suggest there is at least as much divergence, in terms of adaptability, between sectors as between states (cf. Duchene, 1984).

Other variants of determinism

There are some other less general and more explicit forms of determinism which equally serve to absolve policy-makers from blame. One similarly fatalistic idea, particularly common among economists, is that the troubles all started with the 'oil shock' and that this 'oil shock' was an 'exogenous factor' which somehow came from outside to undermine and disrupt the economic system.

R. C. Matthews, for instance, introducing a composite report by British economists on *Slower Growth in the Western World*, asserted that 'Most economists agree that the oil price rises of 1973–4 and 1979–80 had important adverse effects on real demand, both directly and by strengthening inflation, so leading to restrictive actions by governments. In so far as demand was responsible for the productivity slow-down, the oil price rise was thus an important constituent' (Matthews, 1982). Matthews refers several times to the view that the OPEC price rises could be regarded as exogenous shocks, and this view is shared by many fellow economists, especially in the United States where antipathy towards the Arabs is generally stronger than in Europe or Japan, and where the first oil shock produced a highly emotional wave of anger, resentment and hurt pride. In such emotional states, it is natural to look elsewhere for a scapegoat.

Beguiling as this interpretation may be, it does not explain why the world economy proved so resilient at other times to other 'exogenous shocks' – the post-war adjustment in the 1940s, the Korean War in the 1950s. Why did policy-makers then respond so much more readily to a challenge? Why, in the 1970s was it left to the banks and the private sector to adapt to change? From the oil producers' side the story was certainly somewhat different. In two ways, the structures of the world economy had worked against them. For over half a century, and especially during the 1950s and 1960s, the structure of the world's oil industry had allowed the companies to keep profits up to finance new exploration, and other costs and oil prices down in order to expand sales. It was only when demand throughout the world did in fact expand very rapidly in the 1970s, even bringing the United States into the market as a net importer, that the oil-producing governments were at last able to use market forces as an ally in raising prices to the consumers. Having achieved that power through the Tehran Agreement of 1971, they then found that the extra dollars they had managed to wring out of the oil companies were being rather quickly depreciated as a result of US inflation and American domination of the international monetary system. Resort to floating rates seemed like an indefinite licence to Washington to devalue the dollar, while the final slamming of the gold window in 1971 had already put the world on a paper dollar standard instead of a (nominal) gold exchange standard.

This view of the oil price rises of 1973, not as an exogenous shock, but as a rational response to an unstable and inequitable international monetary system, is largely shared by most of the authoritative writers on the oil industry.[6] And John Blair's masterly book, *The Control of Oil*, added the ironic point that it was the United States itself which had done most to make it so abrupt. Had it not pursued for so long the 'Drain America First' policy of keeping US domestic oil prices, and therefore output from US oilfields, so high, the shift in the balance of power in world markets from consumers to producers would have been much more gradual (Blair, 1977). Moreover, the United States had further set the stage for its own vulnerability, first by giving a free hand to the oil companies in their political relations with the Middle East, and secondly by allowing them to treat royalties to OPEC governments as a tax-allowable expense in the United States. Both these factors laid the oil companies wide open to pressure from the governments of oil-producing states in 1971, and even more so in 1973. There is even a suggestion that the oil companies actually encouraged the OPEC price rise, if not the oil embargo on states like the Netherlands considered too friendly to Israel. Certainly, their profits in the mid-1970s were better than they had been when the oil price was lower. At the same time, as Mikdashi and others pointed out, the 'shock' administered by OPEC in 1973 soon lost its force as inflation gathered speed again and overtook and largely cancelled it out in real terms.

Other interpretations

At the risk of grossly oversimplifying all their differences, other commentators on the economic upheavals of the 1980s could be placed, in political terms, into two camps. The protagonists of the first blame governments for making things worse than they need have been – in other words they think governments interfered too much; the market should have played a bigger role, the state a smaller one. Those in the second camp, however, think that governments made things worse by not interfering enough, and by being not too active but too passive in relation to the market economy. There is a more fundamental view still – that of the neo-marxists and radicals – which sees both the state and the economy – in other words the capitalist system itself – as the ultimate source of the trouble. On the whole, since the aim is not to pin labels but to identify opinions and interpretations which overlook the monetary aspect of the problem and those which, on the contrary, ascribe a fairly central place to monetary policies and developments, it may be best to proceed by looking at each of these three approaches in turn.

All share, it might be noted in passing, a common tendency in the great majority of commentators to be wise after the event. As in the roaring twenties, so in the swinging sixties, the warning voices who said *at the time* that times were too good to last were far outnumbered by those who later looked back and discovered the errors that made escaping the depression or learning to live through it harder than it need have been.

A major and obvious exception is, of course, Robert Triffin. His analysis of the international monetary system from the nineteenth century onwards until the 1980s repeatedly and unfalteringly focused on the creation of credit as the central issue. It was Triffin who, from 1958 onwards, steadfastly and patiently explained the weakness and vulnerability first of the gold-exchange system and then of the paper-dollar standard and intermittently-managed floating (Triffin, 1964; 1966). Against the rest of his profession, Triffin argued that floating was neither a panacea nor even a matter of central concern. Rather, it was the irresponsibility of the United States in first allowing the over-lavish creation of credit, and then bringing about its drastic contradiction, that lay at the root of other troubles. His decision to revert from American to Belgian citizenship reflected his concern for Europe's dependence on the United States, and hence for European vulnerability to the consequences of American policy decisions. Triffin was and always has been a fundamentalist among economists. No half-measures sufficed. He was convinced that the only ultimate solution lay in a world central bank and a truly international reserve asset. Like Reinhold Niebuhr's solution to the problem of war, this analysis of inflation and recession was too prophetic and idealistic to gain popular political support or to have much practical influence on the day-to-day discussions of monetary managers.

Although both those who believe the scales have been tipped too far in the direction of the market and those who believe them to have been tipped too far in favour of the state coexist on both sides of the Atlantic and the Pacific, it is probably true to say that pro-market opinion is still stronger in America and pro-state opinion stronger in Europe. The situation in Japan is more complicated because opinions there start from an assumption of state involvement in the economy, and of the loyalty of industry and finance to the state, that far exceeds anything in Europe; yet in international economic relations, the conviction is stronger than in either Europe or America that governments should allow market forces to operate much more freely than they do now.

Pro-market opinion criticizes the state for interfering with markets for goods and services and with markets for factors of production – more especially with the labour market and money markets, with wages and with the money supply which affects price levels and income distribution throughout the system. Individual economists will differ as to which form of interference is the most damaging. Those concerned with international trade, and especially those connected directly or indirectly with GATT, the IMF or the OECD tend to be highly critical of national policies which obstruct or distort trade – with quota restrictions, subsidies, procurement policies, and state support for national industries both privately and publicly owned. They even attack regional policies which they say only make economic adjustment to change more difficult because they introduce rigidities into relative prices. The longer such state interference continues, it is argued, the harder it is for workers, farmers, managers and whole sectors of industry to accept change and for the national economy itself to compete in the world market.[7] The implication is clear that the world depression would have been less severe, and recovery quicker, if all of these self-indulgent practices had been forsworn altogether at the beginning of the decade.

The element of truth in this of course is that protective measures do become harder to change as time goes on. But it does not necessarily follow that the longer they are maintained the greater the inefficiency imposed on the economy as a whole, and the longer the recovery of demand is deferred. Where sectors of industry suffer acutely from cyclical variations in demand, for instance, the economy as a whole might be more damaged by throwing the whole workforce out of their jobs, thus increasing the fall in demand for other sectors, than it would be keeping them at work until the cycle turns. It will all depend on whether the forces of change are permanent or temporary. The point simply is that markets left to themselves can be wasteful and unstable as well as swift in reshuffling the resources that make up the pack of productive cards for an economic system. It may well be that there is a sort of critical threshold beyond which it is dangerous for a national economy to go in matters of protective cushioning for parts of the mechanism.

The problem is, however, that no one knows where that threshold lies. Moreover, the constant emphasis of such argument on the need to compete with others overlooks the fact, already referred to, that the level of demand in the international system is not only affected by market restrictions but also by the rate of growth in global credit and thus the level of confidence in the future.

The error of the state in interfering over-indulgently with markets and trade is seen as complementary to the errors of over-indulgence committed in monetary policy. Broadly speaking, the monetarist economists see depression as the natural, deserved and to some extent inevitable consequence of the previous inflation. Like a hangover after an ill-advised alcoholic binge, it is no more than the victim's just deserts. Thus their theorizing concentrates more upon how the initial inflation was generated than upon the processes by which, when 'correction' is applied, painful consequences for growth, employment, and trade necessarily follow (Friedman 1977; and cf. Mayer 1980).

The monetarist viewpoint blames the incompetence and feebleness of will of the state (or sometimes the 'unnatural' power of organized labour), not the economic system itself. And it does so because it makes the basic assumption of neo-classical theory going back to Walras, and even to Say, that the system has a natural tendency to equilibrium.[8] Hence, perhaps, the tendency to express theoretical propositions and models in algebra, because algebra is a means of communication based on the idea of balance between the right and left sides of the equation.

Much of this conventional 'liberal' theory, moreover, when it is not totally abstract and mathematical but tries to relate the equations and models to the real world, insists on treating national economic systems as if they were (1) totally isolated from the rest of the world, and (2) equally open to it. Each individual government can then be blamed – since it is never the system's fault – for the excesses of inflation or recession. Since market operators act on equal terms and with equal power – or so it is unconsciously assumed – the decision of the market must be fair and just and must not be interfered with. The element of ideology involved, especially in the United States, is of course largely unconscious. But it is nevertheless powerful and insidious – as demonstrated by the evangelism shown by some of its trainees and converts in other countries.

Not only national economies but markets are treated as though they functioned in a sealed box, immune from all but 'exogenous shocks'. The reality (as any political economist is acutely aware) is that each market is at the mercy of others, and in turn its own demand, supply and price affects other markets. This is patently obvious, even though it certainly complicates the task of description let along explanation. I have already discussed this in relation to oil, but it is true also of copper and aluminium, of shipping and insurance, of housing and timber, maize and beef – and would be so, even if each in turn were not *inevitably* subject to the influence, if not the deliberate intervention, of the state.

Another major weakness in much monetary theorizing is the exclusion of all consideration of the nature of financial institutions and markets as generators of money. Much monetarist theory is thus unable – in fact, often does not even try – to explain the recurrence of financial instability in capitalist systems. Money is treated as just another commodity, with a supply that responds to demand, and not as something quite different from commodities. But this is misleading because of the creation of money (especially in the form of credit) confers power as well as wealth on the creator. There is therefore a constant tension between the private creators and the public ones, between banks (and indeed, now, some non-banks) and the state.

This is well understood by economic historians and by a rare few who have spent a lifetime trying to teach students about the working of financial and banking systems. Most notable among these is Hyman Minsky.

Minsky's 'Financial Instability Hypothesis' is worth quoting for it is both succinct and to the point.

> A capitalist economy with sophisticated financial institutions is capable of a number of modes of behaviour and the mode that actually rules at any time depends upon institutional relations, the structure of financial linkages and the history of the economy. (Minsky 1982)

By financial linkages, he is referring to the relation of two sets of prices – prices of current output and prices of capital assets. The mark of a functioning capitalist system is that the relationship between these two sets of prices should be such as to allow a balance between 'money today' and 'money tomorrow', between consumption and investment. With other self-styled 'post-Keynesians', Minsky stresses the importance of bringing time and uncertainty back into the analysis of people's decisions about borrowing and lending (and in what form) so as to direct attention to these two sets of prices.[9]

> Prices of capital assets depend on current views of future profits (quasi-rent) flows and the current subjective view placed upon the insurance against uncertainty embodied in money or quick cash; these current views depend upon the expectations that are held about the longer run development of the economy. (Minsky, 1982 p. 8)

Taking Keynesian theory a step further, it is the flows of funds resulting from past financing decisions through financial institutions public and private that influenced the linkage between the two sets of prices and therefore both inflation and depression. Minsky's argument, grossly oversimplified, is that, by paying attention to the linkage and the intermediating institutions of the market and the influence of historical expectations on people's preferences and judgement, one can trace the route which would lead to financial crisis. The extent and nature of the crisis would then be moderated (or otherwise) by central bank behaviour, government deficits, gross profit flows and the balance of payments. His conclusion is that the way out 'lies through shifting policy from the encouragement of growth through investment to the achievement of full employment through consumption production.'

However, apart from the mention of the balance of payments, Minsky in common with many of his fellow-Keynesians still presents the argument largely in single-economy terms, and the lay reader is not sure whether these plausible arguments still hold when applied to an international economy in which funds flow in response to yet more variables – notably the price of oil, the size of the US deficit and the means currently chosen for financing it, interest rates and investment risks of various kinds including exchange and national debt profits.

In general I think it fair to say that most other post-Keynesians were less inclined than Minsky to find the explanation *within the system* and were inclined to put the blame on governments for applying the wrong deflationary policies, whether for political reasons to curb the power of organized labour, or for economic reasons that recovery could be achieved by checking inflation and avoiding deficits on current accounts in the balance of payments. Michael Bruno, for example, blames the United States, UK and Japan, in particular, for obstructing the necessary adjustment to 'supply shocks'. The observed productivity slowdown is thus directly linked to the choice of short-term and medium-term macroeconomic response strategy (Fitoussi, 1982). Many academic economists, beguiled with elegant theory, also paid far too little attention either to the institutional frameworks within which credit is created, or to the influence of past economic experience or the preferences of government in different countries.

Others are to be found straying further and further still into a sort of post-Galbraithian realm of socio-political analysis, paying much more attention both to his point about the power of large corporations to administer prices (and thus to supplant or distort the market) and to corresponding (but hardly countervailing) power of labour to hold real wages up and to delay the loss of jobs.[10] Yet, for all their shortcomings, it has clearly been the monetarists' explanations which have received most attention in the economic literature, at least in English language journals. During the mid-1970s events and popular perceptions of what was going on both told against the opposite Keynesian view that national economies were in a mess because governments lacked the courage and conviction for decisive intervention. Meghnad Desai, writing mainly of the British experience, says that the tide both for policy and for theoretical interpretation was turned between 1974, when the House of Commons Select Committee on Public Expenditure heard only one monetarist advocate, David Laidler, and 1976, when Callaghan as a Labour Prime Minister addressing a Labour Party Conference pointed to high wages as the cause of rising unemployment, and allowed Denis Healey to override objections in the British Cabinet to the monetarist conditions demanded for an IMF loan. In those two years Friedman and Hayek got Nobel prizes and, according to Desai, 'the majority of younger economists were now willing to admit the relevance if not superiority of the monetarist framework in explaining the hyperinflation of 1974 and 1975' (Desai, 1981, p. 9). Only the older Keynesians (Joan Robinson, Lord Kahn, Nicholas Kaldor and, in America, J. K. Galbraith) stuck to their guns. Although Desai, in common with many economists, believes (1) that sophisticated quantitative techniques can be used to test the comparative efficacy of monetarist policies and Keynesian demand-management policies; and (2) that policymakers will be swayed by the impartial findings of such tests, neither proposition is one which political economists or monetary historians can easily accept. However sophisticated the quantitative technique, there are too many variables in a real economy (some of a non-quantitative nature) to be able to tell for sure that would have happened in the alternative case. And there is also ample evidence that economic theories are like detergents on a supermarket shelf. Politicians decide on other grounds what ends they wish to achieve and will pick on the appropriate legitimating economic theory as a shopper picks off the shelf the detergent that suits the kind of washing or cleaning he or she wants to do.

In the mid-1970s, partly in consequence of volatile oil prices, but partly also because of the resort to floating rates, the British were rediscovering the vicious circle of weak currency – dearer imports – added inflationary pressures – bigger wage demands – more inflation – weak currency, etc. The balance of political opinion shifted – as Jim Callaghan was shrewd enough to see – away from the Keynesian

and toward the monetarist view, away from wages and incomes solutions
to monetary stringency and spending cuts. The same experience and
the same popular and political reaction came in the United States
somewhat later, in 1979. It had nothing whatever to do with Desai's
'objective scientific criteria for choosing between rival explanations
of the same observable phenomena'. People even in the Labour Party,
or the Democratic Party, became convinced that more government
spending, starting from a base already high, would not remedy
unemployment but it would worsen inflation. The Phillips Curve,
which presupposed a freedom of choice for governments to decide
which trade off between the rate of change in wages and the rate
of change in the jobs available, had lost its magic and was subjected
to increasingly critical attack.

But the majority of both monetarists and Keynesians were apt to
look for explanation within too narrowly national a framework. Consequently, their explanations failed to account for the very different
experiences in the mid-1970s of weak currency countries, like Britain
and Italy, and strong currency countries, like Germany or Switzerland,
or between those like Japan, who managed to adjust quickly to their
oil deficit, and those like the United States who found it difficult.
In both camps, the interpretations offered by those who took a global
view made a good deal more sense.

Among the Keynesians, there have been a number of development
economists who took the same view, roughly speaking, about the
1970s and 1980s that Arthur Lewis took about the 1930s. World
economic depression was exacerbated by the lack of purchasing power
of the primary producing developing countries, and especially those
now dependent on imported oil. The lack was made good with credit
from the banking system after the first oil price rise but became acute
with the shrinkage of credit and the slowing of growth in the major
market economies in the early 1980s. Most of these 'global Keynesians'
are to be found in the World Bank and other international organizations, and in academic circles concerned with the political economy of
developing countries. Like the members of the Brandt Commission,
with whose findings many would agree, at least in part, the policy probably comes first – massive resource transfers to the developing countries
of the South, preferably from a World Development Fund set up by
collective international agreement. The explanatory theory follows.

Its strongest feature, in my opinion, is the implied criticism of redistributive countercyclical public policy when it is confined to small or even medium-sized national economies for its inadequacy to the size of the problem. In the 1930s, when government spending constituted around 15 to 20 per cent at the very most of GNP, deficit financing could be undertaken without marked results on the interest rate structure. (Indeed, at the time the British government, like others, was busy forcibly substituting 3 per cent government stock for old 5 per cent War Loan.) And measures of income redistribution could be undertaken (food stamps in the United States, the National Rehabilitation Administration and other New Deal policies) that had a sharp and immediate effect on demand and consumption. Now, for a variety of reasons (defence, social welfare, medicine and education, support of ailing industries), an increase in government spending has unavoidable counterproductive effects – raising interest rates and reviving inflationary forces – all of which serve to undermine confidence and do little to revive investment. Moreover, because unemployment and social security payments run at fairly high levels (not to mention a thriving black economy), redistributive income policies do less to affect demand and business confidence than would a reduction in the rate of interest.

A similar objection can be made to much nationalist or neo-mercantilist reaction to the world depression – that it is too narrowminded and ignores the global nature of the problem. This new nationalism is better represented in the press, the media and in political discussion than it is in the academic literature.[11] Basically, the argument is somewhat fatalistic, like the long-wave determinists: there is little that can be done at this late stage so it is a matter of *sauve qui peut* and *chacun pour soi*. In Britain, the so-called Cambridge school has advocated import controls, and has found some support for the idea in industry and the Labour Party. It is also, I think, implicit in Christian Stoffaes' bestselling book about French policy (Stoffaes 1979) – though that at least takes the point that international competition for markets for manufacturers is now so far gone that national companies if they are to survive cannot do so on the basis of the national economy alone. They therefore need state support and encouragement to be able to hold their market shares abroad, and state control to stop them shifting too much production overseas too fast and too soon. Yet French experience in the 1980s has clearly shown that national remedies are not enough.

Similarly, among monetarists, it is the relative minority, who have adopted a broader definition of money, and have looked at the expansion of credit in the world market economy in the 1970s, rather than at the monetary bases of *national* economies, who seem to have made more plausible explanations of the past inflation and deflation and offered more promising remedies for the depression. They might be aptly described as 'global monetarist'.

One of the best-known and most effective proponents of this approach has been Professor Ronald McKinnon. Much of his argument, though, rests on a restricted view of what constitutes the world money supply, suggesting that it is based on national official reserves of gold, dollars and other foreign exchange, and IMF drawing rights. This gives insufficient attention, in my view, to the flows of funds stressed by Minsky. In the international capital markets these flows have been larger than shifts in official reserves and have borne little relation to the expansion in Euromarket loans. Thus, an argument which rests, as I understand it, on the supposition that when other central banks sell dollars to stop the weakening of their own currencies they will decrease their national money supply base because they will be buying francs, lira or pounds from the private sector, does not necessarily follow.

However, McKinnon is right in observing that there exists in the international monetary system a monetary cycle alongside the business cycle, and that tensions in the two fields have a multiplying effect upon each other; that US interest rates determine Euromarket rates and these govern the largest part of the international capital movements. All this is borne out by recent experience, as is the observation that 'the idea that floating exchange rates would give countries autonomy with respect to their monetary development has proved an illusion' (McKinnon, 1982, p. 23).

Some while ago, McKinnon argued forcibly for a coordination of US, West German and Japanese monetary policy in order to reduce the volatility and disruptive uncertainty in exchange rates and to stabilize, between them, the global money supply and prices (McKinnon, 1974). He has reiterated this proposal and it has been popular among economists. Unfortunately, the political reality is that there is an asymmetry between the vulnerability of Japanese and German financial markets to US policy and, conversely the invulnerability of the United States to German or Japanese policy. This means that both Germany and Japan would have to be prepared to accept a permanent loss of monetary autonomy. Today, they may not have much autonomy but they can still hope one day to regain it.

Politically, therefore, the proposal is naive and pays too little attention not only to the divergence of real national interests, but also to the deeper differences as to what each perceives as the general interest of the world economy and the international community.

A more pessimistic, but also more realistic appraisal was that of the late Milton Gilbert. Gilbert was an American economist who worked for 10 years in the 1950s for the old OEEC, and then for 15 years as economic advisor to the Bank for International Settlements; a posthumously edited book about the evolution of the international monetary system from Bretton Woods to the mid-1970s ends as follows:

> The problem for the monetary authorities in the 1980s and beyond will be how to maintain exchange stability in a fundamentally unstable environment; the march of events has often been described as being the result of impersonal and mysterious forces. But as I have seen it, the force and determination of political leadership, or lack of it, is a key element in the chemical compound of monetary affairs (Gilbert, 1980, p. 236).

In Gilbert's view, the blame for the inflation and, by implication, for the ensuing depression, lay primarily with the United States. This was for two main reasons: first for allowing such a huge deficit 'much beyond the system's reasonable need for liquidity' to develop; and then (when the US did intervene in late 1978), for being inhibited about using temporary direct controls as a shock weapon to restore order and confidence. The United States had also, in Gilbert's view, been wrong to let the Group of Ten consultative mechanism fall into disuse; he thought it should be revitalized.

Another and most recent practitioner's view – that of the former head of the IMF, Johannes Witteveen – also blames the United States essentially for overlooking the international aspect, and impact, of its monetary policy under Paul Volcker.[12] Keeping the monetary target within limits required such large charges in interest rates that it actually increased uncertainty and fostered, rather than restrained, the shift to short-term assets reflecting rational precautionary and speculative motives for increased liquidity preference. He pointed out that the increase between the end of 1978 and May 1982 of chequable deposits (i.e. accounts on which cheques may be drawn) in the United States as a proportion of all deposits from 2 to 20 per cent was a major factor increasing the fragility of the system.

Marxist versions

The marxist literature that directly addresses the question of why depression hit the world economy in the 1980s in the way and at the time it did is neither extensive nor well-known outside left-wing bookshops and journals. But for serious students of international political economy or history, what there is of it should neither be under-rated nor overlooked – and not simply because of its powerful appeal to many victims of that depression. For although Wall Street and Greenwich Village (or the City and Hampstead, the Bourse and the Left Bank) seldom speak to each other – and have difficulty understanding one another's language when they do – the gulf dividing them on this issue is neither so wide nor so unbridgable as ideology on each side would have them believe. When it comes to analysis, some of the more thoughtful and observant of the marxists are not too far distant in their comments from some of the more thoughtful and observant of the financial conservatives.

If this depression is different from others that came before it, it is chiefly because of some radical and rapid changes that have taken place in the last 15 or 20 years in the world credit system and banking, and consequently in the structure of production. Yet many marxists are inclined neither by training nor interest to delve into the intricacies of the Eurocurrency markets and the niceties of foreign exchange markets. Banking is seen as a sordid, despicable and antisocial activity; the politics of international monetary diplomacy or the technicalities of banking innovation and regulation seem distant from the welfare of the working class, and therefore uninteresting.

Taking in the monetary aspects of the world depression – which I believe to be central to the story – is thus by definition a minority pastime on the Left. It is only a few, therefore, that have perceived the main weakness of a modern global capitalist system to lie, not in the exploitation of labour nor in the oppression of the working class, but in the inability of its leading governments to run a monetary system stable and viable enough to sustain a global production system.

And there is a much more fundamental point about Western marxism which has been admirably explained and documented by Perry Anderson. In his *Consideration on Western Marxism*, he traces the divorce of theory from praxis – the 'scission between socialist theory and working-class practice', which Marx always said was so important – to the disappointment arising from the failures of proletarian revolution in Europe after the First World War, and the enforced sojourn thereafter of many marxists in a political wilderness. The gulf opened up by the imperialist isolation of the Soviet state was institutionally widened and fixed by the bureaucratization of the USSR and by Soviet domination of the Comintern under Stalin. The result, he says, was

> a seclusion of theorists in universities far from the life of the proletariat in their own countries and a contraction of theory from economics and politics into philosophy. This specialization was accompanied by an increasing difficulty of language whose technical barriers were a function of its distance from the masses. (Anderson, 1976, pp. 92–3)

This seclusion was accentuated in the United States by the bitter disillusion with the Soviet ally in the late 1940s, and the brutal alienation of the American left in the McCarthy period and since. One might add that this long separation accounted both for the rejoicing – premature as it turned out – at the shortlived reunion of workers and intellectuals in Paris and elsewhere in 1968; and also for the continuing lack of interest of the great majority of marxist intellectuals in the profound and important changes that have taken place in industry, trade and above all, finance. In Latin America, it is true, the 'scission' is far less apparent, and there has consequently been far more lively discussion of the relations between theory and

praxis – particularly marxist, structuralist and *dependencia* theory –
and much more serious empirical studies in political economy than
in any other part of the third world. But the focus has generally been
on the impact of international finance, production and trade on local
political and social systems, rather than on developments at the
international level. (See, for example, Cardoso and O'Donnell in
Collier, 1979; Cardoso and Faletto, 1979. and O'Donnell, 1973.)
Meanwhile, in Europe, most of the leading marxist writers have concentrated on loftier philosophical themes and have shown little interest
in contemporary economic developments (for example, Althusser,
1971; Poulantzas, 1973, 1978).

Little wonder, then, that the Left shares in good measure almost
all the shortcomings of non-marxist explanatory theorizing. It too
is confused, contradictory and uncertain. It too has difficulty escaping
from the mental straitjackets tailored by past experience. And the
majority of those who do write about world depression – like their
conservative or social-democratic counterparts – do not go far beyond
descriptive accounts of a worsening situation, nor do they attempt
to offer a logically satisfactory explanation.

The Soviet literature, so far as I am aware, is even thinner. Although
it is predictably critical of the United States for its exploitation of
the role of the dollar, it shows curiously little interest in such key
questions as why the recession of the 1970s was so shortlived and
that of the 1980s so persistent. Not only is there little technical
comprehension of such important debates as occurred over the use
of SDRs, the deregulation of banking or the limitations of the European Monetary System, but even the general analysis remains on a
very general and superficial level. Possibly marxist ideology, as well
as ignorance, inhibits explanation. For if all capitalist systems are
inherently self-destructive it cannot be admitted that good government
could have overcome difficulties that proved too much for bad
government.

Only a relatively small group of marxist writers, scattered by age,
as well as nationality, are the exceptions to this generalization. In
them can be seen the two great strengths of the marxist approach:
a historical perspective which offers a longer and cooler view of
changes in the world economy; and a systematic vision which tran-
scends the differences in national economies and national experience.

In neither respect, of course, are the marxists alone. Many non-marxists (Hirschman, Arthur Lewis, Paul Streeten, Michael Lipton, as well as Braudel and Perroux) also take a long view, and look at the system broadly, rather than in narrowly national and international terms.

This is true even of a self-styled marxist like Arghiri Emmanuel, whom others repudiate as a heretical deviant.[13] Emmanuel's work has probably been translated into as many different languages as any other. His explanation of the unequal distribution of wealth in the world economy, and the unequal terms of North–South, rich–poor trade is truly systematic (Emmanuel 1971; 1976). His analysis rests on the contradiction between the mobility of capital and credit, moving freely from country to country, and the immobility of labour, prevented by immigration laws from responding to differential wages in national economies. Trade, and incomes, thus become unequal and high wages are maintained in industrial countries, while wages for exactly the same kind of work remain low in the developing countries. When goods are exchanged, the low-wage country is paid for its products at low prices, the high-wage country at high prices. By contrast, liberal economists usually take the limitation of migration for granted, as if it were an inherent, rather than a politically-imposed characteristic of the system; nor do they inquire closely into the explanation of wage differentials.

The acclaim given to Immanuel Wallerstein's work in recent years rests on a similar ability to depict the totality of a world system where others see only a kaleidoscope of states. In *The World System*, a study of European agriculture in the sixteenth century, and then in a book of collected articles, *The Capitalist World Economy*, Wallerstein raised the eyes of a new generation of American students from the post-1945 economic problems with which their current-affairs textbooks had made them familiar, to the more profound issues of social and economic change over long periods of time. (See also Hopkins and Wallerstein, 1982; and Wallerstein, 1974, 1979.) The same applies to the work of Johann Galtung, who has followed Perroux's lead in discussing the world system in terms of core and periphery, but who would probably describe himself as a structuralist rather than a marxist. (Galtung, 1975; cf. Gunder Frank, 1966.) Neither Galtung nor Wallerstein, however, have been much concerned with the origins and analysis of the world depression of the 1980s or the monetary development of the previous decade.

More directly relevant to such questions has been the work of an Egyptian marxist, Samir Amin. His book, *Class and Nation, Historically and in the Current Crisis* directs attention to the major differences between this depression and early ones, which is that is has coincided with very rapid internationalization of production through the preferential access to capital and technology enjoyed by the multinational corporation. The acceleration of change in the international division of labour, whereby yesterday's producers of food and raw materials become today's producers of shoes, shirts, ships, cars and TV sets, is largely attributable to the expansion of Euromarkets and the internationalization of banking. The results in one part of the world economy – structural unemployment, declining industries, uncertainty and failing confidence – are directly linked to the results in the other part – authoritarianism in government, expansion of the public sector, and nationalization of foreign enterprises, urban slums and low wages.

Amin's argument links the relations of international capital (in the shape of banks and multinationals) with governments 'at home' in the OECD countries, with their relations with third world governments. Through the greater mobility of capital and technology they are able to compensate for the falling rate of profit at home by shifting operations to countries where more surplus value can be extracted from low-wage labour. Easy credit and fast growth rates allow the peripheral countries to pay the price for both the borrowed capital and technology, and for the food which they find it increasingly necessary to import.

Amin sees the capitalists engaged in transnational manufacturing, processing or services as confronted both by a militant working class at home and a hostile national bourgeoisie in the periphery. They cannot afford to fight both at the same time. So they avoid open conflict with the former by cooperating with governments in neo-corporatist incomes policies; and with the latter by sharing with them the proceeds of exploitation. They are indifferent to whether those in power in third world states, are democratic or repressive, militarist or civilian, one-party or pluralist, provided only that the regime is stable enough to maintain international financial and commercial confidence.[14]

Amin concludes that as long as these underlying conditions of the new international division of labour persist, there is no possibility of serious North–South negotiations. He does not see the apocalyptic collapse of the capitalist system, but rather its transformation during the long period of slow growth and change that he sees in prospect. The transformation will come about through the break-up both of alliances between states and of alliances of class interests within states and across state frontiers. Like many left-wing writers in Latin America, including Cardoso and O'Donnell, Amin is familiar enough with the realities of third world politics to recognize that not everything can be blamed on the world capitalist system. The inability of so many governments to solve the problem of rural poverty is a major factor ensuring their continued dependency, in one form or another, on the centres of financial, managerial and information power.

More generally speaking, however, there are two aspects of marxist criticism which should be of interest to more conservative minds: their analysis of the inflationary policies pursued by the United States and others from the mid-1960s on; and the critical analysis by some marxist writers of keynesian interpretations and solutions.

On the first point, most marxist writers agree with the monetarists (and with liberal historians like Kindleberger) that the stability of the system was fatally undermined once the United States, exercising what Jacques Rueff and General de Gaulle always called its exorbitant privileges under the gold exchange standard, abused its responsibilities as banker to the world and allowed the financial markets to bring the system down in ruins. The resort to floating rates was another Dunkirk – hardly a victory but a defeat carried off without total disaster. The 'paper-dollar standard' then adopted – the phrase is Triffin's – offered still more exorbitant privileges, and these were also abused as a weak dollar made up for the oil import bill on the US balance of payments and robbed the oil producers of much of the real value of the first price rise. The instability in the foreign exchange and other financial markets was reflected by the instability of commodity markets, exacerbating the impact of the oil price for many developing countries. The third world and the workers at home were the victims, and both were able to perceive the inherent contradictions and weaknesses of the system.

This, with some marxist embellishment, has been the theme elaborated for more popular consumption by Harry Magdoff and Paul Sweezy in issue after issue of the American left-wing *Monthly Review*. Their articles, collected together in *The Deepening Crisis of US Capitalism* (1969), show a lively awareness of economic trends, and an admirable refusal to be taken in by official apologies or by the academic benedictions so devastatingly lampooned by David Calleo in *The Imperious Economy* (1982). But Magdoff's pessimism does not even allow the possibility that the depression is cyclical and sooner or later will end. He sees it as structural and permanent, resulting from the inherent, strong, persistent and growing tendency for more surplus value to be produced than can find profitable investment outlets (Magdoff, 1969, p. 179). Since he believes that no one in the United States who counts for anything has the faintest idea what to do about it, the only possibility is for socialists to continue to work for the overthrow of the whole system by revolution.

In common with many monetarists, marxists see the inflation of 1965-70 as the necessary forerunner of subsequent deflation. But they add a twist to the conventional version. Besides stressing, as that does, the effects of government spending on defence, education, social security, etc., and the increased bargaining power of organized labour, some marxists have added the increasing tendency of governments, whatever their political labels, to disguise – in effect – the falling rate of profit by arranging a variety of covert handouts to corporations, and not only support for what the British call 'lame ducks', but all kinds of subsidy, tax reliefs, and tax deferrals, some of them so complex that only former tax inspectors turned tax consultants can fully understand their significance.

Others are critical of neo-classical literature for grossly underestimating the role of capital accumulation. The collection of explanations of slower growth, referred to earlier, included a marxist view by Andrew Glyn which makes this point:

> Faced with the long run relative constancy of the capital output ratio in different countries, despite varying rates of growth of the capital–labour ratio, they [the liberal economists] have to postulate diverse rates of technical progress which allowed a faster or slower rate of accumulation. Marxists would view the causation as being primarily

in the other direction: diverse rates of accumulation have brought with them different rates of productivity growth. (Glyn, in Matthews 1982, p. 149)

Glyn therefore addresses the question of capital accumulation suggesting (in common with many non-marxists) that the seeds of depression were sown by the inflationary policies of the previous decade. The weakness of the argument lies in the obsolete assumption that investment is governed by past accumulation of capital through profit. The fact is that the modernization and internationalization of banking have effectively divorced both the creation of and access to capital (i.e. credit) from the accumulation of capital. Glyn is stronger on his preferred ground – the consequences for the workers on the factory floor of management's response to the slowdown in productivity. While the 1930s brought in 'Fordism' (the label given to the relentless discipline of the assembly line), modern management has introduced the robot and the 'team production' system – still better methods of enforcing obedience and extracting surplus value from the workers.

Another marxist contribution likely to appeal to conservatives is the criticism of keynesian explanations for the present crisis, and more particularly keynesian prescriptions for recovery from it. A popular French marxist, who has avoided the more usual concern with abstruse philosophical issues, is Suzanne de Brunhoff (see de Brunhoff, 1976a, 1976b, 1978). Her book, *State, Capital and Economic Policy*, shares with Hirschman the perception that capitalism does not function in a totally capitalist context but is shaped by earlier modes and ideas, including mercantilism (Hirschman 1983). Quoting Marx in support, she finds such ideas reappearing from time to time, effectively dividing the capitalist class. Her criticism of keynesian theory and policy correctly (I think) judges the main purpose to have been psychological rather than purely economic or financial, for its aim was to dispel uncertainty about the future by using state policy to compensate for the perverse liquidity preferences of the capitalist. 'The link between the present and the future constituted mainly by credit was underwritten by the state which therefore changed the relationship between certain and the uncertain' (de Brunhoff, 1976, p. 121).

But her conclusions have not advanced much beyond those of the 1930s: the only remedy is to destroy the bourgeois state and with it the capitalist infrastructure. Although she does attribute the crisis of over-production in the world economy to the evolution of the international monetary system and the mismanagement of credit, at the end she can only repeat the conclusions reached over 40 years ago by Maurice Dobb and Michael Kalecki that the system leaves the capitalist class with the choice between renewed inflation, fascism and repression and unemployment.[15] Recently, she says all three have been adopted with the consequent erosion of the capitalist consensus established after the Second World War. Fairly predictably, this is indeed the majority view among marxists. Only here and there is the thought emerging that integration has gone so far now that the establishment of a 'pure' socialist state is no longer feasible.[16]

To my mind, a much more profound criticism of neo-keynesian theories and solutions is to be found in the work of Ernest Mandel, a Belgian trotskyist banned from the United States who is the author of *Late Capitalism* and *The Second Slump* (Mandel, 1977, 1978).[17] Mandel is equally sceptical of both the liberal/monetarist and socialist governments. Like other marxists, he believes that increased capital inputs in production, by recruiting labour from the reserve army of the unemployed (women and *Gastarbeiter*) shrink that army in the long run, while new opportunities for profitable productive investment become fewer, and governments are led to choose policies which postpone or mask the consequent decline in the rate of profit. The classical overproduction crisis was limited in depth and duration by deficit spending and a large-scale expansion of credit, but marked by a clearly declining efficacy of these anticrisis techniques to avert a repetition of the interwar depression.

Unlike many left-wing Europeans, however, Mandel does not think that pump-priming keynesian solutions will work: 'A rise in household incomes really primes the cycle only if it is accompanied by a rise in the rate of profit *and a prospect of generalized expansion of the market*' (Mandel, 1977, p. 177, my italics). But since this market is now global, and as bank lending declines, this third necessary condition frustrates the policy. Nor will liberal solutions work, because in depressions self-interest (for the worker, the enterprise, and the

State) lead each into conflict, not cooperation, with others. Thus, it is a common illusion that national economic recovery can be achieved by export growth in such times. Equally, the 'strength through austerity' policies now propounded by Mitterrand in France, de la Madrid in Mexico and advocated by the late Enrico Berlinguer in Italy, will be no more effective than were those of Stafford Cripps after the war. Galbraithian ideas about neo-corporatist negotiations of incomes policies and 'sharing austerity' only lead in practice, says Mandel, to a reduction in the workers' real living standards. Nor is it true that if consumption is held down by such policies, investment will automatically rise. For, besides consumption and productive investment, there is a third hand dipping greedily into the GNP pot – the unproductive spending of governments and corporate bureaucracies whose pre-emptive power is far greater than either of the other two. The mixed economy therefore is 'a dangerous and disorientating myth', a 'trap for the working class'. Yet, despite the acuteness of his analysis, Mandel like many others clings to the illusion that workers, North and South, share a common interest, and that the solidarity of the international proletariat must still be the goal.

Bob Rowthorn, an English marxist whose work, like Stephen Hymer's, is read in business schools, agrees with Mandel on many points, specifically on the trend of state policies from the late 1960s into the mid-1970s (Rowthorn, 1980). (He also says Mandel's *Late Capitalism* was one of the two most important contributions to recent marxist thought, the other being Harry Braverman's *Labour and Monopoly Capital*, 1972.) Rowthorn is rare among marxists for understanding the role of bank credit:

The key point is that it can increase total purchasing power in the economy. Banks are not merely the funnel through which people's savings are channelled. They can actually create new purchasing power by means of the overdraft system and in this way can provide investment finances in excess of what has been saved by capitalists or anyone else...Like the states, they can create new purchasing power (p. 122).

This perception leads to one basic disagreement with Mandel concerning the 'organic composition of capital' – a marxist term referring to the amount of capital invested per worker in the production process. Mandel, believing it is the key variable in late capitalism and has risen, concludes that profits have not been squeezed. Rowthorn argues that because of the increase in credit, the organic composition of capital has remained stable, so that profits in recent times have taken a lesser share of output because the profits per worker were falling, the state pre-empting some of the proceeds and the workers' share increasing through organization.

He also disagrees fundamentally with Mandel on the reason for the depression of the 1980s.[18] Mandel saw it as the inevitable consequence of the system – the conjuncture, as he put it, of a structural crisis of overproduction with other cyclical crises, including the reversal of our old friend the long wave, the growing militancy of the workers and the redistribution of purchasing power to oil producers. In his view, the global production structure requires both the free flow of capital and its regulation by common rules which allow the 'law of value' which is the logic of capitalism to arbitrate conflicts between states and resolve crises (cf. Gilbert and Witteveen, above). The IMF therefore should not be seen as the malign tool of American imperialism, but as the embodiment of this objective logic.

Rowthorn puts more emphasis on the political imperatives than the economic. His interpretation is that governments have exhausted the power of inflation to arrest the falling rate of profit; 'ever larger doses were needed' and eventually states were faced with just those hard choices that they had tried through inflation to avoid. The imposition of credit restrictions and the adoption of monetary targets caused the rate of profit to fall and this in turn led to a generalized world recession. The system itself was at risk because inflation rewarded the speculator and destroyed faith in the market by rewarding the strong at the expense of the weak.

Rowthorn, like Samir Amin, also sees beyond the depression:

> During the next phrase of capitalist development dynamism will shift from the present advanced capitalist countries toward the underdeveloped countries. . .and will represent a significant extension of the capitalist mode into hitherto unconquered areas.[19]

Compared with either Mandel or Rowthorn, the Italian economist Riccardo Parboni has a much more acute awareness of the background of international monetary history and the place of currency roles and exchange rate manipulations in affecting the way in which different capitalist countries subjectively experienced the world depression (Parboni, 1980). His analysis of the dollar's role in the system leads to the observation that the United States was able to delay that experience until 1979, and to recover more quickly from the recession of the mid-1970s than its European partners. This is an important observation and is in sharp contrast to the perceptions of the American political determinists discussed earlier. While they see the United States sweating, like Atlas, to carry an intolerable burden, Parboni sees the Americans as being in a position to exploit their relative invulnerability and the advantages of their domestic market to suffer later and less, and to recover sooner and faster than other countries. Some comparative (US) figures on the utilization of surplus industrial capacity in the 1970s tell the same story (Strange and Tooze, 1982), and the perception is shared by many Europeans. Parboni's conclusion though, is much the same as Mandel's: capitalism in crisis loses its 'human face' and reverts to the 'wildcat capitalism', the 'unbridled cartelization' of earlier periods. Social democracy has failed to tame it, and the workers of the world should regain their class consciousness, uniting with the socialist countries and the new masses of the third world.

Parboni is typical of many European writers in seeking inspiration from the classical literature of political economy. The present crisis, he feels, has rehabilitated some of the ideas of Marx, Lenin and Schumpeter which had been prematurely declared obsolete. Marx saw crises in capitalist societies as redefining capitalist-worker relations. Lenin saw them as exacerbating conflict between capitalist states. Schumpeter saw them as strengthening oligopolies at the expense of small business. Parboni, anticipating disaster, draws on all three, rejecting Keynes's view that crises were merely an irrational aberration brought about by the perversity of the liquidity preferences of capitalists, and easily overcome by intelligent demand management.

The great weakness of marxist interpretation of the current crisis is the same as the weakness of *Das Kapital*: the anticipation of a revolutionary response on the part of the workers. Marx proved mistaken in the expectation that the internal contradictions of capitalism would bring about the collapse of the system through revolution and its replacement by a socialist system in which money would no longer play a dominant part in human relations. In the 1980s the commonest weakness in marxist interpretations is still the expectation that the collapsing capitalist world economy will bring together the workers of new and old industrialized countries in a common revolutionary cause. Amin and Rowthorn stand out as two writers who do not entertain such fond hopes and who see the internationalization of finance and banking as the Achilles' heel of the system, undermining political cooperation between governments and social classes and disrupting economic order.

Conclusion

Thus it seems that agreement on this key weakness is shared chiefly by those at opposite ends of a political spectrum: those who so object to the injustices of capitalism that they want to get rid of it altogether, and those who value so highly the freedom it promises from political tyranny and oppression that they seek to limit the state's involvement and thus its power to exploit it. Only those who are most keen to preserve it or to abolish it have eyes sharp enough to spot its weakest point – monetary mismanagement. Between them are to be found a few pragmatists: they are mostly senior officials like Gilbert or Witteveen or Schweizer, with a long practical experience of the deterioration of order in the system. Only rarely are they academics.

The landscape of opinions surveyed in cursory fashion in the preceding pages therefore reveals a panorama dotted with individual names, rather than one strongly patterned with greats blocs of defined schools of thought. Looking backwards, I am struck by the contributions to understanding of highly individual men – Minsky, Mandel, Triffin, Gilbert, Rowthorn – all of them essentially loners. None of them belonged to the great intellectual armies. The landscape of recent opinion therefore resembles not so much a continent divided into great plains and massive mountain ranges as it does an archipelago of volcanic peaks, randomly scattered about in a stormy and unsettled sea of ideas.

In sum, the last decade and more has been marked not by the triumph of coherent economic theories, but by the general appearance of disarray. Considering the vast resources devoted in the Western world in the present century to the development of the study of economics, what is striking is that, instead of a rich harvest of convincing, well-documented explanations, we should find such poverty of theoretical interpretations of contemporary events.

This is surely a big change from the mid-century decades – the 1930s, 1940s and 1950s – when the great mass of expert opinion crowded into the middle ground, applauding the mixed economy and acknowledging the benefits of state intervention. Then, even Presidents of the United States could observe, 'We are all keynesians now', without anyone thinking it a remarkable statement. Though there were differences about ways and means of demand management, and about degrees of intervention and state support, large areas of agreement remained for this conventional congregation. It formed the intellectual base on which the centre parties of post-war France, Germany and Italy were built. This was where, in America, Democrats and new Republicans could agree, and where in Britain, Conservative and Labour followers of Butler and Gaitskell could comfortably share the hybrid label of 'Butskellites'.

What happended in the 1970s, to judge by this cursory survey of contending interpretations of economic trends, was the totally unexpected impoverishment of this middle ground. It was not that the middle ground became exactly depopulated, for there were many in active politics or in academic economics who lingered there nostalgically. Like peasant farmers, sentimentally attached to regions of declining marginal fertility, they were unwilling to leave, not knowing where else to go, and hoping, Micawber-like, for something to turn up. The middle ground, however, no longer yielded satisfactory rational explanations for the failures of government intervention and the malfunctioning of the system. It held little promise of permanent and effective solutions to pressing political problems.

There were two major reasons for this impoverishment, and neither is hard to find. One, obviously, was the accelerated internationalization of markets, and the incorporation, directly or indirectly, of ever larger parts of national economies into a world market system. In that system, because capital and technology moved easily across state borders, the assumptions that underlay the keynesian middle ground, about the power of government to order matters within the state, no longer held good. Secondly, and coincidentally, the same assumptions were being undermined by another major change. This was the overburdening of the bureaucratic machinery and the budgets of the state in most of the advanced economies. Mounting demands for social services and welfare systems – and in some cases for defence – often came on top of perceived needs for the state to find money both to support ailing old industries and to invest in advanced new ones. In such circumstances where state spending takes over half the national income, to ask governments to act as countervailing forces to correct the stubborn stickiness or the perverse pessimism of the market operators, is very different from making the same request when the proportion of public spending is down to around 20 per cent of national income. This is a point often reiterated by Milton Friedman and never adequately answered by the neo-keynesians. As with other factors and situations, there comes a point where diminishing returns set in and when the old magic is no longer effective.

It is this intellectual impoverishment of the middle ground that I suspect is the most likely explanation for the resort by so many contemporary writers to different forms of determinism in their explanatory accounts of the events of the 1970s, and especially of developments in the monetary system. For determinism, whether economic, technical or political, is the social and political equivalent of existentialism for the individual. The existentialist writers of the 1950s and 1960s, following Sartre, held that individual choices and actions were shaped by the experiences imposed by the exogenous forces of society. Society, therefore, not the individual, was to blame for whatever consequences followed. The individual was exculpated and need feel no guilt if his or her acts were aberrant or destructive. In much the same way, the determinism that regards the choices made by governments as being conditioned and imposed by Kondratiev long waves, by technological change, or by the loss of some political predominance has the same superficial plausibility and leads to the same convenient conclusion that we need look no further for the source of our present ills.

By contrast, those who *do* look further and who are more familiar with the choices made by policy-makers in the course of the last 20 years (or some would say in the last 40 years) find it hard to see anything inevitable or unavoidable about the present state of the monetary and financial system. Whether the attention to monetary history and to the political debates behind it comes from direct experience in government or banking, or from academic study, it almost always leads to a common rejection, in my experience, of both the determinist fallacies and the exaggeration of trade policies as a cause of economic depression.

Such social determinism has a stultifying effect on the making of economic theory precisely because it always sees the causes of economic, and especially of monetary, problems as lying outside the realm of economics and therefore beyond the theorist's reach. Either it is technology or the Arabs, or else it is the labour unions or the media who have induced exaggerated expectations of non-stop increases in consumption. Whoever or whatever is to blame, economic theory can find no essentially economic answer because the root problem is not economic. That is true enough. But what is striking is the consequent failure even to try to look seriously for the explanation of the determining factor. Why was it that the United States could not or would not adjust to higher oil prices by non-inflationary means? Why was it that financing the Vietnam War could not be done by fiscal means? After all, the higher commodity prices during the Korean War had been met by the United States taking a lead in rationing consumption and controlling prices. And, although the examples are not too many, nevertheless, there have been countries who fought wars without letting inflation rip.

Such social determinism is also consistent with (and indeed is only possible under) two conditions. One is that the element of choice in the management of money and finance (and especially of choice in the regulation of processes of credit creation and supervision over access to credit), is denied or else taken for granted. Whatever is, must be held to be inevitable. And the second condition is that the analysis of production, employment and trade must be divorced and treated in isolation from the management of money. Possibly because different international organizations are involved, and international organizations do not easily communicate with one another, this intellectual separatism is possibly easier to practise internationally than

100 *Some other interpretations*

at the national level. But the separation then allows those who seek for explanations to look no further than the immediate financial circumstances of the firm or the state.

Perhaps that is why both the monetarists, who take a rather moral attitude towards the management of money, and the marxists who assume a totally amoral attitude to money in the capitalist system, find it easier than most to avoid these two pitfalls. Both start from the contrary – and in my view, correct – assumption that the management of credit is necessarily highly political. Both agree that it is the way in which credit is managed or mismanaged in a world market economy which makes or mars the world economy. Both agree that it was political decisions by governments regarding money and finance in the history of the world's monetary system in recent years which, more than anything else, determined the distribution across states and across classes of gains and losses, risks and opportunities.

Notes

1 See, for example, *The Economist*, 13 November 1983, which carried an article, 'Import or die – protectionism would be the surest way to intensify world slumpflation'. Each of the 88 countries involved, it wrote, 'seems likely to believe that if it can improve its trade balance, it will shuffle off some of its joblessness. Since each country's improvement in trade balance is some other country's deterioration in it, this looks a recipe for a mad hatter's tea party, and an ill from which the world has suffered before.' The London *Times*, the *Financial Times*, the *New York Times* and the *Wall Street Journal* all wrote similar dire warnings of the price of failure to stem the rising tide of protectionism.

2 Fatalistic attitudes characterised some of the early Kondratiev litera-ture and paradoxically could be made to fit some present-day economic thinking apparently justifying the view that governments can do very little about the present recession except to follow a policy of monetary restraint and to hope that investment does indeed prove to be suf-ficiently interest-elastic.

Rostow, 1978, p. 189, strongly disagrees and argues that recessions such as this call for more active public policies to encourage and promote technological change, innovation as well as invention.

3 The words are quoted from James March, 'The power of power' in Easton, 1966, Vol. I, p. 54 and are quoted by Robert Keohane in 'Inflation and American power' in Lombra and Witte, 1982. An earlier and better known work, using the same definition, was Knorr, 1975.

4 *International Studies Quarterly*, Winter 1983, for example, included lengthy reviews by C. Kindleberger and two other contributors.

5 See editors' contributions in Strange and Tooze, 1982.

6 Among them, Dankwart, Rustow, Louis Turner, Zuhayr Mikdashi, Michael Tanzer and Edith Penrose. Of these writers Blair was and Rostow and Penrose are themselves American. Expert opinion is not differentiated by nationality.

7 See, for example, the contributions of J. Tumlir and V. Curzon to Strange and Tooze, 1982.

8 Though, as Minsky says, 'The very definition of equilibrium that is relevant for a capitalist economy with money differs from the definition used in standard Walrasian theory' (Minsky, 1981, 1982, p. 3).

9 The post-keynesian critique of the monetarists argues that by leaving out this relationship, the monetarists are led to assume a stable demand for money (again, as if it were a commodity like any other) so that variations in the supply will determine the money value of the total output (i.e. prices and the rate of inflation). But, on the contrary, say the post-keynesians, the liquidity preference of people who have money and can choose what to do with it affects the demand, and it is this unstable demand which also influences the price level of current output.

10 Notably among some Scandinavian economists. See also Tibor Scitovsky, 'Market power and inflation', *Economica*, August 1978; and Scitovsky, 1980.

11 A notable exception is Wolfgang Hager's 'Europe and protection', *International Affairs*, Summer 1982.

12 Johannes Witteveen, interviewed in *The Banker*, November 1982.

13 What and who is marxist, and who is not, is an insoluble question and the source of much fruitless debate. In my view 'marxist' is a status – like 'liberated woman' – that can only be self-defined. In either case, you are one, if you think you are.

14 The argument in more concentrated form can also be found in two interviews given by S. Amin, reported in *Politica Internazionale* and published in Amin, 1980.

15 Dobb was a Cambridge economist: Kalecki, whose work anticipated Keynes's *General Theory*, was a Pole who emigrated to Britain but returned to Poland in 1955. The same view was taken by Nicos Poulantzas, whose early death by suicide removed a potential leader in marxist thought.

16 Perhaps more commonly hinted at now in Eastern Europe, but see also such writers as Jacques Attali, 'L'acception des regles de l'economie mondiale est irreversible', *La Parole et L'Outil*, Paris, 1977.

17 *The Second Slump* was originally published in German as *Ende der Krise oder Krise ohne Ende* – 'the end of the crisis or crisis without end'.

18 Both refer back to the same study: Glyn and Sutcliffe, 1972. The falling rate of profit was also documented in a Brookings Institution study, 'The falling share of profits' by W. Nordhaus in A. Okun and Perry, Brookings paper No. 1, Washington 1974.

19 Rowthorn, 1980. The quotation recalls Marx's prescient vision of 'the entanglement of all peoples in the net of the world market and with this the growth of the international character of the capitalist regime' (*Das Kapital*, Vol. 1).

CHAPTER 4

Betting in the Dark

Instead of offering some protection against the uncertainties of life, money has itself become the cause of new uncertainties. Not only is there uncertainty over the duration of the world depression, we do not know when or if inflation will ever return. We can only guess what will be the divergence in the exchange rates between the dollar and other currencies. Oil prices in 1990 are anyone's bet. At a time when the most secure jobs are apt suddenly to vanish and still more people are made redundant, the capacity of the monetary system to offer – as it should – a secure store of value that people can use to cushion themselves against such misfortunes or against illness or old age, seems less than ever it was.

Why this matters – as I believe it does – and not only to those who have money or who make their living by handling or dealing in it, but to the whole of society, is not a question to which there is a quick or simple answer. It calls for some thought to be given to what the use of money does to human relations, and to human behaviour in society. And this more philosophical side of money is one that has rather been lost sight of and overlooked in recent decades. Most contemporary discussion of money and monetary problems has been highly mechanical, focusing on the technical details and the rather arcane minutiae of the subject. The social and political issues behind the machinery were seldom mentioned. Yet this was something which several of the early sociologists had thought hard about and which had also figured in the writings of the classical political

economists from Adam Smith to John Stuart Mill, and from Karl
Marx to Max Weber.

One of those who gave it most thought was a German Jewish
academic writing at the very end of the last century. His name was
Georg Simmel and he was not at all sure that the general use of money
had been all to the good.[1] For one thing, it replaced the subjective
appreciation of objects, goods, services, with an objective valuation
of them in terms of their monetary value, and in the process had
often debased them. It quantified, as he put it, the qualitative. It
equalized what was essentially unequal and not truly to be compared.
At the same time, the use of money instead of barter or subsistence
production vastly extended the network of human relationships. But
in doing so, it also dehumanized the relationships and made them
more mechanical, putting people, as we would say, at arms' length
from each other.

Simmel did not deny the advantages that the use of money brings
to society. It is not just – as every introductory textbook of economics
soon explains – that using money instead of barter or subsistence
production greatly increases the production of wealth through the
division of labour. It also adds a political value in that it gives people
more choice over what to consume, whose services to use, and –
perhaps most important – whether to enjoy the consumption of goods
or services today or to save them for the future. Without money,
it is just possible, of course, to store grain and other non-perishable
commodities like wool or timber, some metals, even wine. But many
other things like meat, fish or fruit and all services, cannot be stored
for later consumption. Thus, the lack of money restricts our freedom
to choose between consumption today and consumption tomorrow.

To Simmel, the balance of advantages in the terms of wealth and
freedom of choice against the loss in the quality of human relationships was by no means clear. Whereas for Marx, it had been plain
that the use of money and the accumulation of capital by one class
– which the use of money made possible – was the very basis for
the detested capitalist system of production and the exploitation of
man by man that it entailed. In perceiving the debasing of the relations
of production brought about under capitalism and through the use
of money to direct a man's labour, Marx undoubtedly romanticized
a little the relations of production in pre-capitalist society, both in

Europe and elsewhere, where what he called the Asiatic mode of production prevailed. And this may be why, to non-marxists, there has always been something rather vague and unreal about the marxists' notion that a society in which people who have once enjoyed the freedom conferred by the use of money would easily give it up and be content with the dependence on the decisions made by others that is implicit in a socialist state.

A property of money of which Simmel made much in his great study was its essential neutrality. Instead of having to trust a person, you could trust this neutral, stable medium of exchange and store of value. Its stability, he thought, allowed people to put their trust in values expressed in money. To us, that seems a rather naive notion. But writing in 1900, it was hardly surprising that he should think of money as a source of trust and confidence. It would be hard to think of a date – at least in Europe – when the recent experience of monetary stability had been greater.

Yet Simmel was very much aware of the social consequences of changes in the value of money and of differences in individual re-actions to it. If, he argued, the amount of money in everyone's pocket were to be suddenly magically doubled, while the supply of goods and services remained the same, different reactions by people to this magic change would bring about a realignment (as we would say) of real prices. Suppose, he said, that among three people to whom this happened, one has 1,000 marks, one 10,000 marks and the third, 100,000 marks. The consumption patterns of each would not be exactly reproduced if their nominal income or wealth in money were suddenly to double. For the poor man would be emboldened to buy more food; the rich one would put aside more saving for investment in land or property; and the middle man would feel free to spend more on small luxuries and inessentials. Magnified in society, these choices, induced by what today would be called money illusion, would actually alter the relative prices of various goods over some sort of short-run while the money illusion lasted. Even this very moderate degree of uncertainty about the value of money would therefore undermine the stability of a society based on money. For even though the relative shares of wealth had not been changed, a monetary change would have brought about a change in real prices, the value of some goods in terms of others. It was important therefore that trust be put in the unchanging value and supply of money itself. For if that changed, other real values would be indirectly changed.

For Simmel, money was therefore an expression of trust; but trust could only be established by faith and experience. It could not be created by fiat. Like love, any effort to ensure it by legal forms was more apt to destroy it than to assure it. There was a paradox about money in that, despite its mechanical, dehumanizing, neutral character, it could only function at its best and confer its greatest benefits if it rested on something as irrational, and even emotional, as faith.

People who work in financial markets will understand the relevance of Simmel's ideas better than the theoretical economists. They know that the London Stock Exchange's motto 'My word is my bond' is a declaration of the same belief, and that everyday dealing in Eurocurrency markets could not be done without the vital element of trust. They too are aware that, while trust takes time to build, it can very quickly be destroyed. And once destroyed, it takes even longer to rebuild. 'Once bitten, twice shy' applies to money as to other things. The attachment of Europeans, and especially perhaps the French, to gold, bears testimony to long tribal memories of the betrayal of trust by governments, just as the horror of inflation in Germany reflects the collective trauma of the 1923 hyperinflation.

Moreover, it seems that trust betrayed or made questionable in the realm of social relations can have a kind of contagious effect on trust in other realms, whether it is the security of property or confidence in the conscience of politicians, the discretion of officials or the impartiality of the police.

It is the recurrent argument of this chapter that the global monetary system has been an important source of just such a contagious spread of distrust, reaching far beyond the limits of financial centres and affecting relations between states and even relations within states; and that a vicious circle of uncertainty was begun as much by the kind of key decisions of governments referred to in chapter 2, as by increased uncertainty in markets. Indeed, the key decisions of governments have often increased the uncertainty arising from the markets. They have even, as was shown, created new markets dominated by uncertainty, of which the Eurocurrency market is probably the most important and the various futures markets the most numerous.

But before explaining in more detail how this vicious circle of uncertainty has developed, there are some other political and social aspects to uncertainty itself which are another neglected part of that no man's land that still lies, so inadequately charted, between politics and economics.

The trend of most liberal economic analysis over the last 40 or 50 years has been toward the sophisticated theorizing about market-based behaviour, and in particular about behaviour on the basis of rational expectations. Some of this theorizing claims intellectual descent from a seminal work by Frank Knight first written as a thesis for Cornell University in 1916 and published in 1921 under the title, *Risk, certainty and profit* (Knight, 1933). The chief purpose of Knight's work was to explain why the capitalist system, depending as it does on risk-taking by individual entrepreneurs, was actually socially very efficient, despite some tendency – as noted by the marxists – of the rate of profit to decline. It was efficient, he argued, mainly because entrepreneurs, being human and fallible, were not good judges of their own judgement. Men, he said – and, not to be sexist, one might add, women too – 'have an irrationally high confidence in their own good fortune'; and on top of that they tend to overestimate the statistical probabilities of success in any business in which they are personally engaged. To lead up to that thesis, it was necessary to distinguish, as Knight did, between risk, or as he called it, *a priori* probability, on which there was long-rooted literature relating to games of chance and mathematical odds, and *statistical probability* which involved the application to particular instances of statistical data regarding probabilities to a group of events, cases, firms or whatever classified as having things in common. The one was the basis for most insurance, but almost never occurred in ordinary businesses; the other did, but the usefulness of statistical probability depended on the accuracy with which the classified instances were grouped together. Moreover, though the statistical probability of one house in a million burning down might be known, uncertainty would remain concerning which of the million houses it would be. Both *a priori* and statistical probability had to be distinguished from *estimates* which, in real life, were the basis for almost all business decisions.

Take as an illustration, any typical business decision. A manufacturer is considering the advisability of making a large commitment in increasing the capacity of his works. He 'figures' more or less on the proposition, taking account as well as possible of the various factors more or less susceptible of measurement, but the final result is an 'estimate' of the probable outcome of any proposed course of action. What is the 'probability' of error... in the judgement? It is manifestly meaningless to speak of either calculating such a probability *a priori* or of determining it empirically by studying a large number of instances (Knight, 1921, p. 226, in LSE Reprint Series No. 16, 1933).

Not only, moreover, were business decisions based on estimates not really rational, they were inclined to overestimate and not underestimate the prospects of success because, as Adam Smith had observed a long time before, men will work, on average more cheaply for an uncertain than for a fixed compensation. The main aim in life, as Knight I think rightly observed, was not – *pace* liberal economics – to maximize profits or to 'satisfy' a lot of rational ambitions.

'Man's chief interest in life is after all to find life interesting, which is a very different thing from merely consuming a maximum amount of wealth' (Knight, 1933, p. 269).

However, since any economic process of production or trade involves uncertainty, because it has to be begun before either the state of demand for the product or the full costs of supplying that demand can be precisely calculated, it follows, as Knight says, that 'rational conduct strives to reduce to a minimum the uncertainties involved in adapting means to ends...' (p. 238). Knight therefore devoted a whole chapter of his book to examining the structures and methods for meeting uncertainty.

Of these, he pays particular attention to insurance in all its forms, from the actuarial side of it to mutual associations like the P and I (Profit and Indemnity) clubs to which shipping companies belong. He also includes under insurance, speculation which sounds like a very different business but (in relation to uncertainty) is actually its complement. For while one spreads risk among a number liable to similar uncertainty, the latter shifts uncertainty from the entrepreneur to the specialist. And specialists in speculative business have two advantages which allow them either to reduce the costs of uncertainty or to make a profit out of it, or perhaps to do both. One is that while a single entrepreneur will be in the market once, the speculator will be in it hundreds or thousands of times and 'his errors in judgement must show a correspondingly stronger tendency to cancel out' (Knight 1933, p. 256).

This is precisely what happens in foreign exchange or Eurocurrency dealing. The banks' foreign exchange dealers are able to match one person's uncertainty as to whether he may lose if D-marks appreciate against dollars, against someone else's uncertainty as to whether he may lose if dollars appreciate against D-marks. The other reason is that familiarity with an uncertain market and specialization on decision-making in relation to that alone will usually lead to the speculator being better and more quickly informed than his clients.

Knight also foresaw that in such circumstances, one likely result of uncertainty would be a greatly increased demand for information and statistics; and that consultancy services, processing the available information and statistics would expand in answer to the demand. In fact, in the course of the argument he identifies the three main responses to increased systemic uncertainty as being diversification, insurance and an increased demand for information to reduce the uncertainty. Writing in a neutral isolationist America, still basking in the warm afterglow of pre-war stability, he refers at one point to 'an environment as little subject as our own to progressive and capricious change' (Knight 1933, p. 335).[2] Knight was not concerned directly therefore with the question that arises in our own times of the social or systemic consequences of progressive and capricious change. Yet his observations about the irrationality of entrepreneurs in handling uncertainty, and about the characteristic responses to it, provide an extremely useful corrective to much contemporary economic theorizing based on concepts of rational choice and rational expectations. Whatever this may have gained in 'rigourousness' and internal logical consistency, it has lost much more in the accuracy with which it approximates to real human behaviour, both collective and individual.

Speculation

Knight saw speculation as the complement to free enterprise, and another way in which, through specialization of function, society could

achieve economic progress despite uncertainty. By allowing speculation, a society could allow a further degree of specialization, allowing
uncertainty-bearing to be carried out by persons most willing to
assume that function. Even within industry, uncertainty produced
a tendency to separation of function in industry so that 'promoters'
– who, I suppose, correspond to the property developers and venture
capital financiers of our own day – tend to move on once an enterprise,
a product or a development has become safe and established.

What little Knight had to say about speculation was highly
consistent with the observations made some 40 years before by Walter
Bagehot when he explained the workings of the City of London. In
Lombard Street, Bagehot found three conditions necessary to the
efficient functioning of the world's trading system. They were that
(1) a loan fund of money should be available for investment; (2) there
should be a speculative fund; and (3) a supply of young men should
be available eager to exploit the latest opportunities to make a fortune.
Of course, as another commentator on profit and speculation as a
phenomenon, H. von Mangoldt (1855) had also observed, there were
always more who lost money than those who made it – but it was
the hope of making a fortune that mattered and the greater readiness,
percipiently observed by Adam Smith, of men to risk a little for a
slim chance of making a great gain than of men to risk large amounts
to make a much more likely gain. In our own day the foreign exchange
dealers, the commodity market brokers and financial futures operators
are more likely to be making money for their employers than they
are to be making it directly for themselves. But they do not do so
badly, and in a few years can accumulate sufficient capital that their
future choice of occupation is greatly increased.[3] Today, it is still
true that the combination of youthful optimism and enterprise, and
the availability of a speculative fund, ensures that the opportunities
for speculation opened up by capricious uncertainty are quickly and
efficiently exploited. That exploitation of course necessarily involves
the expansion and growth of markets that by their specialized nature
are essentially speculative.

But the point is that this expansion does not come about by
accident. It is the direct response to uncertainty of those who are
averse to bearing the risks attendant on capricious change, and of
those who are eager to make a fortune by responding to a widespread

demand for greater certainty than is to be found in the market. A speculative market therefore actually *requires* uncertainty. It also needs risk-aversion on the part of others, a speculative fund and a supply of young men eager to work hard for above-normal gain.[4]

A speculative market can be defined as one in which prices move in response to the balance of opinion regarding the future movement of prices, as distinct from normal markets in which prices move in response to objective changes in the demand for, or supply of a usable commodity or service. In this respect, a speculative market most resembles a racecourse, where there is a market for bets on the horses (or dogs) that will win or get a place. The more people, through their bets, express their opinion that one particular horse is going to win, the lower the odds that they will get from the bookmakers. Their opinions may – and often do – turn out to be wrong; but it is the opinions not the objective prowess of the horse that moves the prices.

Yet, whereas people who go to racecourses or bet on the races actually enjoy gambling, the great majority of participants in the speculative financial markets of our times are there involuntarily because they are risk-averse and do *not* want to gamble. They are afraid of uncertainty and they are keen to hedge against it. And the speculative markets allow the risk-averse operator or his agent to take out a converse bet to the outcome feared in order to protect himself against it. So if the uncertainty damages the real business in which he is engaged, he will at least win on the converse bet. Making that bet is not without cost, however, and the price is paid to brokers who will live well, as explained earlier, by reason of their ability to match the opposed fears of risk-averse clients and their superior knowledge of the forces that move the market. Thus, importers who want to hedge against the increased uncertainty of the foreign exchange markets will try to cover against the risk that their invoice in a foreign currency will cost them more in their own currency; while exporters, hoping to be paid in a foreign currency, will similarly (and conversely) take cover against the risk that the payment will be worth less in their own currency.

Such a market will inevitably attract, among the more careful brokers, some gamblers and, from time to time, some operators who will see the chance of swinging the market to their own advantage – usually by acting in such a way that only they have the information as to which way prices are about to move. The gamblers will be more numerous the smaller the margin required by market rules for them to deal in it. In the authoritative and detailed monetary history of the United States which Milton Friedman wrote with Anna Schwarz, he pinpointed the margin-dealing allowed on the Wall Street Stock Exchange in the 1920s as an important contributory factor in the boom that preceded the crash of 1929 (Friedman and Schwarz, 1963). Afterwards the rules were changed to stop margin dealing in shares. But the futures markets that have proliferated in recent years and which suffer the same weakness still permit it. So, as H. C. Emery observed in 1896, commodity dealing is liable to the same abuse:

> The possibility of making quick and large gains from fluctuations in prices leads thousands into the speculative market who have no real knowledge as to its condition and no real opinion of the course of prices. They depend chiefly on chance for their success. Such speculation is mere gambling in spirit. The evil is still further increased by the margin system. The speculator need not have enough capital to make his purchases but only enough to put up 5 or 10 per cent with his broker (*Commodity Exchanges*, 1896).

It was for this reason that, until the end of the nineteenth century, California, Texas and 10 other mid-western and southern states maintained a strict legal prohibition against futures trading in commodities where there was no intention to deliver. But the dyke had been breached in New York in the Civil War when uncertainty over cotton prices produced the same risk-aversion that nurtures hedging operations today, and its necessary complement, speculative future trading. And once speculative markets exist, they inevitably offer the opportunity for sharp practice in cornering the commodity so that those caught by margin dealing on the rising market will have to unload at enormous loss to themselves – and profit to those controlling the supply – when it falls.

The most famous example of this in recent times was the Hunt brothers' almost successful attempt to corner the world market in silver. This is well described in Michael Moffitt's book on the global monetary system (Moffitt 1984, pp. 180–93). It is evident that the greater the uncertainty and the greater the need for futures contracts and covering options in a highly volatile financial system or a highly volatile commodity market, the greater the opportunities open to speculators and large-scale operators like the Hunt brothers to exploit the market to their own advantage.

Some of the volatility of the markets in grain, soybeans, pork bellies, frozen orange juice and 90 or so other commodities produced in the United States is undoubtedly due to the widespread participation in futures trading by the farmers themselves, even though since 1974 there has been strict supervision by the federal Commodity Futures Trading Commission. Unlike most European farmers, American producers use the futures markets very extensively to insure themselves against poor prices. That the Europeans do not do so to anything like the same extent is due not so much as Americans might think to their lack of sophistication, as to the greater security of prices afforded them by the Common Agricultural Policy (CAP) and national market management. Those who attack the CAP do not always understand that the protection it has given has been protection against the uncertainty of volatile world prices as much as protection against more efficient foreign producers. It is not entirely accidental that the two commodities in which the CAP has been most protectionist – grain and sugar – have also been those marked by the most violent changes in world prices.

In the 1980s, futures trading in commodities has been completely overtaken by trading in financial futures.[5] This is a direct result of the increase in financial uncertainty and dealing is far less stringently supervised than the trading in commodity futures. In the 1960s and 1970s the practice grew up of dealing in foreign currency 'forward' (i.e. a sale to be completed at an agreed price three or six months ahead) as well as 'spot' (i.e. an immediate sale). But these forward markets were somewhat inflexible from the customer's point of view. Contracts to buy or sell were tied to a specific date and were between particular buyers and sellers. Starting in the United States in 1972, the financial futures markets on the other hand have allowed much more general trading of futures or options on any currency's exchange rate, on government securities and therefore interest rates or – the latest development – on stock-exchange indexes (i.e. the general up or down movement of corporate stocks and shares).[6] As with commodity futures, the contracts are for very large standard quantities to be completed on fixed delivery dates, but in the meantime, the contracts can be retraded on the market. London belatedly followed the American example, setting up the London International Financial Futures Exchange (LIFFE) in 1982. Business in both has grown quite phenomenally (see figure 4.1). In 1983, 20 million contracts on US treasury bill futures were traded in the Chicago market; this was 20 per cent more than the year before. In the same year no less than 800 million deals were concluded in Chicago and New York alone in stock-exchange futures (i.e. bets on the future level of the Standard and Poor share price index for the top 500 companies) – nearly twice as much as in 1982.

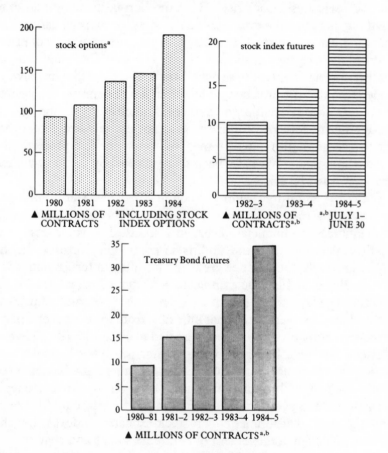

Figure 4.1 Growth of options and futures trading.
(*Source: World Development Report, 1985.*)

The explanation of this last explosion is easy, but makes nonsense of the claim that financial markets behave rationally. Any fund manager or financial director – whether for a bank, a corporation, a municipality or a trade union pension fund – is naturally afflicted today by the fear of making the wrong choice of where to place the funds. Should he (or she) invest in treasury bills or gilts, or in corporate stocks? In dollars or in yen? How can he tell? Yet the wrong decision exposes him (or her) to ridicule, criticism or worse. Hedging with financial futures is relatively easy and protects the manager from the unforeseen disaster – even though it also cancels out any windfall profits he might have made by making the right decisions. As Richard Lambert wrote:

> Financial markets everywhere have become much more volatile and fund managers – even of long-term assets – have become increasingly concerned with short-term performance. As a result, they have adopted the strategy of taking small profits whenever they present themselves rather than take the chance of building up bigger gains by staying with their successes. These days a buy-and-hold policy would be considered distinctly *passé* (*Financial Times*).

The consequence, however, is that trading in stocks and shares and all sorts of new financial innovations like interest rate swaps and options and futures rate agreements (FRAs) has grown apace even in the depressions of the mid-1970s and the 1980s. The slowdown in growth, surplus industrial capacity and flagging demand has not stopped. Everyone is busy chopping and changing their portfolios, as Lambert says, to make a small quick profit. The abolition of fixed commission rates for brokers on Wall Street in 1974 led to increased competition for business. The general uncertainty created eager customers. Share trading in New York increased by *five times* in ten years. The technology also helped. Mechanical limitations used to put a top limit on daily share trading on Wall Street at around 20 million deals a day. It now allows as many as 200 million. Moreover the moment is rapidly approaching when for all financial dealing, there will no longer be 'financial centres' in the old sense, but one widespread global market in financial futures, government stocks and shares. Already the financial futures markets have arranged to link up with each other so that dealing can go on around the clock, for 24 hours a day, linked only by satellites and computers. The Amsterdam options exchange is linked with Montreal, Vancouver and Sydney. Chicago and Singapore, New York and Sydney have linked to make one market for financial futures. It can only be a matter of time before the operators run so far ahead of the regulations that this global financial casino will be working non-stop – but with rather hazy and indeterminate rules and few prudential controls.

Market economists in recent years have rushed to the defence of these proliferating futures markets with subtle theoretical arguments about their function in ensuring 'market-clearing' as a significant contribution to the greater efficiency of the system. The plain implication is that the system was less efficient before there were so many futures markets. But that is only true – if at all – if 'efficiency' takes no account of risk or the external consequences of volatility of price on production and distribution. For it can be demonstrated historically that prices have in fact been more volatile since futures trading became widespread, and that there has been waste consequential on that volatility. Not only must the overhead costs of maintaining the markets and their operators in existence be taken into account, but also there are wasteful – because exaggerated – adjustment costs for labour and management in productive sectors.

Market economists are also apt to make the highly questionable claim that futures markets offer a similar facility to all who may be afflicted in the conduct of their business by uncertainty, since information is readily available to all who need it. This claim is highly unrealistic. The same was said of British courts of law before the state provided legal aid to poor litigants – a claim which at the time provoked Harold Laski to retort 'Ah yes, like the Ritz Hotel, open to rich and poor alike!' For it must be obvious that, in a market moved by opinions rather than by objective changes in supply and demand, anyone with ready access to the opinions of operators will have better information – and that must surely be other operators. Gossip, hearsay and rumour move these markets, and those who hear the latest whisper first or, nowadays, keep the closest eye on the computer screen, will be at an advantage when dealing in the market, while those who hear or see it last will be at a disadvantage.

This was another point appreciated 80 years ago by Frank Knight.

He foresaw the close connection between uncertainty and the demand for information and advice. What he could not have foreseen was the immense enlargement in the opportunities for marketing information that has been produced by recent advances in communications technology. This has made it easy for the supply of information to expand in step with the growing demand for it in conditions of continued financial uncertainty. For example, in the field of commodity markets, where financial uncertainty and volatile prices have led to a greatly increased demand for futures and options as a hedge against uncertainty, there has been a corresponding growth in dealing and broking in commodities.

A clear indication of expansion can be found in the mushrooming of information systems available to those who can pay the quite substantial costs of using them. A recent trader's guide to commodities futures, for example, lists no fewer than 27 wire services, data banks and on-line computer services almost all of which are relatively new, and most of which use computers and satellites to store, retrieve and communicate to desk terminals in offices around the world the latest market information (Nicholas, 1985). The same publication lists no fewer than 68 newsletters, printed and/or on-line just on commodity trading. The average subscription can be as high as $7400 a year for Quarterly Market Service reports on five major metals, or as low as $5 for a collection of quarterly charts of commodity price trends for 40 commodities.

A similar explosion of competing information systems can be seen in the field of bank lending and currency dealing. Political risk analysis may have a rather poor record in predicting major events like revolutions, military takeovers and other *coups d'etat* in developing countries. But that seems only to whet the customers' appetites for more and more sophisticated instant information.

The not inconsiderable costs of this large information system must be paid by someone. In the first instance the brokers, banks and corporate finance departments will buy the databases and newsletters. But these in turn will add these costs to their overheads, so it will be the shareholders, the customers and the consumers who ultimately foot the bill.

It is not only the cost that is at issue. It is the opinion of some experienced observers in business, and the financial press, that these overgrown futures markets themselves add to instability. Nicholas Colchester, for example, has commented:

> Today's instant information, instant transaction markets behave like mechanical systems devoid of friction or of damping. In each market large weights (speculative capital) are linked by weak springs (the fundamentals of supply and demand) and the whole shuddering blancmange is subjected to the impact of unfolding events (Colchester 1983).

The consequences for the real economy, for production and trade and employment can only be guessed at. Clearly, the financial managers of companies, even though they are working in the dark, have become much more important than the engineers and the personnel managers. The advice of bankers is more readily sought than that of scientists and technologists. And the big established international companies who can make regular use of these financial hedging devices are at a substantial advantage compared with small, national enterprises.

That this is true is borne out by some recent surveys. One such study in recent years was conducted under the auspices of a body called the British North American Council and was directed specifically at the question of what effect floating or flexible exchange rates had had on business behaviour by large companies (Blin et al., 1981). From a questionnaire supplemented by interviews, data was collected from a fairly large sample of British, US and Canadian corporations. The authors concluded that the larger companies had in fact been able to make themselves comparatively invulnerable to exchange risks. But they had done so only by directing far more of their executive manpower into financial management, and by making much more deliberate efforts to match ingoings and outgoings in different kinds of foreign exchange, and finally by resorting to futures markets when risks could not be managed internally within the company.

Unfortunately – and perhaps unavoidably – the study made no overall estimate of the additional overhead costs which these efforts added to the enterprises' operations. Still less did it make a quantitative assessment of advantages which the large corporations consequently enjoyed over their smaller competitors. The latter would have found it less possible to find managers who could spare time to specialize in purely financial decision-making. They would also have found it harder either to match foreign exchange incomes and expenditures, or to keep reserves in the major trading currencies or to resort to hedging in the futures markets.

The same conclusion about the invulnerability of large-scale international business to financial uncertainty was also reached in another study for the Royal Institute of International Affairs (King, 1982). The implication again is that uncertainty is manageable (at a price) by the big enterprises. But the increased risks and/or costs handicap the small enterprise against the large, and the producers of real wealth as compared with the financial operators.

Conclusion

It would seem that uncertainty, in the sense used by Frank Knight, has substantially increased in the past decade or so, as the number of volatile variables in the monetary and financial structure of the international political economy has multiplied. This has often been as the result – direct or indirectly – of certain specific political decisions or non-decisions taken by the leading financial authorities, especially in the United States. The uncertainty has started a vicious circle of risk-averse responses, which in turn have added to the volatility of the variables and consequently to the general sense of confusion and the faltering confidence in the long-term viability of the global financial system. This erosion of social trust and confidence has been exacerbated as human and other resources have been diverted either to gambling and speculation, or to self-defence against them. Thus, far from stabilizing the system by damping its ups and downs, the devices such as futures markets – developed to deal with uncertainty – have actually served to exaggerate and perpetuate it.

Notes

1   The book was long and meandering. Published in 1900 it was called *Die Philosophie des Geldes* and was only recently translated by Tom Bottomore

and David Frisby as *The Philosophy of Money* (1978). The fact that Simmel was never given a proper German University Chair, Frisby suggested, could have been due to the prevailing anti-semitism of German society. Without professional status, Simmel had a rather limited influence on other writers. Subsequent neglect of his work has recently been somewhat remedied by Professor S. Herbert Frankel's stimulating little book *Two Philosophies of Money* (1979).

2   Knight makes a useful distinction between *anticipated change*, as between night and day or from demographic trends, say, and *capricious change*, which is much more difficult to respond to, and which characterizes a good deal of the behaviour of markets.

3   In 1983, for example, Merrill Lynch set aside several million dollars from its annual profits to pay out as bonuses to its middle-rank executives.

4   In 1985, salaries of $60,000 were commonly being paid by banks in Wall Street to recently qualified students from major business schools – about four times the starting salary in industry.

5   In 1984, markets in London, Chicago and New York recorded over 53 million contracts in financial futures, against 5 million energy futures and 7 million futures contracts in coffee, cocoa and sugar (J. Edwards, *London's Commodity Markets*, 1985).

6   A financial future is a promise to buy or sell a financial instrument like a bond, a currency or a basket of shares at a market-fixed price on a given delivery date. An option is a contracted right – which need not be exercised – to buy or sell at a market-fixed price on a given delivery date. While US regulations require 50 per cent of the price of a stock or share, a stock option, traded in Chiacgo since 1973, can be bought for a down payment of only 6 per cent.

CHAPTER 5
The Guessing Game

When does ignorance matter? This is a very important question when it comes to organizing an efficient and stable system for the world's money and finance.

The whole notion of ignorance thus deserves a moment's thought. There is more than one kind of ignorance. There is, for instance, unavoidable ignorance – all the things we cannot possibly know, like the hour and day when we shall die, and which therefore we can do nothing about. And there is insignificant ignorance – all the many things that we do not know, do not need to know and are not even interested in knowing. What we are concerned with in the present context is the large, undefined area that lies between these two extremes. In it there are all the things we ought to know and which we need to know, but do not know. We could call it the area of significant ignorance.

What lies within that area is entirely relative; there are no absolutes. If, for instance, you intend to drive home from work, then, for you, the information in the bus or train timetable lies outside the area. But if you were intending to take a train and did not know that the timetable says that the particular train you meant to catch does not run today, then the timetable is important to you; for you, it lies in the area of significant ignorance. It is the same with the business of government. What rulers and authorities need to know is a relative matter, depending on the environment – physical, political or economic – that they are in, and the responsibilities which they assume towards society. Different circumstances will carry with them different risks, and to guard against these risks, different kinds of knowledge will be needed. There was a time, not so long ago, when governments managed quite well without population censuses, and without detailed statistics about the national income or the balance of payments with the rest of the world. Now all these things are regarded as essential to good modern government. The question, however, in the context of a disordered monetary system is whether there are other things which now lie – as they did not before – inside the area of significant ignorance for national governments.

Assuming this to be the case, it could be the result of technical change or change in the nature of markets, or the result of government decisions – or some combination of these factors. More than likely, the experts will not be altogether agreed as to whether such a change has taken place at all.

Two such questions of considerable importance to discussions of the international monetary system and its future management are (1) whether the Eurocurrency market has an independent capacity for creating credit, and is thus able to add to inflation by affecting the global money supply; and (2) whether there has been a significant change, largely as a result of technological advance in banking transfers, in the velocity of the circulation of money.

Are Euromarkets inflationary?

The inflationary implications of credit-creation in Eurocurrency markets have been the subject of much searching discussion among the economists. Some years ago, a helpfully comprehensive survey of conflicting opinions (Swoboda, 1980) identified no less than four main schools of thought on the question. All appear to rest their conclusions on some very shaky assumptions and one rather dubious concept. This concept is that there is an identifiable 'multiplier', i.e. a numerical factor by which the monetary base has to be multiplied to find the aggregate money supply. The notion of the multiplier is very prominent in the literature. It assumes that the only variables are the total amount of bank deposits and the monetary base; everything else including exchange rates, interest rates, exchange controls, government debt, etc. are fixed. What it is doing, however, is applying to Eurobanking the same analytical process that might be applied to domestic credit creation in a closed and regulated system.

The 'multi-stage banking' approach draws a different but equally inappropriate analogy, likening the relation of Eurobanks or offshore branches to their home-based banks to the relation between 'city' and 'country' banks in the American banking system. It therefore assumes all sorts of fixed ratios which do not in fact apply at all in the Eurocurrency business (e.g. of deposits to reserves). It complacently concludes as a result that Euromarkets cannot increase the amount of credit available in the US economy. (This, indeed, since so much of the literature is American, is the dominant question: not so much what Eurobanking does to the world at large, as what it does to the United States!) The conclusion is surprising. For the Bank for International Settlements (BIS) and the Federal Reserve Board figures for 1981, for example, show that US residents in that year increased their borrowing from Eurobanks more than they increased their deposits by $23.6 billion. In the same year, American corporations raised $20 billion on the Eurobond markets – though how much of this they spent in the US there is no way of telling. Plainly, the empirical facts show that the amount of credit available in the US economy is very substantially affected by Eurocurrency transactions.

The 'initial deposit' approach is even crazier. It assumes that Euromarkets exist *in vacuo*, so that Eurobanking must have started with an initial deposit of uncertain provenance, and has continued to exist in inexplicable isolation from national banking and credit systems.

Swoboda's clear preference was for what he calls the 'world money stock' approach, even though this was developed (partly by himself) in the early 1970s, and apparently still rests on the assumption of fixed exchange rates and uniform rates of inflation and deflation throughout the world money system. Despite this rather heavy handicap, Swoboda claimed that this model was the most realistic of the four.

It does in fact lead to some general conclusions that actually accord with experience in the real world. One is that Eurobanking, because its lending practices do not have to conform to reserve requirements that restrict national banks, 'economizes' on high-powered money[1] and therefore serves to expand the world money supply above what it would have been had the Eurocurrency business never been invented. It also finds that because the Eurocurrency markets facilitate switching of financial assets and liabilities between currencies, and from national currencies in and out of Eurocurrencies, this also tends to swell the world money supply and to exacerbate the asymmetry between the United States which is comparatively little affected in its monetary management, and the European countries which are much affected.[2]

Even this school, Swoboda said, would agree with the others that 'unbridled' credit creation does not take place in the Euromarkets. This comforting conclusion may be aided by the shared assumption that the world money stock is governed by the sum total of domestic assets of national central banks and their reserves of gold, foreign exchanges, IMF drawing rights and SDRs, inferring that it must therefore be under control. Yet the facts are that world reserves in SDRs grew from $92 billion in 1970 to $310 billion in 1983; that an increasing percentage of these reserves consisted of funds that had been borrowed through the Eurobanking system; and that the IMF agreed on successive increases in quotas and drawing rights (i.e. credit creation) on the basis of fractional deposits of gold or other convertible assets. There is the further fact that 'domestic assets' and reserves in the United States – which are naturally the largest single component of the global aggregate – are rather different to what they are elsewhere. The United States does not need to hold dollar reserves as others do; and of the total increase in its domestic assets (i.e. government securities) over the decade of the 1970s, some 60 per cent had been bought by foreign governments and central banks. Moreover, this amount of officially-held US government securities has been apt to vary rather widely from year to year, according to other governments' perceived needs to defend their currencies against a depreciating dollar and/or high US interest rates.

Moreover, there is a strange omission from all these approaches to the question. This is the extent and effect of the interbank market, which is generally estimated to account for some 40 per cent of Eurocurrency transactions in any year, although (as the BIS freely admits) it is quite impossible to be accurate in netting out interbank deposits from the figure for gross loans to arrive at some sort of estimate of net transactions. Not surprisingly, a more recent – and rightly more sceptical – assessment of the situation by Marcello de Cecco concluded that nobody knew how much the Eurodollar market was adding to any national money supply (let alone the global money supply) and that considering the variations in individual assumptions about the multiplier, it would be wise to nurture 'a healthy disrespect' for any assertions that it was not inflationary or, for that matter any estimates of just how inflationary it was (De Cecco, 1982). In short, credit-creation through Eurobanking is not simply misperceived as being negligible, it actually belongs in the domain of ignorance, of things we do not properly know (Spero, 1980; Cornwell, 1983).

The velocity of money

The second uncertain question, it will be recalled, was whether the velocity of money was constant. (This also relates to the issues just discussed of credit-creation through the Euromarkets. But it also affects monetary management within national systems as well as between them, and could therefore be more important still.) If it has been misperceived, this will be partly because attention in monetary theory has been directed at prices, the monetary base, and at the money supply, and very little at the other component in the classic equation $MV = PT$; and partly because it has been the subject of very rapid technical change.

This whole question of the consequences of technical change, and especially the extensive use of computers, in banking is a long and complex story. But, to be as brief as possible, some of the relevant facts are that in 1981 money in the United States was moving through the writing of cheques to the tune of $15 trillion a year, while something of the order of $75 trillion was moving through the Fedwire system first introduced in 1973 and subsequently much improved. These funds are called Same Day Funds. And a further $165 trillion is transferred through the New York Clearing House Interbank Payments Systems (CHIPS) (Mayer, 1982). Some of this – but no one knows how much – consists of Eurocurrency transactions. These used to be known as Next Day Funds. But in October 1982 Same Day Funds and Next Day Funds were 'merged' and both are now cleared through CHIPS. Yet no one can distinguish, as they move, which is which. What this adds up to is that the widespread use of computer networks, private as well as public, by the banks immensely speeds the transactions velocity of money (i.e. how quickly money changes hands). It also, most likely affects the more important income velocity (i.e. how quickly credit is used for purchases). In a recession, as people postpone spending, or paying their bills, income velocity falls. But if, at the very same time, credit instead of cash is increasingly being used for purchases, and funds are being transferred electronically by banks through CHIPS and by enterprises and individuals through automatic transfer systems, then it seems more than probable that income velocity is increasing.

It seems to me that we have here something like those terrible sums where you have to calculate how quickly the bath fills with the hot tap full on, the cold half on and the plug out. Yet in this case, one can only guess at what change is taking place at any given moment in both the transactions velocity and the income velocity. It is another case of misperception really adding to the area of significant ignorance.

The above changes in technology clearly do something – though it is by no means clear what – to the Friedman concept of high-powered money. This has been cynically defined by Martin Mayer as 'that portion of the banks' funding requirements that they have been unable at the close of day to get out of the type of liabilities that the Fed requires them to keep as a reserve' (Mayer 1982). So has the implementation of the 1980 Depository Institutions Deregulation and Monetary Control Act. This piece of American legislation was expected to allow US bank reserves to fall from $40 billion (or $28 billion if you deduct the $12 billion held in bank vaults) in 1981 to $15 billion by 1986. But how fast the reserves will fall, and what that unknown quantity will do to velocity and the concept of high-powered money, and thus to the ability of government to control the money supply, no one knows. Small wonder the British have given up guessing and the Americans are fudging the issue!

If the credit-creating capacity of the Eurocurrency markets and the velocity of monetary circulation when aided by advanced technology are still open questions, it means that the limits of the area of significant ignorance are still open to doubt and debate. It may also be true that some current misperceptions draw these limits more narrowly than they should be drawn.

There is no need to labour this point unduly for it is perhaps less important than the much larger areas of acknowledged ignorance in the system. All the same, it has to be pointed out that some of these misperceptions have proved highly dangerous.

One memorable misperception was the conviction – very prevalent among American economists some ten or more years ago – that international loans were appreciably less risky than domestic loans. In 1975, an economist called Ruckdeschel compared the figures given by a sample of large banks of loans lost or loans past due for domestic as compared with foreign loans. He found that domestic loans had been riskier. He also found that only three banks then had had foreign loans which had proved worse risks than the domestic if US banks were to diversify and that their foreign lending they would reduce their loan loss rates by 20 per cent. 'Little support can be found', he concluded, 'for the argument that international or Eurocurrency lending activities are riskier or less profitable than is domestic lending (Ruckdeschel, 1975). Five years later, on the very eve of the debt crisis, the figures were still telling the same highly dubious story. All the lessons of history gave a very different verdict.

Yet as late as 1977, Governor Henry Wallich was still testifying to the House of Representatives that the losses of the seven largest US banks in the four years 1971–5 on foreign loans in proportion to their portfolios, were only a third as large as their domestic losses. With hindsight, we can see that it was highly dangerous to take so short a view of foreign lending. A little refresher course in nineteenth-century indebtedness would soon have corrected this misperception. Unfortunately it was made rather worse by the legal provisions of the American system. This decreed that loan contracts should have a cross-default clause, providing that a borrower defaulting on any one loan would be held to have defaulted on all. Partly for this reason many of the bad foreign loans by US banks were for far too long just reclassified as 'non-performing loans'. The banks, moreover, did not wish to advertise their mistakes to the stock market any more than was necessary. However, the loss in 1983 by most of the leading American banks of their AAA rating on the Moody index of risk to stockholders, drew unwelcome attention to their worsening debt–capital ratios. And there is little doubt that but for the Brazilian case, the US banks' records for 1982 would have diverged rather sharply from the 'trends' suggested so reassuringly by the earlier figures (Dufey and Giddy, 1979, p. 253).

Areas of ignorance

More important matters on which the rapid changes of recent years have opened up wide areas of ignorance concern what is going on in the markets, and whether the levers of control over financial institutions operated by governments are really working.

How much it is necessary to know about what is going on in a financial system depends a good deal on the system of control. One effective way of keeping control is to limit severely the freedom of action of financial institutions to create credit on their own initiative. In Eastern Europe, for example, the government does not need to be told what the banks are doing because it is the government rather than the banks which makes the major decisions about investment, inputs and costs of capital and labour. The role of markets is slim; access to credit is strictly and directly controlled. What may go on in the peripheral markets for personal services, like hairdressing, or for perishable commodities, like vegetables, is not going to upset the Five-Year-Plan. Only when the command economy becomes involved with a market system by borrowing heavily, as Poland did from Western banks, does it become important for the government to gather more information about the vagaries of the international financial markets. It then has to extend its net of controls widely enough to make sure that its exchange controls cannot be evaded, and that only those who have government approval can get access to credit and thus play a semi-independent role in the production structure.

Another system is to have very firm rules about the kind of external involvement that national financial institutions can have, and to attach very severe and personal penalties to any discovered infringement of the rules. The Swiss, for example, had the rule that national banks might take in deposits in foreign currency, but were strictly bound to make corresponding outward deposits while crediting to the depositor the equivalent sum in Swiss francs. Provided that rule was kept, the national central bank acting for the state did not need to know who the depositors were, how they acquired their funds, nor how the Swiss banks invested the counterpart to the deposits. The bankers were aware that any transgression of Swiss banking law would be speedily and severely punished, and that bank officials responsible would be held personally responsible and possibly sent to gaol.[3]

The British system

Or there was the British system which also laid emphasis on personal responsibility but did so indirectly by first imposing a statutory separation of function on operators in financial markets and then depending on an indirect system of control over them through autonomous self-regulation of each group by their own chosen group of peers. In the stock market, the Stock Exchange Council was the executive authority, and the buying and selling of shares by the brokers was functionally separated from the floating of shares by the stockjobbers. In the insurance market, Lloyd's was the authority, and the function of underwriting risks was separated from insurance broking. In the same way, in non-financial professions, the surgeons were functionally separate from the physicians and each was governed by its own Royal College of senior practitioners; while in the legal profession the solicitors were functionally separate from the barristers and were subject respectively to regulation by the Law Society and the Bar Council. In each case, the purpose was to remove the incentive for acting in the market out of self-interest instead of in the interest of a client, so that the market would respond as far as possible to the demands of the ultimate consumers of the professional service and not to the self-interest of the professionals. Without such separation, the system supposes – and not without reason – that practitioners will tend to abuse their position. Thus, by contrast in the United States the lawyers' self-interest in litigation has led to a flood of cases against manufacturers for 'product liability'. As the lawyers are allowed to take for themselves a percentage of any damages awarded by the judge in favour of the plaintiff, it is hardly surprising that manufacturers (like doctors) now have to insure heavily against the risk.

The principle of functional separation was also applied by the British to their financial institutions. Joint stock, commercial or 'high street' banks were not allowed under the old rules to lend their depositors' money abroad; neither were the trustees of minors or the executives of estates. Overseas banks were a separate category, as were the acceptance houses who dealt in the short-term credit market for bills of various kinds and maturities, and who, being more vulnerable to sudden market changes, were also offered resort to the Bank of England's support in its role of lender of last resort. The support however, was available only against the collateral of good securities and on 'onerous conditions' (i.e. high interest rates).

Under such a system it was not necessary for the Bank of England to keep under constant supervision all the activities of the various institutions. It could leave disciplinary action to the autonomous self-regulatory councils who had a strong collective interest in hanging on to their power and privilege and in being seen to be resolute in punishing offenders against the professional rules. Doctors were fairly often struck off; lawyers debarred. Stockbrokers were hammered and could never again practise their profession. So long as state employment of the professionals and government participation in the markets was limited, the system worked comparatively smoothly and economically. All that the monetary authority had to do was to monitor trends in the market, both at home and (after the First World War) in New York, and the major European financial centres. It did not need detailed and up-to-the-minute information on the day-to-day operations of each of the banks. The slightest hint or nudge by the central bank to the operators produced self-interested responses. Yet, for such a system to work reliably, the circle of banks had to be small and closely tied to the central bank by social as well as functional links. Individual responsibility had to be clear and unequivocal. And the authority had to be impartial and rather indifferent to the fortunes of any individual bank or banker in the system.

Once the door of the City of London was opened wide to foreign banks dealing in foreign currencies, and 'Welcome' put on the mat, this system of monetary supervision and control was probably doomed. Its decline has taken nearly a quarter of a century, and is now practically certain. For the Bank of England can no longer apply the system to some of the most powerful market operators in the City who are not British-based; and the operators in the stockmarket can no longer afford to maintain the separation of function if they are to compete with the big American and Japanese investment houses. Hence the Goodison–Parkinson deal, negotiated in 1983 between the head of the London Stock Exchange and the British Minister of Trade and Industry. By this deal, the government agreed to drop its prosecutions against the Stock Exchange before the Monopolies Commission for maintaining fixed fees, and in return the Stock Exchange agreed to accept new statutory regulation on the American pattern.

The American system

The trouble has been, however, that the American system, which is mainly responsible for the erosion of the British system, is itself the eroded relic of yet another system of financial regulation. It was a system that had some features in common with the British one and which, 50 years ago, seemed better adapted to a vast continental country in which the main financial centres were far apart in time and space, and in which regulatory power was dispersed through a federal system from the central government to the individual states. Thus, the small saver and depositor was protected by a federal law giving special support (at the price of specific restrictions) to savings banks – and Loan Associations or S and Ls – and by a federal agency from New Deal days – the Federal Deposit Insurance Corporation (FDIC) – which guaranteed deposits up to $10,000 (now raised to $100,000) against bank failure. Meanwhile, by the Glass–Steagall Act of 1933, commercial banks were not allowed to operate across state borders. Thus, the Bank of America based in San Francisco could operate in California, but not in New York. Conversely Chase Manhattan was excluded from California, and Continental Illinois confined to that state. The idea was to prevent a concentration of financial power and also to leave responsibility for supervision and discipline with local authorities more likely than distant federal bodies to know when things were going wrong. The security of the major banks was assured from 1913 onwards by their participation in the Federal Reserve System which was essentially voluntary, but which gave those who joined access to ready and substantial liquidity when they needed it.

Opinions differ somewhat as to which factors have been most important in bringing about change in this system, but most are agreed that there have been several contributory causes and that they have combined to undermine both the effectiveness of control and the adequacy of support where it is needed. One factor was that while banks were confined to state banking, neither their clients nor the depositors who fed the major financial centres were so limited. Neither were non-banks – those enterprises that had started as investment houses like Merrill Lynch, or as travel agents like American Express, or even as mail-order retailers like Sears Roebuck. Competition from these in recent years has pushed the banks to press for deregulation so that they could compete with the newcomers on more equal terms. Moreover, while the US authorities had freely allowed both the corporations and the banks to operate without restriction overseas, it seemed somewhat anachronistic not to let the latter do so within the United States across state lines. Technology, too, was rapidly undermining the system. When the courts were ruling that automatic debiting by computer state-to-state was legal, it was no longer logical to forbid the same operation conducted by the old-fashioned cheque. And whereas local stock markets and exchanges had been fairly important, even as recently as the post-war years, now four or perhaps five major centres dwarf all the others; by comparison with New York, Chicago, San Francisco, Dallas and possibly Atlanta, the volume of funds for investment or speculation in any other provincial centre is trivial. Reliance on a federal system of control no longer fitted the facts of the financial system.

Thus the argument here is, first, that it is the American system which has dominated the development of international banking over the past 25 years; and, second, that the areas in which the US authorities are ignorant when they cannot afford to be, have become progressively more extensive as the years have passed. And this is because the economic system of control has progressively relaxed its rules through various kinds of deregulation. It has also allowed the necessary dependence of the banks on the authorities to weaken, while the dependence of the system on at least the largest of the banks has destroyed the necessary indifference of the watchdog over the fate of any individual institution.

Hayek, Keynes and Simmel

An alternative argument which has been put forward by Professor Hayek is that the system has become so impossible to control that we should give up trying. It is his view that the illusion that governments are in charge of the money supply – or even that they wish to be – is highly dangerous. It fosters a false sense of security while permitting governments still to be tempted – as, Adam Smith observed, they always had been – to cheat people and thus to bring about 'a greater and more universal revolution in the fortunes of private persons than could have been occasioned by a very great public calamity'. But Hayek's solution – that money should be subject to the discipline of the market, and that like any other commodity in the market, anyone should be free to offer it for sale – is politically rather naive. Indeed, however persuasive the logic – given certain assumptions – the solution proposed as a result is no solution at all. What is to happen to existing contracts in particular currencies? Are we to be free to pay taxes in any money we choose? Do we have to negotiate, every time we buy or sell goods or services which money the other party will accept? The very idea that states in the international political system would even entertain such an apolitical system, or that business could function in such conditions of financial anarchy, is totally preposterous. It is based on two fundamentally false assumptions: first, that money has nothing to do with politics and government; and second, that confidence in money does not need time to develop. Whereas the lesson of history, surely, is that while governments have often abused the powers conferred by control over money, it has also only been through governments that economic systems have enjoyed all the benefits that sound money and well-regulated financial systems have been able to confer.

This observation leads me to the other reason why areas of ignorance in the present situation are so politically significant. Economic systems with sound money and well-regulated financial institutions certainly produced wealth, but were also apt to produce two other things both of which were socially disruptive – depressions at the trough of an economic cycle, and greater disparities than before in the distribution of the new wealth created by a more efficient system of economic exchange. It was the recognition of these tendencies at a time when both had become painfully obvious in Britain, that led Keynes to offer an ingenious explanation of why the system behaved in this cyclical way, and to propose a solution which would make good the deficiencies of the system. Paraphrasing rather brutally the famous *General Theory*, Keynes argued that the capitalist system did not function evenly nor efficiently; that is to say, it was liable to slumps and depressions and it did not always keep up enough real investment in production to maintain economic growth. Nor could it be saved from its own inherent weaknesses by the use of merely monetary policies. Although governments had the power to control the rate of interest and could make it act as a brake by raising it, and as an accelerator by lowering it, that would not work because the changes that would be politically practicable in either direction could never be big enough to offset in the one case the enthusiasm of optimistic investors nor, in the other case, the reluctance of pessimistic ones. Since in a depression, a deficiency of investment (and thus of growth and jobs) could not be accounted for by a deficiency of savings – on the contrary, the capitalists and rentiers were saving too much – the problem was how to get the rest of society to consume less and invest more – to prime the pump, as it were, and thus to get the famous multiplier to work to restore the economic *élan* of the system.

> The only radical cure for the crises which afflict the economic life of the modern world would be to allow the individual no choice between consuming his income and ordering the production of the specific capital-asset which, even though it be on precarious evidence, impresses him as being the most promising investment open to him (Keynes 1936, p. 160).

In an authoritarian system this can be done quite easily by decree, across the board and over the workers' heads. In a free society where wages have to be bargained, it can still be done, not by decree but by the state cheating the workers of their wages by changing the quantity of money and relying on their 'money illusion' so that the deception is undetected until it is too late.

The logic of Keynes's thought has, from the beginning, and understandably, exercised an immense and broadly based appeal, especially with those who, as economists or students of economics have been trying to think clearly and logically about economic problems. The two objections that can be raised against the argument therefore are not directed at the logic but at the basic assumptions on which the logic rests. One is a moral assumption, and the other is a practical one.

The moral objection has been expounded by Professor S. H. Frankel in his book, *Money: Two Philosophies*, in which he contrasts the Keynesian view of money as a tool of politics, something that can be manipulated by government for the long-term good of society at large, with that of Georg Simmel, the German sociologist referred to earlier. Frankel suggests that Simmel rightly sees the management of money not as a technical aspect of government, somehow separate from the rest of politics, but, on the contrary, as an integral part of the whole philosophy of society. The implication he finds in Simmel's rather long and rambling work is that if you damage or undermine the trust which it is essential that people have in money, it may continue to function as a means of exchange and a store of value, but you will also have risked undermining and damaging all the other forms of trust in authority and in the social institutions and relations which are essential to bind a society together.

Simmel, he says, had two profound reasons for being pessimistic about even the fairly stable monetary system of his time. He did not believe that people would indefinitely accept the increasingly abstract ways of thinking required by the growing complexity of monetary systems. Secondly, he feared that serious misconceptions would accumulate about the unlimited power of money, and that these would ultimately destroy a free monetary order. Frankel, a deep conservative who sympathizes with Hayek's comparable distrust of the power of reason in human affairs, sees the contemporary belief that problems will be solved by applying more money to them, as similar and comparable to the other belief that problems can be solved with the application of more research and study. Keynes, by contrast, was essentially optimistic, an intellectual mandarin who believed that intellect could triumph over capitalist caution and risk-aversion. This is why he advocated the deliberate practice of deception: 'The motives and the movements of the economic actors on the stage are to be influenced by simply deflecting the mirror of money so that they may be led to apprehend a *distorted* image of reality' (Frankel 1977, p. 72; his italics).

Although, according to Frankel, Keynes himself did not use the word 'moral' and prided himself on being a progressive, free-thinking and thoroughly modern man, Frankel suggests that Keynes's argument was nevertheless predicated on his own explicit and essentially moralistic disapproval of the love of money, and of the materialist values exalted in capitalistic society. Whether for tacit and undeclared moral reasons or simply because of a kind of intellectual snobbery towards people who had and used money, Keynes freely used pejorative terms in writing about the system and about capitalists. But since Keynes never shared the naive illusions of some of his contemporaries (notably Sidney and Beatrice Webb and Bernard Shaw) about the achievements and attractions of the socialist alternative as practised in the Soviet Union under Stalin, the only serious question was how to remedy the defects of the existing system. Perhaps Keynes could see a rough ironic justice in using deception to correct the weaknesses of a system which itself proclaimed a good many half-truths (if not downright lies) about the impartiality of the market, the openness of opportunity, the harmony of interest and so forth. At any rate, Frankel argues that Keynes knew exactly what he was advocating, but believed, cynically, that the ends justified the means.

Keynes also believed that he understood the working of the system and that governments had at their disposal enough information about the moving parts of this complex machine to be able, with spanner and screwdriver, to manage demand to the point of 'fine-tuning' the entire engine. It is this, it seems to me, which is a much more doubtful assumption in the 1980s that is was even in the 1930s. And one does not have to go all the way with Simmel to see that Keynesian demand management is very much less likely to work if those who are running the system do not in fact know all they need to know, and if in addition they cannot be sure that their interventions will have the results they expect. Thus, if we are to remain optimistic – whether with Friedman or with Keynes – about the possibilities of managing the system, we have to be convinced either that the rules and the penalties for breaking them are tough enough on all those involved to keep the system running smoothly and to maintain social trust in it; or else that some combination of regulation and informed intervention can do the same. And since, as everyone now recognizes, we are talking about a highly integrated international banking and credit structure, the information needed will be about the operations of credit-creating institutions *outside* their respective states, as well as those within them – or at least within the most important ones.

We need, in short, to ask a variety of new questions. Are the collections of international statistics that we have good enough? Are there any serious gaps in information about the monetary flows between national systems? What effect do these flows have on the domestic money supply? Are the boundaries between national monetary authorities clearly enough defined? Between the various national systems for exerting authority over money markets and financial institutions, have any yawning gaps or holes developed through which control can slip away?

What do we know?

On the question of the adequacy of information, a first step might be to look at the Manual of Statistics published by the Bank of International Settlements (BIS) in Basle, which summarizes the information compiled by international organizations on countries' external indebtedness. This gives an overall picture of the primary sources of all the main statistical series on which central and private banks (and academics) rely when tracking changes in the creation and flows of international credit.

The BIS itself is responsible for making the best available guesses – they do not claim to be more – about the external claims (loans made) and liabilities (loans taken) of banks operating inside the BIS reporting area and in certain offshore centres. The 'reporting area' consists of the territory of 14 industrial countries. These are the original Group of Ten[4] plus Switzerland, Austria, Denmark and Ireland. Excluded are such countries as Australia and New Zealand,

South Africa, Spain, Portugal, Greece, Turkey, Norway, Finland, South Korea, Taiwan, India and Pakistan, not to mention the whole of Latin America, the rest of Africa, the Middle East and East Asia. The tables also include the external claims and liabilities of US banks (but not Japanese or other banks) in Hong Kong, Singapore, Panama, the Bahamas and the Cayman Islands. The totals are consequently by no means complete, though they are probably comprehensive enough for any general trends to show up in them. They are published quarterly and so they do give some rough indication of the rate of change (e.g. the switch of bank transactions away from the Caribbean tax havens and back to New York in the wake of the International Banking Act).

Some of the other BIS statistical series, collected from the member central banks are a little more extensive. For instance, the tables showing maturity profiles of bank loans outstanding or committed, country by country, includes loans contracted by foreign banks in Lebanon, Liberia, Bahrain and Barbados, together with some of the minor Caribbean centres.

The BIS has always been – and still is – the source of such information as is available from the reporting area about the growth of Eurocurrency loans, the source of deposits and the currency denomination of the loans. Most of the statistics published by the OECD in Paris concerning foreign bank lending, issues of foreign bonds, and on the maturity and spreads of international bank loans are derived from the BIS. In addition the OECD has published for over 20 years a table of financial flows to developing countries which is widely used and quoted. Yet this tends to overstate net North–South financial flows since it does not count the return South–North flow of profits, dividends and financial fees of all kinds. The information it gives on investment generally is moreover extremely sketchy. The fact is that statistics collected by international organizations are only as good as those collected and published by their member states and apart from the United States (and, on matters like investment, Britain), most countries have not thought it necessary to require banks and other private corporations to divulge the necessary information about their foreign financial transactions.

It is thus not surprising that the BIS Manual regretfully concludes, 'There are no countries for which full information on the outstanding stock of external indebtedness is available' (p. 96).

Specifically, the BIS study revealed that although the World Bank's Debt Reporting System collected data about government borrowing and major foreign borrowing by state enterprises and large private ones, this data did *not* include long-term debts incurred by private individuals or corporations to lenders outside the country *if such debts were not guaranteed by the government.* Individual borrowing is probably not very important statistically, but corporate borrowing certainly is. Yet no comprehensive figures are available to indicate whether it is rising or falling.

Moreover, even if foreign direct investment were being fully monitored, which, as pointed out, it is not, this would still leave us in the dark about the growing number of joint production arrangements where the foreign partner supplies for instance, the technology, the capital equipment and the managerial and marketing knowhow, and in return eventually – perhaps five or ten years later – takes a share of the output. The capital goods will show up on the import side of the country's trade balance and the ultimate exports on the other side, but the finance involved need not show up anywhere. This sort of arrangement has become fairly common in East–West deals in Europe and is now becoming more so in the Third World, as transnational corporations (TNCs) continue to relocate production in order either to profit from cheap labour or lower taxes, or to be sure of securing permanent access to LDC markets. Nor is it only production that is relocated. Just as intra-firm trade is coming to account for a substantial portion – varying for different countries from 25 to nearly 50 per cent – of all international trade, so intra-firm transfers of money are likewise growing – but only show up in the statistics to the extent that they pass through the banking system, or at least through certain visible parts of it.

A comparable blind spot in the monitoring of long-term liabilities of LDCs concerns the foreign-owned share in a corporation which goes bust, as happened in 1983 to the Banco di Fomento in Chile. Several foreign banks, encouraged by the regime change and by a currency supposedly pegged to the US dollar, had taken shares in Chilean banks and other enterprises. But the generally deteriorating situation of all developing countries in the 1980s put many of these at risk, and the foreign shareholders, banks especially, were apt (as the Chilean case showed) to use their political leverage to claim the return of their investment.

Also excluded from official data, according to the BIS, is a mass of short-term debt. The statistics show the short-term borrowing by banks inside the country concerned from banks outside it. But they do not show credit from non-banks; for example, short-term trade credit whether this is given by foreign governments or state enterprises or by foreign suppliers. We know that when a country looks as though it may be heading for financial difficulty, the banks are apt to go cold on requests from importers for financial cover, so it is only to be expected that their first reaction is to look elsewhere for credit. But whether or not they are successful, it seems no one knows. More particularly, their foreign creditors (including their bankers) do not know how deeply they have gone into short-term debt from others and thus what chance they have of being able to repay their short-term loans when the time comes (Stewart 1985).

Rather more surprising is the fact that while each of the major industrialized countries has made its own arrangements for providing insured credit – and often insured at subsidized rates – for its own exporters, the national export credit agencies do not pool their up-to-date information on how much each has increased its lending, and at what maturities, to Country X. The most comprehensive aggregation of this sort of data presently available appears to be made by Caploan, a private consulting agency in London.

The real problem here is that for historical reasons of convenience banking statistics have been habitually based on a 'location' basis rather than on a 'charter' (i.e. nationality) basis. The result is that the loans made by a US bank branch in London to an Australian bank in Hong Kong show up as British assets and Hong Kong liabilities, and that loans made by an American or a British bank outside the reporting area do not show up at all. This is a convention which flagrantly ignores the political reality underlined by the post-Herstatt 1976 Concordat that left the final responsibility for regulating – and if necessary rescuing – banks with the government that had chartered them, not with the one whose territory they happened to work on.

And there are other lacunae in the BIS data. Not all the countries even within the area report everything. For the loan maturity series,

Canada ignores investment banks, Italy some of the large institutions that make only long- and medium-term loans, Switzerland the often large investments made by trustees in foreign currencies. Neither Italy nor Luxembourg bothers about loans made by their banks' foreign affiliates – as became painfully obvious in the wake of the Ambrosiano affair (Cornwell, 1983). In the statistics on foreign borrowing from the banks, there is no knowing how much is 'real' and how much is interbank borrowing. Indeed, perhaps the most important weak point in the whole information picture is the absence of information about interbank lending.

The BIS's best guess is that interbank loans make up 40 per cent or thereabouts of total lending in Euromarkets, though the total volume of interbank borrowing and lending is known to be much greater (i.e. gross transactions rather than net). But how much a particular bank is depending at any point on the interbank market, either for deposits or for the profit from loans, is a dark secret. (Even the data that does exist is at least five months old by the date of publication.) And the importance of this is easily seen when any bank begins to get into trouble – Franklin National, as described by Joan Spero for instance, or, more recently Penn Square and Continental Illinois. And the extent of ignorance on this point is important for its relevance – as pointed out by Marcello de Cecco (1982) to the whole tangled question of the global money supply.

The fact is that some information is pooled and much more could be. The BIS has not only long been aware of the problem, but as far back as the early 1970s started to prepare to take advantage of the possibilities of centralizing financial information opened up by computer/telematics technology. It set up a Working Party of Economic Statisticians and Computer Experts which by now has devised a system linking all central bank computers by satellite and telephone to Basle. Through this the central bank can have instant access to all the data possessed by the IMF, plus the BIS's own statistical series on Euromarket transactions. But obviously, information that is never collected cannot be shared. Moreover, there is the rather astonishing fact – given help being brought into the negotiations – that because the BIS is a central bankers' club and not a conventional international organization, neither Finance Ministries nor commercial banks have access to its centralized computer system.

Weakness of another kind lies in the fact that the banks themselves do not publicize the limits they have set themselves on lending to any one country. It is true that since 1974, and especially in the last three or four years, these limits have become tighter and more detailed; sometimes under pressure from the US Comptroller of the Currency in the case of US banks, sometimes out of simple self-preserving prudence. And since the mid-1970s the US regulators have insisted that loans to any one borrower must not exceed 10 per cent of the bank's capital surplus plus retained earnings. But it would be wrong to infer from the existence of the rule that it is universally observed. In the letter, it probably is, but in spirit it is not, since the total of loans made to a variety of borrowers in Country X is not added up, even though it is the country and not the individual borrower which may eventually have to ask for rescheduling.

In this game of Blind Man's Bluff, it is not only the creditors and their governments which are blindfolded. Borrowing LDC governments also do not know what limits the system is setting on their overall foreign debt. In the Eurocurrency market, banks come in and go out all the time, and quite unpredictably. Up until the mid-1970s the market was dominated by the US banks, with each of these big fish trailing a shoal of minnows behind it; then they are increasingly joined by the European and Japanese banks, and later still by the Arab banks.[5] But in 1978/79, the Japanese Finance Ministry put limits on Japanese banks' participation in the market, and in 1982/83 almost all the banks substantially reduced their Euromarket operations.[6] Not only can the credit available shrink in this way without earning, but the market for medium-term credit or the bond market (or both) can quickly be pre-empted by big industrialized countries (Britain, France and Italy, for example) or by a spate of corporate borrowing. Either or both can easily 'crowd out' the hapless LDC borrower, or arbitrarily and suddenly raise the spread over LIBOR charged to them – regardless of their objective circumstances.

Conclusions

Summing up the important conclusions emerging from this statistical jungle, we can say that the central banks of the major countries and the international organizations who publish the data they provide know some things for certain (official grants and loans, loans from multilateral agencies). They can make informed guesses at others, such as the volume and direction of international bank lending and financing from the international bond markets. But of the amount and nature of foreign direct investment, they can only make a rough guess.[7] And on two or three extremely important components of international financial flows – trade credit from non-banks, very short-term credit and financial transfers carried out across frontiers within large corporations – there is absolutely no reliable information.

This highly partial information picture is clearly important when it comes to the effective management of what I would call the credit crisis, but which is usually referred to as the LDC debt crisis (Strange, 1983). It is also important for the domestic monetary management of the United States and other major industrialized countries, if it means that they do not know for sure what money is coming into the country or flowing out of it through the banking system. These 'errors and omissions' as they are called on balance of payments accounts, are by no means trivial and have been steadily increasing in size. In 1982 the OECD announced that it had calculated that the total for all its members had risen above $20 billion a year. It is well understood in financial circles that these unknown quantities arise from short-term money moving in and out of banks and the accounts of large corporations in one country and into another.

As mentioned earlier, the interbank market is a very important grey area so far as accurate information goes. Table 5.1 gives the estimates made by the Bank of England – others do not even attempt to make any – of the percentages of total interbank claims and liabilities lent and borrowed by London banks in foreign currencies in 1973, 1976 and 1981.

The extent of one bank's dependence on others is not at all clear, even within one country. In the United States for example, in the summer of 1982 an obscure Oklahoma bank, Penn Square, was found not only to have lent lavishly and unwisely to oil ventures in the region, but to have borrowed funds to do so from some of the major moneycentre banks and specifically from Continental Illinois, one of the two biggest Chicago banks. The whole intention of US banking

Table 5.1 Percentages of non-sterling interbank transactions in London

	1973	1976	1981
British banks	81	59	81
American banks	85	85	75
Japanese banks	98	95	94
Other overseas banks	88	85	78
Consortium banks	95	94	86
TOTAL	85	86	81

[a] includes claims and liabilities of Commonwealth banks which after 1975 were counted among other overseas banks.

regulations prohibiting inter-state or national banking had been frustrated when a bank like Penn Square was able to operate under the control of a man apt to appear in his office in a Mickey Mouse mask, without either the US Treasury or the officers of the Comptroller of the Currency being aware of this 'eccentricity'.

In considering these aspects of the system together, we have seen that increased uncertainty has produced a marked hypertrophy of financial markets and financial dealing, much of it speculative in character. It has also increased the inequality in competition between large enterprises and small ones. And it has altered the balance – so vital to any stable market system – between authority and market, with the result that authority has been undermined and markets made more volatile.

Yet these consequences were masked for too long by some important misperceptions, mostly promulgated by academics, about what was really going on and what consequences followed. Some of those misperceptions have been shown up. Other persist. But the general effect has been gradually to extend the area of significant ignorance – significant, that is, from the point of view of political control and supervision of the economic and financial system. That control and supervision requires knowlege, and as change accelerates and the markets and national monetary systems become more integrated into a global system, the nature of the required knowledge increases and changes.

It is in the light of these broad conclusions that we have to review and weigh the various remedies and reform plans that have been put forward to bring the system under better control.

Notes

1   High-powered money was the term coined by Milton Friedman and Anna Schwarz for the monetary base which determines the money supply, however calculated, see *Monetary History*, p. 55.

2   Not everyone would agree. In recent years it can be argued that the United States has been liable to violent change in borrowing and lending by foreigners and US residents in the United States, or in Eurocurrencies, and that this has only been apparent with a time-lag that has made monetary management a matter of guesswork (Jane d'Arista interview).

3   Paul Erdman, author of *The Billion Dollar Killing* and other financial-thriller bestsellers, was in fact sent to gaol.

4   The Group of Ten was the name given to the signatories of the General Arrangements to Borrow (1962). The are the United States, Canada, Japan, West Germany, France, Britain, Italy, Belgium, the Netherlands and Sweden.

5   These now account for as much as 10 per cent of all Eurocurrency transactions (T. Wohlers Scharf, OECD, Development Centre, 1984).

6   The annual growth of international banking credit was 21 per cent in 1980 and 1981, but only 8½ per cent in 1983 and 7 per cent in 1984. Instead of providing $67.5 billion in net credit to the rest of the world, as they did in 1981, banks in the industrial countries were net takers of funds from the rest of the world to the tune of $18.5 billion (BIS *Annual Report*, 1985, p. 111).

7   One such semi-official guess was that this had increased from $33 billion in 1977, $37 billion in 1978, $40 billion in 1979 and $43 billion in 1980. But how much of this was local capital raised by foreign corporations in the country in which they were investing was not at all clear – nor could it be.

CHAPTER 6
Some Prescriptions

There are people who believe that there is nothing much that can be done about the weaknesses of the world's money and financial systems. Those whom I have called the technical determinists agree that there is not much of a policy nature that can be done to remedy the situation, but they do not regard the condition as fatal or incurable. They are like Christian Scientists, imagining that God, or Nature – or in this case, Kondratiev long waves – will sooner or later come to the rescue and in the meantime these is not much else to be done but wait for it to happen.

Another pessimistic group consists mainly of marxists or neo-marxists who regard the whole capitalist system as incurably doomed, so intrinsically and inherently sick that only death and resurrection through revolution, bringing about a fundamentally different socialist society, can cure its ills. There is also, of course, quite a substantial body of opinion that accepts the marxist diagnosis but refuses to follow its logical progression to so fatalistic, pessimistic and violent a conclusion. Instead, its exponents look for some interim strategy to limit or modify the social and economic damage that results and to the extent that they have ideas that must be regarded as solutions, they too deserve consideration.

There are also those who prescribe the wrong remedies because they have misdiagnosed the basic flaw or weakness in the system. Chief among these are those liberal economists whose passionate, practically evangelistic, faith in the blessings of free trade lead them to locate the seat of the infection in the global political economy in misguided trade policies, and the cause of poor economic growth, international conflict, unemployment and much else besides in protectionist measures against foreign competition. The preferred remedy, therefore, is to be found in more liberal trade policies. Some liberal economists will say that a concerted effort to reform and liberalize the trade policies of the major trading countries, though necessary to restore the world to economic health, is not sufficient and that a concurrent effort must be made to tackle the monetary and financial disorders as well (Camps and Diebold 1983; Tumlir 1983; Corden 1984). The argument developed in earlier chapters leads to the somewhat different conclusion that even if it were politically and technically possible to liberalize trade and make world markets for most goods and services truly competitive, that would still leave untouched the more serious and damaging aspect of world economic disorder which concerns (as argued in a previous chapter), the chronic instability of the world's financial system, the invitation that it offers to speculation and an ever-increasing disparity and inequality in the social distribution of risk and of opportunities for gain.

The only other important kind of misdiagnosis to my mind is the one which is more popular with some political scientists than it is with the economists. It is expounded by those I labelled in chapter 3 as 'political determinists' – those who believe that the root cause of world economic disorder lies in the loss of American hegemonic power to lead, guide and to some extent govern the world economy. Looking back nostalgically to the Bretton Woods system as a golden age of stability and growth, they see the reason for the abandonment of rules in the loss of American power. In chapter 3 I tried to sketch the reasons for thinking that there was nothing predetermined or inevitable about the policy choices made by the United States which have led to a condition of increased monetary and financial anarchy. It surely follows that if there was nothing inescapable about the path to greater anarchy, there is equally nothing impossible about a return journey towards greater order and stability. But it does not require, as some of the political determinists are inclined to argue, a major renascence of manufacturing industry in the United States or a return to surplus on the US balance of visible trade, or indeed the handicapping of Western Europe, Japan or any other participants in the system with larger defence budgets or restrictions on their export industries (Cline 1983; Keohane 1984).

Impossible remedies

Prescribing the wrong remedy through diagnosing the wrong problem is far more excusable as a genuine understandable mistake than prescribing remedies that are – and are known to be – quite out of the patient's reach. The doctors do the first all the time. How many patients have undergone surgery that turned out to have been unnecessary? How many sufferers from *anorexia nervosa* have been sent off to see psychiatrists when – some experts say – all they needed was something to correct a dietary deficiency of zinc? How many electric shock treatments were discovered afterwards to have been inappropriate? But at least the medical profession does not indulge so often as the academic profession in the other error of 'discovering' a solution that experience has already shown to be unattainable.

In my view, this is by far the commonest error in the whole literature of international political economy as it applies to contemporary troubles. And the main reason for it is a persistent inattention to the history of international relations and more particularly to the history of international organization.

This has shown quite clearly and unequivocally the limits set to international cooperation and conflict resolution by the nature of the international political system. There may still be some disagreement on the basis of past experience about where the precise divide lies between the conceivably practicable and the probably unattainable: there is no doubt whatever about the large domain of the impossible that lies beyond that borderline area. Here lie all the remedies that are simply not practicable so long as political authority rests with states functioning within defined territorial limits, and so long as that authority is supported by the willing (or unwilling-but-effectively-coerced) loyalty of its inhabitants.

Those experts, therefore, who propose these beguiling but impracticable remedies for the problems of the monetary and financial system are like the supposedly wise old owl to whom the other animals went to ask how they could stop the lion from killing and eating them.

'Well', said the owl, 'if you knew when the lion was coming to attack you, you could run away or hide. So you must arrange for every lion to have a warning bell round its neck.' 'But how', they persisted, 'do we do that?' 'Ah', said the owl, 'I've told you the principle behind the answer: it's for you to work out how to put it into practice.'

The fable applies in this case to those who prescribe the coordination of national economic policies. It applies also to those who prescribe any 'reform' of international organization that is so far beyond the limits of what is conceivably acceptable to the chief governments of leading states that there is no way that the principle can be translated into the practical. It would be different if either were ready to admit that theirs were counsels of perfection, ideal goals to be aimed at over a long period of education and gradual step-by-step advance towards a different international political system, and if, at the same time, they could tell us what to do in the long meantime until the happy day dawned when the ideal remedy at last lay within our grasp.

Coordinating national policy

The better coordination of national economic policies has been a recurrent theme of many international conferences, private and official. It was first given a big push in 1977 when the United States propounded what it called the 'locomotive theory' as the solution to the weakness of the dollar and the exchange rate instability that went with it. But it is now seen that what Washington really wanted when it pleaded with Germany and Japan to put their weight behind a push for better growth rates in the world economy was that both would inflate their economies in step with the United States thus arresting the distressing fall of the dollar in the foreign exchange markets. To the extent that both did so while the US growth rate slowed down, 'coordination' may have helped to stabilize exchange rates and keep the dollar stronger in 1979. But, the coincidence was partly accidental and as a general rule it would be very rash to rely on Germany and Japan always finding it consistent with their own national political and economic objectives to keep in step with the United States. This is particularly so because the United States hardly maintains an even steady pace from one month to the next. In the past decade, it has gone from the pursuit of lower inflation to lower unemployment and back to the pursuit of lower inflation, and it has passed from enjoying the trading benefits of a very weak dollar to enjoying the financial benefits of a very strong dollar without ever consulting other governments or giving them notice of sudden changes of policy direction.

One of the leading exponents of the proposition that the world's monetary system would work more smoothly if it were subjected to coordinated tripartite management by the monetary authorities of the United States, Japan and West Germany, has been already mentioned. Professor Ronald McKinnon first developed the idea of this prescription more than ten years ago in a Princeton Essay in International Finance (McKinnon, 1974).

At that time many fond hopes were still being entertained about the possibility of international monetary reform through the deliberations of the IMF's Interim Committee. McKinnon's point was that the key for the health of the system (as in the mid-1930s) lay not in multilateral agreement between 20 or 100 different governments, but in close collaboration between the major monetary powers – a point John Williams had stressed in vain at the time of Bretton Woods. It was therefore sensible and timely. Since then, he has elaborated his original ideas from a technical point of view. He has explained how a central monetary authority like the Federal Reserve Bank, in setting its monetary targets, can give less emphasis to purely domestic indicators and more emphasis to the stability of the exchange rate with its major partners and thus to the stability of the relative purchasing power of each currency compared with others. For the United States this would mean decelerating growth in the money supply whenever this surged too far ahead of the money growth in the partner countries (McKinnon, 1974, 1984).

There are some technical and economic objections that could be made to the scheme, but the major objections are political. The basic assumption is that governments accept stability as a prime value having priority over any other policy goals such as national security, lower unemployment, a free hand in foreign relations, and so on. Stability comprehends, moreover, both stability in the long-term value of money ('a common long-run money growth target') and stability of exchange rates between the three major currencies. Now this may be desirable, but it is not at all realistic – least of all for the United States whose record of exploiting the system rather than governing it in a stable fashion is plain for all to see. Secondly, it discounts, to the point of ignoring, the possible conflict of these tripartite arrangements with any other major policy considerations that may inspire the two junior partners in the troika.

For Germany, there is the commitment to the European Monetary System and to the aim of creating in Europe a 'zone of greater monetary stability'. The differences that emerged in 1978–9 between the ideas of the Bundesbank and those of the German government showed the priority which the latter gave to political objectives – and this has not changed with changes of government in Bonn. In addition, there is a German interest in trade and peaceful co-existence with Eastern Europe which Washington does not share and which could easily lead to differences of opinion on monetary policy. And for Japan, there is the consistent Japanese concern both to insulate Japan as far as reasonably possible from the vagaries of US policy and to build closer bilateral links with neighbouring Asian countries, including China. Both of these long-term national interests could easily upset the tripartite applecart.

To meet some of these political objections, McKinnon has suggested that the ultimate goal of fully coordinated policy should be approached gradually, by stages, so as not to alarm politicians overmuch and to give time for habits and techniques of collaboration to develop. But this is precisely the neofunctionalist fallacy that the Europeans fell for in the early 1970s with the Werner Plan and the early ideas about European monetary union. Surely the whole experience of the European Community has shown that playing 'grandmother's footsteps' with the nation state is no easy game. For as soon as national autonomy and freedom of action are seriously threatened, the pace of 'supranational' decision-making slows to a crawl, and resistance, instead of weakening, begins to harden. Thus, in McKinnon's scheme, the adoption of Stage One would be more likely to alert politicians and officials to the interests threatened, and so to heighten resistance to any further advance.

It would be recognized by Europeans, however, that the notion of tripartite or international coordination of macroeconomic policy-making among the major industrial countries is very popular among American liberals and internationalists. For instance, James Tobin, a prestigious Yale professor and Nobel prizewinner, suggests that 'macro-economic policy coordination is a good place to begin both with the repair of the Atlantic alliance and the recovery of the world economy' (Tobin, 1984, p. 112). But the argument for it is based on the doubtful assumption that the subjugation of national to common interest is of equal benefit to all, because any country that expands home demand depreciates its currency. But, in practice, the United States can flout normal economic logic by raising interest rates and drawing in enough foreign capital to compensate for its very large trade deficit. This points to the inherent asymmetry of economic autonomy in the system – and thus to the unlikelihood of American politicians of any party being any more heedful of European or Japanese grumbling at American economic unilateralism than they have been already. Marina Whitman in the same collection of essays is more politically sophisticated, suggesting that a new 'implicit bargain' between Europe and American is a necessary prerequisite for any progress in the direction of coordinated monetary policies'.

> In such a bargain the United States might take greater account of the
> transAtlantic spillover of its economic policies and curb its tendency
> toward 'global unilateralism' – efforts to assert extraterritorial jurisdic-
> tion and impose universal rules of behaviour that have long been a
> source of irritation to our allies – in return for an increased willing-
> ness on the part of the European nations (along with Japan) to share
> responsibility for maintaining Western security, the viability of the
> international trade and financial system and the health of the global
> economy. (Whitman 1984, p. 51.)

Jacques Polak, veteran international official, research director for over 20 years at the IMF and subsequently an Executive Director, is even more sceptical of the constraints set by the art of the possible. Writing on the same theme for the Group of Thirty in 1981, he observed with dry understatement: 'Confidence that national levels of demand could be negotiated at summit meetings must rely heavily on the ability of heads of state to make international comparisons of utility, an ability that lesser mortals lack even on an inter-personal basis' (Polak 1981, p. 13). He pointed to situations requiring adjustment by one or other country for which coordination 'involves not so much the exhilarating pursuit of a common goal but the invariably messy search for a compromise of conflicting national interests'. The difficulties of policy coordination in the field of aggregate demand, he concluded, are so formidable that nothing is gained by overlooking them or pretending that they do not exist. Indeed Polak ended by suggesting the converse – that since integration has brought so much instability with it, it may be better to look to 'decentralized decision-making', to 'controlled disintegration' in Fred Hirsch's words, for a solution (Hirsch and Doyle, 1977). This seems to be another way of saying that it would be better to put back some controls to insulate national economies from the transnational consequences of financial markets and the impact of other countries' policies upon them (Polak, 1981). But whether this is possible is open to question.

To be frank, it seems that the popularity of macroeconomic policy coordination in American circles reflects an unconscious form of American imperialism, more than a real wish to change American attitudes. It is a remedy that allows the Americans to do as they please while others do as they are told. It is not a feasible cure for our economic ills (Calleo, 1983).

The Brandt solution

Many prescriptions for economic reform seek, in one way or another, to increase the power and resources and to extend the activities of international organizations. This is especially true of those who broadly concur with the diagnosis and conclusions of the Brandt Report on North–South relations (Brandt, 1979). They subscribe to the basic proposition that the rich North and the poor South countries have some fundamental interests in common. It is in the long-term interest of the rich countries to help the poor ones to develop economically, and it is in the long-term interests of the poor countries – so the argument goes – to sustain and not to disrupt a world market economy in which capital and technology for investment, goods and services for consumption move relatively freely across frontiers. To this end, the Brandt Reports recommend a large and immediate increase in the resources transferred to developing countries channelled through a World Development Fund – far larger and more ambitious than the World Bank. Arms sales and defence policies, being wasteful of resources, must be cut, and the resources devoted to civil development. The large corporations operating internationally have too much power and should therefore be controlled. Authority to tax should be given to international organizations to free them of dependence on national contributions. Given the sort of broad commitment to social democratic ideas about the need for countervailing political power to redress the failures and inequities of a market system, there is an internal logical consistency about these sort of proposals.

Although these ideas are held commonly enough in Europe, they are by no means so generally accepted in America (Strange, 1981). There the Brandt Reports got little publicity and raised few echoes of agreement. And in other continents, while governments are content to complain about the injustices of the capitalist system, it is extremely doubtful if in practice many would willingly forgo their freedom to buy arms, both Western and Soviet, or would be happy to concede far-reaching powers over their economy to an international development agency. Experience with the IMF missions hardly endears Brazilians, Argentines, Nigerians and many others to that idea. Indeed, when it comes to the point, it is not only the rich and powerful countries who have been reluctant to let international bureaucracies make the decisions that shape the country's future. One big reason why this is so is that these bureaucracies are not properly accountable to anyone in particular. The servants of many masters heed none. There is a premium on being inoffensive, and though provocative speeches can be tolerated, provocative actions or obstructive behaviour cannot (Archer, 1984). The result is that instead of leading the vanguard of progress, many of the best-known international organizations – the UN itself, UNESCO, the European Commission – are increasingly regarded by anyone who has much to do with them as backwaters of inefficiency, the haven of quiet-lifers and of people who would rather push paper than policies. This is not true of the organizations with a specific technical function – the International Maritime Organization, the International Telecommunications Union,

Intersat and Inmarsat – whose operations are necessary if states are to enjoy the benefits of a world economy integrated by technology and finance. The organizations dealing with transport and communications especially are taken seriously and allowed for the most part to get on with their necessary work without fuss. As to the rest, for the organizations dealing with matters of political sensitivity concerning security or money, it would seem that governments only call them in to take on new tasks when there seems no alternative, as the IMF is called in to do whatever is necessary to restore the creditors' confidence in an indigent near-defaulting debtor.

But the sort of permanent transfer of power and resources from the nation-state to international bodies that is implicit in the Brandt proposals, and many other reform plans, is not something that is going to be seen as unavoidably necessary for a long time to come. It may be that new generations of voters and politicians will one day come along who think differently, and who are readier than voters and politicians and their officials are today to dismantle the state in favour of some international authority. And it may be that analysing problems and the working-out of possible ideas for reform are a useful contribution to the necessary process of education and attitude change that will be required if that day is ever to come.

If and when it does come it is not likely to be in this century. And meanwhile, we have to live in a world economy caught in a dilemma over the management of money and consequently dogged by economic depression. In that context, reform proposals have to be looked at with a good deal of political scepticism. Some questions we might ask are:

1 How do proposals for reform help with the here and now?
2 Is there any way in which they can be made to appeal to the self-interest of those with power to take decisions?
3 Do they offer the basis of a bargain that could be negotiated?
4 Is the analysis of the problem correct but the solution proposed impractical?
5 Is it impractical because almost all governments would reject it, or just because the United States, which has the greatest power to veto and reject reforms, is unconvinced that it is in US national interest?

Reform proposals

With these questions in mind, let us consider three examples of proposals for reform which at least address the problem from an international and not from a narrowly national point of view. Each is directed at the problems of credit and financial management. There is, for instance, John Williamson's plan for a mammoth issue of Special Drawing Rights (SDRs). There is a proposal from Michael Lipton and Stephanie Griffith-Jones for an International Lender of Last Resort (Griffith-Jones and Lipton, 1984) and there is Herbert Grubel's suggestion for an International Deposit Insurance Corporation as a life-jacket for international banks (Grubel, 1983). We might also examine the suggestions for rate-capping – that is, the direct and indirect subsidization of interest rates for developing countries – made by Felix Rohatyn and others, and the argument that the only escape route from present dilemmas lies in long-term loans or investments in place of short-term bank credits (Rohatyn, 1983).

Williamson's argument for a massive $43 billion issue of Special Drawing Rights by 1986, $4 billion of it to be made in 1985, more than doubling the total issues made so far, is based on the argument that the debt problem is eventually one of illiquidity rather than insolvency. It is not that the debtor countries are inherently so poor that they cannot find the resources to service their debts, but rather that they lack the foreign exchange necessary to make the payments on it. The reason, he argues, is that trade and other transactions have run too far ahead of the capacity to lay aside monetary reserves. The solution therefore does not lie in cutting their imports – Latin America's were cut by 30 per cent from 1981 to 1983, or $30 billion in value – but in building their own reserves so convincingly that confidence in their credit-worthiness would return, to the benefit of all. Although he grants that after years of debate economists are still not agreed on how to calculate how much a country needs in the way of reserves, because factors other than the size of its import bill enter into the question, he argues that the traditional rule of thumb which says that a reserves/imports ratio of 1:20 is asking for trouble, and that 1:30 is a desirable norm in most circumstances is not seriously challenged. This leads to the conclusion that the reserve shortfall for non-oil LDCs alone – leaving out of account any industrialized or oil-producing countries who might need larger reserves than they currently have – amounted to $21 billion by 1983 and was increasing at a rate of about $9 billion a year. His analysis of the problem suggests that the heavy borrowing from the banks in the 1970s was taking care of the problem, but that once this began to shrink the problem was likely to reappear. Williamson's proposal is not the same as the 'Link' idea, favoured for so long by the Group of 77 – the third world alliance – in which reserves would be created as a means of deliberately financing economic development, and it would not free the major debtor countries of dependence on the IMF. Brazil for instance would get only just over $0.5 billion for its reserves, compared with $1.5 billion it agreed in 1984 to draw under conditional IMF facilities and the $6.5 billion it proposed to borrow from the banks. Williamson also proposes that the original reconstitution provisions about which there was so much debate when the whole SDR scheme was being negotiated in the late 1960s, and which was dropped in 1981, should be reintroduced. This would tend to discourage LDCs from just spending their new SDRs and would encourage them to hold them in reserve except in a temporary emergency. The Keynesian analysis that lies behind the proposal argues that the creation of 'paper gold' international reserve assets became superfluous almost as soon as the ink was dry on the original agreement on SDRs in 1970. This was because credit expanded so fast that the world economy then entered a highly inflationary period. Later in the 1980s, however, SDRs are needed to correct the deflationary situation of the early 1980s. The logic can hardly be contested. The problem, however, is purely political. SDRs cannot be allocated except by the agreement of the US government, still the weightiest voter in the IMF. There was little outcry from American public opinion against President Reagan in 1984 when at first he resisted the increase in IMF quotas. And though he subsequently pushed the necessary Bill through a reluctant Congress, it was only out of fear that without larger quotas the IMF would be unable to prevent a collective default by Latin Americans and possibly an unmanageable banking crisis in the United States itself. As Williamson and others – notably the French – suggest, the allocation of SDRs would smack of handouts to the improvident and corrupt, as much as to the deserving countries of the third world. Economic depression in the United States would have to be far worse and hopes of economic recovery 'around the corner' would have to be severely dashed before the Americans are likely to agree to any allocation of SDRs large enough to have an impact on the subsequent behaviour of creditor banks and debtor governments.

Bitter experience of near-miss banking failures in the past decade or so has brought forth a growing number of studies which focus on the disparity between the international character of the banking system and the limitations on the jurisdiction and knowledge and supervisory influence of central banks. It is more difficult for them to function as lenders of last resort (LLRs). With only minor divergence, all the studies are agreed on the inadequacy of the present arrangements and on the dangers to the whole structure of credit on which markets rely (Kaletsky, 1985; Dale, 1984; Cline, 1984; Moffitt, 1983; Delamaide, 1984). In this, their analysis of the nature of the problem is, in my view, incontestable. Some of the weak points in the present arrangements that relate to inadequate knowledge on the part of central banks, have already been reviewed in chapter 5. They are inadequately informed about the full extent of their own banks' lending to other banks (i.e. lending by banks whose registered headquarters are within the state to others whose headquarters are outside); and they are inadequately informed about short-term export credit and the commitments of their banks to joint ventures and syndicated operations. Their information about major debtors is incomplete, as is their ability to assess the financial and moral limits on the debt-carrying capacity of major debtors. Other weak points relate to the loopholes in the powers of the central banks acting as national LLRs and to the loopholes between their respective jurisdictions. For instance, they do not always fully control the operations of subsidiary branches of their own flock – as witnessed by the refusal of the Bank of Italy in 1983 to honour the obligations of Banco Ambrosiano's Luxembourg holding company. Except for the monetary authorities of the United States which have unlimited power to create dollars, the ability of other central banks to pay their banks' debts in foreign currency is not unlimited. And there are still yawning gaps between the jurisdictional reach of the banks who belong to the BIS and who have agreed to the Basle Concordats, and the banking operations conducted in other parts of the world.

An important point is that the holes in the safety net are not simply due to temporary technical oversights. The essence of the LLR function in a secure banking system is that the bargain between the LLR and the commercial banks is contingent on a bargain between the latter and its customers. The LLR will provide support, on certain conditions, but it is on the strict understanding that the commercial bank continues to lend to solvent borrowers. This is because these customers are part of the national economy to which the central bank has a social responsibility. In international banking, however, the customer may be solvent in his own currency, but he may not be solvent in dollars or marks. Even if he is solvent, the willingness of the central bank to sustain a foreign bank that is lending to him cannot be taken for granted. It is apt to be affected negatively as well as positively by considerations of foreign policy.

Some of the writers who have tackled this crucial subject have concluded that effective LLR facilities are highly desirable in these circumstances, but that they are unfortunately unattainable (Moffitt 1984; Lever and Huhne 1985). The system is thus still vulnerable to a credit shock that would make major banks insolvent. The best that can be hoped for is thus a confessed second best in which central banks ask for more information and in which, instead of fudging the extent of their responsibilities, they are much more explicit about where they stop. Central banks should also try harder to discourage banks from operating beyond the range of the Basle network, and wherever possible should encourage private systems of mutual support on a contractual basis between major banks.

An international support system

Some other writers agree that the system will still be highly vulnerable, but conclude that it is necessary, somehow, to create an ILLR – an international lender of last resort. This is the argument developed by Michael Lipton and Stephanie Griffith-Jones for a 'formal, transparent, swift international lender of last resort'. Their argument – that recovery alone does not solve the problem, because 'more lending on the same pattern as before will only mean bigger problems later, while less lending either destroys recovery or precipitates default' – is convincing. But when it comes to suggesting *how* this can be done or who should act as ILLR, they are strangely silent. 'Let us assume a tin-opener', as the economist says in the old story of the engineer, the biologist and the economist on a desert island with nothing to eat but a large case of unopened cans of beans. Neither the IMF nor even the BIS has the resources, and therefore the authority, to do a job which might require the provision of funds greater than $11 billion provided for Continental Illinois in 1984.

An alternative idea is to resort to the insurance principle, not so much for the sake of the banks themselves as for the economy they serve. In the 1930s the Roosevelt administration had been threatened, almost as soon as it took office, by financial panic, starting with a wholesale run on the banks, as depositors rushed to demand cash. A banking moratorium closing all banks was the government's first emergency measure. But for the longer term the New Deal Administration imposed a compulsory insurance system on all banks, guaranteeing all their small depositors against loss in case a particular bank failed – as many did. The Federal Deposit Insurance Corporation set up in 1935 did not stop some banks from failing, but it did introduce some stability into the sytem. The danger that many small depositors responding all together to some whispered rumour could bring down a perfectly sound and solvent bank, and perhaps even start a spreading bushfire of collapse among other banks, was thus averted.

The same idea has been proposed by Professor Grubel and others for the international banking system (Grubel, 1983). But the analogy drawn with the American system in the 1930s is not a close one. There is no world government equally concerned for the health and viability of the whole global credit system as the Roosevelt administration was for the whole of the American economy. And there is no international authority able to impose the insurance principle on all the major banks in the world nor powerful enough to make them pay the premiums. Nor does the major threat to the system come from small depositors who might take their money away from a particular bank, but rather from the other banks who, when rumours begin to fly, refuse to extend interbank credit lines to it. Insuring all the other banks against the loss they might suffer by overlending to a failing bank would be a great deal more expensive than insuring US depositors for losses less than $10,000. Most decisively, there is little chance of getting international agreement to achieve some such end. The chief danger to the system has come, and still comes, from the American banks who have lent most heavily to LDCs, but been made to make least provision against loss through bad debts. The authorities in other countries like Switzerland or West Germany with banks heavily exposed to sovereign risks have made the banks write off their bad debts or insisted that they set aside large reserves to cover them, and have sugared the pill by allowing them to pay lower taxes in compensation. Provident and prudent governments, like provident and prudent companies, are not going to be willing to pay large insurance premiums to protect the improvident and the imprudent. Recall that a comparable proposal was made in the mid-1970s to cope with the sudden catastrophic fall in tanker freight rates. An organization representing banks, shipbuilders, shipping companies and insurance companies proposed that all should contribute towards buying up and scrapping old ships so as to reduce the oversupply of world tonnage and improve the price both of tankers and of freight rates. The scheme, admirable in intention and workable in theory, came to nothing because the provident saw no reason for saving the improvident from the consequences of their own over-confidence, either in building, buying or chartering very large tankers. Moreover, the biggest operators – the major oil companies – were large enough to cope with the situation out of their own resources. In the financial system today, the United States is effectively in a similar situation. At a pinch, as with Mexico or Brazil, or even with Continental Illinois, the US government knows it can act to protect its own national interests. It is up to others to protect theirs.

Another idea that enjoyed some popularity for a while was that of 'rate-capping', or finding the difference between the current high real rate of interest and the rate which a developing country could manage to pay. Better, it was argued, to find the necessary subsidy to bridge that gap than to take the shock of writing off an entire loan as a bad debt because the service charges on it were more than the debtor could pay. This idea was advocated by Felix Rohatyn of the New York investment bankers Salomon Brothers, and was again

based on a false analogy. Mr Rohatyn had become famous outside
Wall Street as the wizard responsible in the 1970s for restoring
a bankrupt New York City to financial respectability. That was
a goal in which many people in the local financial community
and many people in the American political system had a very
strong interest. But the international system is very different. The
United States has a strong interest in preventing the long-term
bankruptcy of Mexico and of Brazil. Japan has a strong political
and economic interest in preventing the bankruptcy (or even the
financial embarrassment) of the Republic of South Korea. The
Federal German government has a similar concern for East Germany.
Each therefore has an incentive to find some disguised form of
'rate-capping' for its particular clients or protégés. For example, the
rescheduling arrangements finally agreed with Mexico have allowed
the loans to be made longer and also easier, and 'easier' means adding
grace periods in which no payment at all is required so that the average
interest paid on the loan is effectively reduced while the risk is
extended with the maturity.

The extension of such a system to all developing countries would
be another matter altogether. For one thing, it would rob the IMF
of some of its teeth in coercing LDC debtor governments into the
sort of deflationary behaviour that seems necessary to reassure the
banks. For another, it raises the difficult question of who is to finance
the subsidy inherent in the proposal. There is little sign that the
United States would do so on a large enough scale, given the general
American attitude to foreign aid and despite the substantial shift in
American policy at the IMF meeting in 1985. And as for the banks,
the same objection would apply as to the insurance proposal – that
is, that the prudent should not have to pay for the follies of the
imprudent. Moreover, it would probably be unacceptable even to
the developing countries themselves, some of whom would see their
competitive position in financial markets and in the aid game impaired
if the same relief were given to all. And finally there is the problem
of all subsidies – how to stop the temporary becoming a permanent,
built-in part of the system, with all the distortions and difficulties
that that entails.

The danger of debt

The conclusion which a great many observers have reached – and it is undoubtedly correct, analytically – is that a good deal of the 'debt problem' would never have occurred but for the difficulty of raising long-term finance for economic development and the relative ease in borrowing short-term money. Just as the debt problems of countries became progressively more acute – Mexico is the prime example – as they were obliged to refinance old loans at shorter and ever shorter maturities, so the debt problems can be at least partially solved if only developing countries could find ways of raising money for investment that did not have to be quickly repaid. This is a conclusion reached by the Commonwealth Secretariat in their 1983 study of the international monetary and financial system and by a large number of professors of economics (Commonwealth Secretariat, 1985).

But once again the problem is to find the means to the end. One major consequence of the multiple uncertainties now present in the global financial system is that there is a plentiful supply of funds deposited short-term or on demand, because the risk from one uncertain variable or another is thereby minimized. There is a corresponding strong demand for short-term credit – from governments, from corporations and from traders. Where governments used to borrow from bondholders and holders of long-term securities, they now borrow far more in the form of Treasury Bills or other short-term securities – or from the banks. Where corporations used to borrow from shareholders, they too now borrow far more from the banks. Where individuals used to provide (if they could afford it) for their own sickness or old age, this is now provided to a far greater extent by governments or by large institutional pension funds, building societies or investment trusts. But pricked by inflation and by violent changes in property and financial markets, all these institutions have had to become highly mobile financially. In self-defence, their strategy has had to be to spread their risks as widely as possible, to make as few long-term commitments as possible and to take as much advantage as they can of the comparatively high return on short-term lending. An examination of the bond markets shows that they are dominated by the governments and public utilities and other enterprises of the industrially advanced countries. Not many of the LDCs are able to float successful issues.

The only readily available alternative is foreign investment, either directly by corporations or indirectly through the foreign acquisition of shares in joint ventures or local enterprises. In the late 1970s, this prospect was discouraging. In mineral development especially, the big corporations were badly scared by OPEC's example of nationalization followed by collective price-maintenance. Wherever they had the choice, therefore, they cut back on investment in developing countries and expanded their investments in stable, rich industrialized countries like the United States, Canada or Australia. The experience of this instinctive reaction by developed countries imperceptibly brought about a significant change in the host governments' bargaining posture. To persuade the foreign corporation to risk its time, expertise and money, many host governments became much readier to share the risks and to take a share of the costs of new ventures, whether oil exploration in Indonesia or steel and engineering plants in Brazil. In the long run, there seems little doubt that the symbiotic relationship between the state and the foreign corporation holds out the best hope of providing the finance necessary for economic development. But there is also no doubt that the process is a long one, that the opportunities to attract foreign capital vary immensely between countries, and that it is therefore only a partial and distant solution to the problem of international debt.

A choice of scenarios

Perhaps, though, partial and distant solutions to this (as to other problems of the international system) are all that can reasonably be hoped for. Just as there is no quick or easy solution to the problem of nuclear weapons, the population explosion, or the pollution of the seas and the skies, so it is hard to envisage a quick and easy solution to the uncertainties of a precarious financial system. As with the other problems, the known solutions fail when political authority is diffused among so many, and when the competitive spirit among the groups of humans who think of themselves as nations is so often apt to triumph over their inclination to cooperate.

And as with the other insoluble problems of the international system, a survey of the possible scenarios for the future tends to the gloomy conclusion that the best scenario is the least likely and that the most probable outcome is the least satisfactory.

However well-meaning or well-informed they may be, the history of international relations and of all the major attempts to extend the power of international agencies tells us that governments have always been uniformly unwilling to hand over to international organizations any of the fundamental powers of the state. They will not let them decide independently to go to war. They will not allow them to raise taxes and thus to become independent financially. They will not allow them to make binding rules and apply them through courts of law with power to impose penalties on the guilty. They will not even allow them to claim the undivided loyalty of those who run them and work for them. The only alternative to an international authority, therefore is a national one. The only national authority in any sort of position to influence the behaviour of major banks and financial institutions, and to set rules governing the major markets for credit, is that of the United States.

The United States occupies that unenviable position primarily because of the unquenchable preference of buyers and sellers, creditors and debtors, traders and bankers for dealing in dollars rather than in any other currency or even in the various possible hybrid units of account like SDRs and ECUs (see note 2, ch. 1). The slow inroads that these have made into the dominant position of the dollar is an indication of the virtue of convenience in any monetary medium. The more people use it, the more other people have to do so too. Preference for the dollar has survived both extremes of the volatile foreign exchange markets, both the years when the dollar was objectively (i.e. in terms of comparative purchasing power within the national economy) far too weak, and the years when, objectively, it has been far too strong.

The second reason for saying that only the United States has the political potential for governing the system is that it is there that the biggest, most innovative and most active financial markets are to be found. In recent years it has become clear that any bank, whatever its national origin, that aspires to truly international status must be prepared to operate in the US markets because it cannot afford to do otherwise. In the same way, the United States dominates the world grain market and the world art market. Whatever their national origin, no grain broker can afford to stay away from Chicago any more than any operator like Christies or Sotheby's can afford to stay away from New York.

The important point to grasp here is that it is not necessary for an agency of the United States government to set rules for every bank in the world that borrows or lends in Eurodollars. As in 1913, when the Federal Reserve System was introduced, it need only make rules, exercise supervision over and demand information from the major operators; in return it must hold out for them the possibility of support against a liquidity shortage in dollars – which only the United States can convincingly offer. The New York Clearing House for bank transactions in dollars and Eurodollars is a gate at which the US government could act as toll-keeper – if only it chose to do so.

It might be objected that if the United States were to act as toll-keeper, it might choose to favour its political friends and to discriminate against its political opponents. The truth is that it does so already: leaning on British or French banks to help out in Mexico: making life difficult for German banks who lent to Poland. The only difference would be that the banks would at least know where ultimate responsibility lay; and rules and norms could be established among banks dealing in dollars which they could take as being reasonably stable and unchanging.

A further objection is that the political constitution of the United States, subject to presidential elections every four years and to somewhat violent changes of political mood, would not provide the stable regulatory environment which is so much needed for a healthy global financial system. But though there is something in that objection, it is also true that history has shown the capacity of the Americans, when necessary, to set up agencies and authorities that are remarkably immune from changes in the White House or Capitol Hill. Besides the US Supreme Court, there are bodies like the Federal Reserve Board, the Securities and Exchange Commission, the Tennessee Valley Authority, the International Trade

Commission and the Federal Bureau of Investigation – not to mention the Central Intelligence Agency. Only provided that the United States were to recognize the advantages in its own national interest of having a stable and reliable international financial system, it would not be too difficult to work out the means and mechanisms for the purpose.

The trouble is, as Whitman, Calleo and others have pointed out, that at present the United States is more aware of the costs and difficulties of taking on this responsibility than of the rewards and benefits to be gained by doing so – and of the risks of not doing so. The second scenario therefore would involve the Europeans putting some pressure on the Americans to moderate its unilateralist tendencies in finance, as in military, strategy. It would call for a new 'implicit bargain' in which the United States took on greater responsibility from the European central banks for the support of non-American banks dealing in dollars – while the Europeans took on greater responsibility from the American forces for the security of Western Europe. The requirements of a coordinated European defence policy would surely include some steps toward a common system for financing it, whether by taxation or by borrowing. Inevitably, this would both necessitate and facilitate the more extensive use of a common currency unit, the ECU, and the advance towards a common monetary policy.

At the time of writing and contemplating the agonies of the budgetary debate within the European Community, it is almost as hard to visualize the Europeans taking the initiative and putting some pressure on the United States in the financial field as it is to visualize the Americans doing so voluntarily and unilaterally. Yet, there are, broadly speaking, only two alternative scenarios. The first pursues the path indicated by Jacques Polak – a retreat from internationalism in finance in order that national authorities can once again assume control over their own banks and their own economies. The implications of such a strategy for the United States particularly, are extremely far-reaching. It would surely require a very radical change of banking policy – if not the complete closing down of Euromarkets, at least the restriction of the right of US banks to transfer funds to and from their foreign branches and thus in and out of Eurodollars. Or else, American banks would have to choose between operating at home, or operating in a much riskier and unprotected environment in international finance. Whatever the means chosen to accomplish the end of 'controlled disintegration', the cost to international trade and investment of lopping off, so to speak, the major branches of bank activity would leave the structure of credit much reduced in size and capacity. Indeed, so difficult is it to envisage quite how 'controlled disintegration' could be brought about, that it raises the question whether, in fact, it is possible in the 1980s to put the clock back 30 years or more. More damage to confidence and enterprise would result from this strategy for limiting risk than would be gained in the long run.

The only remaining scenario is that in which we continue to muddle through. More of the same is very often the most likely outcome of any situation and this is no exception. Yet even though it seems unlikely now to lead to total collapse and financial catastrophe, the costs of carrying on as we have been doing are by no means inconsiderable. They are indeed almost all more political in the last resort than economic. At home, the United States' actions in rescuing Continental Illinois bear out the judgement of many experienced bankers that no American government could afford to let any of the major American banks close its doors and stop trading. The damage to the economy at large would be too great. But the alternative either to having a system (as under the third scenario of controlled disintegration) which you can control, or of extending control over the whole system and imposing discipline on the banks in it, is to move, as the United States now has moved, towards nationalizing the major financial institutions. Perhaps the example of Continental's managers being ousted in favour of government appointees will encourage other banks to be more cautious and less eager to pursue profitable but risky business at home or abroad.

But this in turn raises the prospect that world economic recovery will be a long time in coming. And in that case more of the same is going to mean that the system survives more or less intact, but that the costs of adjusting to a smaller shrunken credit structure are predominantly borne by the politically weak and the economically dependent, both within the industrialized countries and in the international system. Many developing countries are going to have their IMF missions around for a long time to come. Awareness of the high price of regaining the confidence of foreign bankers is going to grow. What the political consequences of that awareness will be, no one can tell, but past experience of the 1930s and of debt situations in the 1970s suggests that the choice lies between two unpleasant alternatives. Either, government becomes stronger and thus more repressive of opposition, more authoritarian and militarist – in which case the prospects of peace, democracy or of free economic enterprise diminish. Or, government remains weak and unstable; foreign confidence in the country flags, leaving it in a continued state of debt, depression and disorder. This too holds little attraction for the still prevailing Western liberal cast of mind.

In the short term, the United States could, it is true, continue to enjoy certain privileged immunities through the use of its considerable bargaining power as military protector (or interventionist) and as trading partner. But in doing so it would risk a dangerous alienation of large areas of the world economy. In the long term this would damage its own economic future no less than the rest of the system.

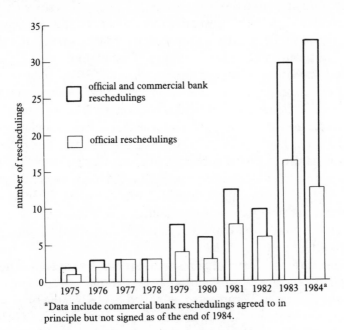

ᵃData include commercial bank reschedulings agreed to in principle but not signed as of the end of 1984.

Figure 6.1 Multilateral debt reschedulings, 1975–84. (*Source: World Development Report*, 1985.)

CHAPTER 7
Cooling the Casino

The problem of managing and stabilizing a financial system that is fundamentally out of order and control is a global one. But the solution is a national one. It is absolutely no use looking to international organizations to wave a magic wand and restore financial order and with it world prosperity. Any survey of recently proposed solutions (as in the last chapter) leads to the conclusion that the reform must start with a change of mind in Washington.

There have been plenty of times in the last 20 or 30 years when the staff of some international organization has dreamed up some very pretty schemes for powerful new agencies. There was the International Seabed Authority; there was the UN Environmental Agency; and the Integrated Commodity Stabilization scheme. The IMF even has had its dreams for a substitution account, or a world in which every country held its reserves in SDRs. A long time ago, Sir John Boyd-Orr drew up an impressive blueprint for a World Food Board – a body that would have been standing ready to deal with famine in Africa – if only the United States had not turned thumbs down on the scheme 40 years ago.

In short, international organizations are not free agents. They are created by, and are forever dependent on national governments. And of all the national governments the United States has the biggest veto in organizations dealing with money and finance. Nor is the United States peculiar in opposing any extension of the power of international bureaucracies. The whole history of international relations tells us that governments have always been extremely careful not to take even the smallest step which would let an international organization usurp any of the fundamental prerogatives of the state. The record of UN peacekeeping shows how jealously governments have kept from the UN the power to decide to go to, or to get involved in, a war. Nor will they allow the UN to raise taxes and thus become financially dependent on the member states. They will not allow the UN to make binding rules and apply them through courts of law endowed with the power to impose penalties on the guilty, nor yet to claim the undivided loyalty of its employees.

Drawing up blueprints for new international authorities, therefore, is a waste of time. The inspiration for any new policy has to be national. The power to act through an international organization can only come from the authority and legitimacy of the state. And of all the states pulling the strings that move the limbs of international organizations, the United States is by far the most powerful. This is most particularly so in matters of money and finance. Here the United States is the only state in any sort of position to influence – for good or for evil – the behaviour of banks of all nationalities and in almost all other countries. No other country's policies – diplomatic and commercial as well as monetary – produce comparable reverberations beyond its borders. The United States, therefore, is the only country with a decisive power either to deregulate (and risk destabilizing) the international financial system, or to set rules that would govern financial transactions in the major international capital and money markets.

The United States has to recognize its own true long-term national interest in exercising a wise hegemony over the world market economy. Americans, and especially young Americans, must be persuaded to take up the reins of economic power again – not out of altruism or because they owe it to the rest of the world in any way, but out of simple self-interest. Ever since the First World War, whenever the United States has been tempted to turn its back on the world outside its frontiers, to be isolationist and indifferent to what goes on there, it was not only the rest of the world that suffered. In the long run, it has been young Americans too who paid the price of this indifference. They lost their jobs in the Great Depression; and many lost their lives in the Second World War. In the current economic crisis, if the United States carries on acting unilaterally and continues to take what one American academic has called 'domesticist' decisions (i.e. decisions that take into account only domestic, national considerations) it is not just the third world or the Europeans and Japanese who will suffer (Nau, 1984). American society too will be affected if an end is not put to the casino capitalism which we see developing all around us and in every major city in the world. Some parts of American society have already suffered – the young black unemployed, the dispossessed farming families, the blue-collar workers made redundant in middle age. Many more will suffer in future. They will suffer because, if things go on as they are at present, the world depression will go grumbling on for a decade or more, and in the long run they cannot be insulated from it. The sort of sticking-plaster tinkering we have witnessed in recent years will not get either the world or the United States out of it. Nor will solutions that deal only with national symptoms have much effect.

The 1984 recovery in America disguised the gravity and the deep-rootedness of the depression. It proved, as a few farsighted observers said it would, to be a false dawn, a temporary boost to business produced by some clever tax changes which helped to revive a flagging construction industry, and by heavy defence spending sustained through an inflow of funds from abroad. But the effects of such quick-fix shots in the arm do not last for long. And you cannot go on finding tax changes to get investment going without either so starving the public sector that you lose on the swings what you gain on the roundabouts, or else reverting to the inflationary policies that were tried in the United States in the mid-1970s. Experience has shown that course to be no solution. The security of the United States is at risk if confidence in the dollar begins seriously to fail once more as it did in 1978; once again, drastic measures would have to be taken which would land the economy back in a cold turkey deflation.

The truth has also to be recognized that America cannot exist – however it might hope and wish to do so – as a prosperous island in a sea of debt and depression. Far too many American corporations, not to mention banks, depend for their long-term survival on the profitability and growth of their operations not inside but outside the United States. If the uncertainty over exchange rates and interest rates and over general economic prospects continues, the tendency to gambling and speculation, to chasing the fast buck by fair means or foul, is going to persist too. Serious long-term investment is going to suffer, as in some respects it already has. There will be a few high-technology sectors that will do well, but the general economy will stay in the doldrums. As before, politicians will promise that prosperity is just around the corner, but they will be proved wrong.

It is possible too that things will get a lot worse, the longer the system drifts from one 'crisis' to another with only temporary patchwork measures taken to deal with the problems. Indeed, the very use of the word 'crisis' is misleading. It implies that if you can get over the crisis, you will be on the mend. The danger will be past, as in a Dickensian sick-bed scene.

Actually, in recent international monetary history, it is the crises that central banks have been particularly good at dealing with. It is the chronic problems that have always been dodged and avoided. And the longer you put off dealing with them, the worse they are apt to get. Take the debt problem. In the crisis of Mexican debt in 1982 everyone rallied round, and a collapse of the banking system was averted by rescheduling and refinancing.

But to conclude that the problem is solved because the crisis has been survived is to overlook the politics of the situation. For debtors, the longer people have to go on putting up with the stringencies imposed by the IMF, the harder they are to endure. Pain is bearable if it is not going to last long. It gets harder when there seems no end to it in sight. And for debtors, if new bank loans are still not forthcoming after months or years of lower wages, shortages and unemployment, the risk grows that some politician will be tempted to think that the risks of failing to pay the interest on past debt may not be so great after all. It may well be that the longer the debt problem goes unsolved, the worse relations will become between the debtors and their creditors. Those creditors, moreover, are mostly American banks.

The same may be true of the three other problems that are closely related to the debt problem. They are the instability of banks, the depressed state of world demand and the deteriorating relations among the Western allies. The latter certainly has been getting visibly worse in recent years. There was a time when summit conferences of Western heads of state papered over the cracks and those assembled all smiled at the cameras. Now there are scowls and open disagreements. Every year, bills before the Congress show growing American resentment not only against the Europeans but also now against the Japanese. Such feelings are surely mutual. Like all family quarrels, it would be better (and easier) made up sooner rather than later. As for the instability of the banking system, that too does not get easier but harder to put right as time goes by. It is not only that new credit instruments are thought up every month, and new assets 'securitized' – which means that the banks find new ways of passing on to a speculative market the loans they have made to houseowners or businesses. The boundaries dividing the markets, and keeping one set of operators inside one regulatory fence and another set of operators inside a different fence, are getting progressively weakened and broken down. It is not only a matter of computerized information systems abolishing time and distance between the great financial centres so that national financial markets no longer exist in isolation from each other. The old distinctions between financial institutions on which many regulatory systems depended are also being progressively broken down. And the longer nothing much is done about it and the problems are swept carefully under the mat so as not to upset confidence, the harder the reform is going to be.

The world depression itself, it can be argued, will get harder to put into reverse, not easier. The Kondratiev long wave, after all, is only a guess. Other historical experience tells us that there are some problems which actually get worse and harder to deal with the longer those in power put off grasping the nettle of radical reform. This is true of restructuring obsolete industries or regenerating depressed economic regions. In politics it has been true of negotiating an Arab–Israeli peace, as it was in the 1930s of resisting Nazi intimidation and expansionism. The debt problem could be the same.

The United States must act

Time is running out. What, then, must the United States do?

The most important thing is that the Americans should restore some stability and predictability to their own domestic economic management. The world's financial system has become unstable and unpredictable in direct proportion to the increasing instability of American economic policies at home. If one were to imagine US interest rates staying as level as they were early in the 1960s; and if one were to imagine the level of US Government spending to stay roughly the same from year to year; and the lurching flow of funds in and out of the United States to stop, a good deal of the problem would disappear. In short, no one is asking the United States to sacrifice self-interest to the good of the world, only to put its own house in order. For if the value of the dollar were as stable in terms of the goods and services it bought at home as it was in the 1960s; and if its value were to be unaffected by the monetary shifts which cause such turbulence in the foreign exchange markets, then many of the economic problems which are secondary consequences of either an unduly weak or an overly strong dollar would melt away.

But putting the economic management of the United States in order is clearly a task easier said than done. It requires first, the political conviction that it has to be done. Then it requires some institutional changes that will make it easier to accomplish.

The banking problem

These institutional changes are of two kinds. One relates to the management of the real economy – industry, agriculture, savings, investment, tax and so forth – of the United States itself. The other relates to the management of transactions conducted in United States dollars, whether they take place in New York, Kalamazoo, the Cayman Islands or Hong Kong.

The first goes beyond the scope of this book. But it is already clear to many Senators and Representatives in Congress that the division of authority over financial policy and monetary management gives the White House and the Administration too much power, and leaves the chairman of the Federal Reserve Board at the mercy of any President with a political axe to grind. At the time of writing, with Mr Paul Volcker in control of the Federal Reserve System, this is not so acute an issue. But in the long run the constitutional checks on the power of an Administration to go in for deficit financing and sudden changes in monetary management have to be elaborated and made stronger. How this is best done is a matter for the Americans; probably it cannot be done in a hurry or without due consideration of all the possibilities. The United States may need a central monetary authority with the constitutional independence equal to that of the West German Bundesbank. Or it may need a constitutional amendment similar to the British Bank Charter Act that would require perhaps a two-thirds vote of the Senate or the Joint Economic Committee of both Houses before certain credit-creating and spending limits could be breached.

Meanwhile, there is the more immediate question of controlling banks that deal in dollars, for they too create credit. The dispersion of authority that results from the Office of the Comptroller of the Currency operating with the US Treasury, while the business of intervening in the capital and foreign exchange markets is left to the Federal Reserve Bank of New York suggests strongly that it is time for a major reorganization. But it is a reorganization that must reach further than just the major banks with headquarters in New York, Chicago, Dallas or San Francisco.

The United States is the only country that is in a position to regulate the operations of international banks, whether they are British, German or Japanese. This is primarily because of the unquenchable preference of buyers and sellers, creditors and debtors, traders and bankers for dealing in US dollars rather than in any other currency. Dollars are preferred to Japanese yen or German marks, or even to Swiss francs, despite the much greater stability of all three in terms of real purchasing power. Dollars are also preferred to the various hybrid or 'basket' currencies like the International Monetary Fund's SDR or the European Community's ECU. None of them is so convenient or so universally accepted. As pointed out earlier, preference for the dollar has survived both extremes of the volatile foreign exchange markets, both the years when the dollar was objectively (i.e.in terms of comparative purchasing power within the national economy) far too weak and the years when, objectively, it has been far too strong.

Table 7.1 The interbank market in international banking at end 1984 ($ billion)

Transactions	Assets	Liabilities	Net position
With non-banks	703	422	281
With related offices	505	504	0.8
With non-affiliated banks	940	935	4.4
With central banks	21	125	–104
Certificates of deposit issued	14	101	– 87
TOTAL	2183	2087	95

Source: Bank for International Settlements, May 1985. Note that the figures relate to the situation three or six months earlier. No one knows the situation at any given moment.

Table 7.2 Shares and net positions of banks' interbank transactions in major countries at end 1984 ($ billion)

	Assets	% of total	Net positions
US banks	614.3	28	55.5
Japan	513.7	23.5	20.5
France	197.1	9	20.5
Britain	161.4	7	–3.3
Germany	142.1	6.5	13.8
Italy	88.2	4	0.6
Canada	88.9	4	–9.1
Switzerland	75.3	3.4	7.0
TOTAL BIS banks	2022.6		93.6

Source: Bank for International Settlements, May 1985. Note that the figures relate to the situation three or six months earlier. No one knows the situation at any given moment.

Not only is the dollar the unchallenged international currency in the system, there is also the fact that the largest and most active financial markets are to be found in the United States. It is there that all the major innovations that have subsequently spread to London or Tokyo have been thought up. Just as the United States dominates the world market for grains, or the world market for fine art, so it does in banking and finance. And just as any grain broker (whether the original enterprise started in Switzerland or Argentina) cannot afford to stay away from Chicago, or just as Christies and Sotheby's if they are to stay in the lead in the art world have to operate in New York, so the major banks throughout the world have to operate in, as well as outside, the United States – and that usually means in New York.

When it conducts transactions in New York, whether these are simply transfers from or to other banks or corporate enterprises or wealthy individuals, and whether or not they involve the transfer of funds into or out of dollars from another currency, the transaction is cleared through the now highly mechanized New York Clearing House system. The introduction of this up-to-date system gives the United States a unique opportunity to develop the role of international lender of last resort. Financial markets, as the experts increasingly agree, and experience is showing ever more clearly, do need some kind of authority to fill that role. The experts are agreed that the authority must be backed by the political and economic power of the state. And they are coming to doubt whether the agreement between central banks in the Basle Concordats to take responsibility for supporting their own national banks is really sufficient (Griffith-Jones and Lipton, 1984; Kaletsky, 1975; Lever and Huhne, 1985). It is neither extensive enough, efficient enough or fast enough to be an adequate substitute for a single lender of last resort.

Nor would any lawyer doubt the right of the United States – should it wish – to develop such a role. As far back in economic history as the princes of mediaeval Europe, rulers have reserved the right to tax, control and regulate the operators in any market taking place within their jurisdiction. That right was sometimes delegated, often abused, but never abandoned. Today there is nothing to stop a new authority backed by the power of the United States government from requiring any bank conducting business of any substantial volume in New York (or any other major US city) to register with it for a licence to do so. The conditions attached to that licence can be as extensive as the US agency chooses to make them. In fact, all the requirements that an international lender of last resort might make could very simply be done in this way. The New York Clearing House system can be seen as a sort of toll-gate to the US financial market. To use it as a device for licensing operators other than native banks would not be new. For it now deals impartially with domestic dollar transactions – the sale of shares for example – and with international Eurodollar transactions, such as bank loans in dollars by, say, a Geneva bank to a Brazilian company.

Banking experts agree that in a well-regulated system, banks should be required to show that they have sound and well-established systems for assessing the risks they take on when they lend – whether to a government or a corporation, a local authority at home or a state enterprise abroad. They should be made to hold in reserve capital assets in a defined ratio to their worldwise assets and liabilities. They should accept limits on the amount they can lend to any one borrower – or to any homogeneous group of borrowers, whether they are all shipbuilders or all enterprises in the same country. Either group is likely to be afflicted by the same unfortunate coincidences of misfortune that would run them all into financial trouble at the same time. Banks should also be in a position to take decisions in the light of as much information as is possible about what other banks are doing. Otherwise they are shooting in the dark, and are apt to multiply the consequences of their own risk-taking by the risks taken in equal ignorance by other bankers.

For an American monetary authority to demand all these requirements all at once and for all foreign banks as a matter of right might meet with immediate resistance from both the foreign banks and their governments. But what it could easily do instead would be to offer a bargain to the big international banks. They would be offered access to support from the Federal Reserve System – at a price and on fairly hard conditions, of course – if they should have a liquidity problem in dollars. The price of such access would be conformity with the requirements of the US monetary authority on risk assessment, on disclosure of balance sheets and open positions, on reserve ratios, and on diversification of lending not only in New York but anywhere in the world.

For the United States to take a step like this would be no more than to take a leaf out of its own monetary history. In 1913 when the Federal Reserve System was first set up, no bank was obliged by law to join it. The deal was basically the same: 'Come in, and we will provide liquidity if and when you need it. But you will have to observe the reserve ratios we lay down and give us full information about your operations.' Once again, it would be perfectly open to some banks to turn down the offer. The Japanese banks for instance might well decide that their major risks being in yen, they did not need the American safety net. Some requirements on disclosure, however, could still be demanded as the price of their transactions being cleared through the New York system. In this way, the United States would operate a kind of two-tier supervision of the international banking system. And as in the original Federal Reserve System, there would be no attempt to supervise or to support all the little banks in the system. Their collapse has only ever been a danger to the system when they were being heavily backed and underwritten by the big banks, as in the Penn Square–Continental Illinois case. But if there had been better controls over the commitments of Continental Illinois, the situation could not have arisen in the first place. Penn Square could have gone bust and the repercussions would have been limited and local.

The idea of making banks an offer which they could accept or refuse would also get over the thorny question of national pride and conflicts of jurisdiction with other states. For whenever the United States has asserted its right by virtue of a Statute of Congress arbitrarily to *sub-poena* any foreign witness it chose, or to demand disclosure of information by a foreign corporation, it has met with smouldering resentment, if not with outright resistance or retaliatory legislation. When, however, it has allowed US courts to be used by foreigners, if they wish to do so, to sue an airfraft manufacturer, a group of airlines or a chemical company, for instance, no one has raised a whisper of objection. National sovereignty was never even mentioned. It would be the same in this case, since it would be perfectly open to any bank not to take the offer and to rely instead on the formal commitment of its own central bank under the Basle Concordat of 1976 to come to its assistance, should that ever be necessary.

Moreover, in making the first offer, the United States could easily invite other governments and central banks to do the same for banks dealing in their currencies in their financial centres. The Bank of England could offer – at a price – to back foreign banks dealing in sterling and in Eurosterling. The Bundesbank could do the same for banks dealing in D-marks. A network of such arrangements, basing authority not on the *territorial* principle of where the operator's headquarters building happened to be, or where the branches happen to operate, but on which *currency* was being used for its dealing, would make a lot more sense in the modern world than the present rather precarious agreement under the Basle Concordat which promises that each central bank shall look after its own national banks wherever they operate and in whatever currency. For the fact is that only the United States has – and is recognized by the markets as having – an unlimited supply of US dollars to back an institution that is in trouble through its lack of an immediate supply of US dollars.

The debt problem

The main focus of this book is not on the economic development of poor countries, but on the sorry state of the international financial system. Yet it has been emphasized again and again throughout the book that this cannot be separated from broader political and economic issues. The instability of the banks, the stubborn persistence of economic depression, the debt problem[1] and the strains within the Western alliance all interact all the time with one another. Thus, the sorry state of the financial system is undoubtedly aggravating the difficulties in the path of economic development for poor countries, while conversely the difficulties of the deeply indebted developing countries, so long as they persist, will aggravate the instability in the banking system. Thus, there are two immediate questions. They are: (1) 'What can be done about the so-called debt problems of the LDCs that will improve the prospects for the world's financial system?'; and (2) 'How can the financial system be improved or changed in such a way as to relieve in part at least the difficulties of managing economic development?'

The answer to the first question does not require solving *all* the problems of the developing countries. That would be to ask too much. In every country, in every century, economic development and industrialization has been a difficult and, for certain generations and certain social classes, a highly painful process. This harsh fact of life is unlikely to change. The grandiose solutions outlined in the Brandt Reports (Brandt, 1980, 1983), involving a massive World Development Fund and a wholesale switch in spending from arms to welfare are going to remain a pipedream. Nor will political realities permit a solution by means of a massive issue of new official credit in the shape of vast amounts of SDRs.

But this does not mean that nothing can be done through international organizations; only that action channelled through the World Bank and the International Monetary Fund is still subject, as explained earlier, to rather severe limitations. This is still the case even after the welcome change in US policy towards the two organizations expressed by Secretary of the Treasury James Baker at the 1985 annual meeting at Seoul in September 1985. Baker then proposed a 2–3 per cent growth in bank lending to Latin America – where the American national interest is most directly concerned – over the next three or four years. This would add some $25 to $30 billion in new bank loans. A rescue operation for Africa, meanwhile, would be mounted from a combination of $2.7 billion from the IMF's Trust Fund and a matching amount from the World Bank.

It is still unclear at the time of writing whether the change of US official attitude will bring results. Will a workable bargain with the banks take this blueprint off the drawingboard and into reality? For two points have to be remembered. First, resistance in the United States, especially in the Congress, to any major extension of the role of international agencies has not disappeared. Mr Baker still did not dare suggest that the World Bank should be allowed to double its capital by issuing more bonds. Second, while official policy and action through these multilateral financial institutions (and their regional counterparts) is necessary and may help the situation, such action cannot possibly offer a sufficient solution to the problem. For even if some of the suggested reform measures were to be taken, the ultimate dependence of the system on private lending through the banks cannot be escaped. It would remain even if corporate investment in the third world were to equal or exceed even the most optimistic current forecasts.

Specifically, some of the most constructive of these reform measures build on the idea (discussed in chapter 6) of 'rate-capping'. One idea is to use the IMF to operate a compensatory financing fund, similar to the ones it has set up to make up for unexpected and unavoidable shortfalls in export earnings from commodities or for sudden increases in the cost of oil imports, to relieve debtor countries of at least part of the burden of interest payments. This could be done by making grants or by adding the cost of the extra interest rate burden to the total repayable capital. This device would make the debt problem less immediately dangerous to the banking system, but, like the Multi-Year Rescheduling Agreements (MYRAs) negotiated with many LDCs since 1984, would exchange a chronic risk for an acute one. The political risk of inviting a default would be increased while the financial risk of bank failure would be diminished. Much the same objection, limiting its usefulness, applies to the World Bank's Structural Adjustment Loan (SAL) strategy. This gives debtors more time than IMF drawings to repay but generally offers too little support to them to restore the banks' confidence in making long-term loans available. In the present context of an unstable and precarious international financial system, that is no easy task, and is certainly beyond the present capacity of any international organization.

By far the most promising proposals for reform build on the familiar concept of insurance as something that offers the greatest contribution to the problem. Insurance of loans to developing countries would not remove the inherent risks, but would spread them more widely, and would transform the risk – as insurance always does – into a cost. The cost to governments, however, would be very much less than the cost of themselves providing enough official 'aid' to take the place of bank lending, and would be well repaid in the extra export orders (and therefore jobs) thus created.

The proposal for a collective insurance scheme has to be distinguished from the idea behind several proposals that 'bad' loans should be bought up from the banks at discounted prices in order to remove the 'overhang' of third world debt on international capital markets.

The banks, in return, would be obliged to hold long-term 'world development' bonds or something of that kind. But the snag with this, it is argued, is that the transaction would only reveal to public gaze the extent of 'bad' loans held by the banks and the risks attendant upon them. At present, these risks are hidden from view by the banks' (undisclosed) provisions against bad debts in the form of contingency reserves of one kind and another. It would be better to let them remain so.

Collective insurance, however, would be no great departure in principle from the practice, prevailing among all the industrialized countries, of insuring export credit in order to promote the country's exports and thus sustain employment. Instead of the present rather messy competition among national export credit agencies, inadequately regulated by OECD guidelines and a succession of gentlemen's agreements, the proposal would institute a multilaterally insured guarantee not of the exports but of the loans to finance them (Lever and Huhne, 1985, pp. 138–9).But loans to any single debtor would be guaranteed only up to a ceiling negotiated by each debtor country with the IMF. And the total amount of loans guaranteed would be varied from year to year according to good Keynesian demand-management principles in accordance with the value of the dollar and the rate of growth in the world economy and in international trade.

The key to the problem, this proposal insists, lies in the power of governments to act as guarantors, while exacting a price for their guarantee. A similarly helpful proposal based on the same idea would have national governments of the major creditor countries offer a guarantee to holders of long-term bonds issued by developing countries – the United States for Latin American countries, Japan for Asian countries, the European Community for its African, Caribbean and Pacific (ACP) associates. But the guarantee would not be open-ended. The debtor would suffer a reduction in the value of the guarantee if bad economic management brought the traded value of the bonds down below a certain limit and kept it below that limit for more than a stated period.

Other forms of guarantee are also worth inquiry. In the old British Empire, certain colonial bonds were added to the list of safe securities which could be held by trustees and other non-profit institutions.

Such a dispensation would help agencies like the highly successful and enterprising Inter-American Development Bank to raise more money for productive long-term investment. Indeed, the question of better tax incentives for LDC bondholders, for banks engaging in co-financing deals with the IADB or the World Bank, even for corporations that devised joint ventures in debtor countries that could be shown to create jobs at both ends, in Latin America and at home, calls for more careful consideration. The idea of counterpart funds, as developed in the Marshall Plan, might also be looked at again to see if it could not be used for the sort of social schemes – education and school meals, for example – that are a long-term investment in human capital, yet currently impossible under IMF conditions.

The defence issue

Again, defence and the defensive strategy for the Western Alliance are not the subject of this book. But they cannot be left out altogether for two very good reasons. One is that cooperative monetary relations are very hard to develop between allies embittered with each other's lack of cooperation on military matters. And the other is that it is the cost of the defence budget to the United States that puts out of reach the sort of imaginative vision sketched out above of how the United States might change its present tarnished image in Latin America and once more play the good neighbour, as in Roosevelt's day.

It is generally agreed that the defence budget has made a mockery of President Reagan's devotion to monetarism. It is the defence budget which has been the main reason for the mounting US budget deficit. The popularity of the dollar made it easy for the United States to bring about an inflow of dollars from US banks and corporations, and from foreign governments, corporations and individuals sufficient to finance the deficit. Doing so, however, kept real interest rates high and thus weighted the dice once more in favour of speculation, short-term gains and against long-term productive investment, whether in America itself or in the rest of the world.

The Europeans are frustrated at the slow pace of superpower discussions on arms control. They want both the Soviet Union and the United States to slow down the replacement of old missiles with new ones. A sign of readiness in Europe to take over from the United States more of the NATO bills for European defence, including the stationing of US troops in Germany, would give the Europeans much more leverage on the arms control question. Against the cost to the European taxpayer, however, there might be set the benefits of some job-creation. For example, if the American PX shops were to be closed down and the American troops were to be paid partly in ECUs or D-marks, they could be supplied with local food and drink replacing stuff brought over at much great cost from America.

The main point here, however, is a much more general one. It is that agreement on these security matters between the United States and Europe will ease the financial predicament. Failure to do so will make it that much harder. There has to be a meeting of minds between the financial and economic experts on the one side and the strategists and the military experts on the other.

A nudge from Europe

The former President of France, Giscard D'Estaing, has shrewdly observed that the Americans have always been more inclined to contemplate change in international monetary arrangements when the dollar was being challenged in some way.[2] He is right. In the early 1960s, for instance, when Professor Robert Triffin was already pointing out the inherent weaknesses in the dollar–gold system when run with a persistent US payments deficit, the idea was discussed of replacing the dollar as a reserve asset which governments kept in case of a payments deficit with a Composite Reserve Unit, the CRU. It was proposed that even the United States would have to settle its accounts out of its reserves of CRUs which would be linked to gold. At the time, that challenge to the dollar was more notional than immediate. Nevertheless, it brought Secretary Fowler to the negotiating table and the eventual outcome three years later was the Stockholm agreement of 1968 that the IMF would issue SDRs to all its members and that these would be treated in some measure as an international reserve asset. It was not quite what Triffin had wanted but it did represent a shift in US policy.

The next challenge came at the beginning of the 1970s and was the result of the increased strength of the yen and the D-mark. The American response was violent, abrasive and perhaps ill-advised. But the unilateral devaluation of 1971 and the decision in 1973 to float the dollar (downwards) was certainly radical. By legitimizing floating rates, the United States abolished the Bretton Woods system of fixed exchange rates supervised by the IMF which had been its own pet creation in 1943.

More striking still was the effect on American thinking of the Schmidt–Giscard agreement, at Bremen in 1978, to set up a European Monetary System. This, they hoped, would create in Europe a zone of monetary stability immune to the dollar's weakness. The US Treasury did not much like the idea, but in time the United States responded with the Carter measures and then with the sterner stuff of credit restraint through monetary targetting and higher interest rates introduced by Paul Volcker.

What ex-President Giscard D'Estaing, and other Europeans, are now suggesting is that Europe should try once again to nudge the Americans into taking steps to manage their own economic affairs more steadily and responsibly, and to show more concern for the gyrations of the dollar in the foreign exchange markets. His proposal aims – without saying so in as many words – to build the ECU into a rival to the dollar. At present the ECU is an imaginary currency. That is to say, it is not in use on the streets of Europe. But it is possible to have a bank account in ECUs. An ECU is a basket of European currencies weighted according to their importance. Deposit so many francs in your ECU account and their future value will depend on the weighted sum of the constituent currencies in the basket. The ECU has also come to be used increasingly by bankers and their clients as a denominator for bond issues.

So far the Europeans have dithered about proceeding as fast as originally planned to the second stage where the ECU begins to take over from the national currencies. The British would not join. The Germans were reluctant to allow prices in Germany to be quoted in anything but D-marks. The French clung to the exchange controls limiting free movement of funds in and out of France which they have brought back to check the capital outflow of 1982. The Italians insisted on their right to a wider margin of fluctuation for the lira before they had to intervene.

Nevertheless, by and large, the markets have clearly been impressed by the determination of the European Community governments to keep their exchange rates with each other under control, even though there have had to be realignments from time to time. A prolonged or precipitous fall in the dollar could still make the markets unstable again, as funds fled from dollars into the stronger but not into the weaker European currencies. More and more frequent realignments within the EMS would erode its credibility.

So the only alternative to sinking back into the bad old days of 1976 and 1977, when the European currencies were polarized in this way by a weak dollar may well be, as Giscard D'Estaing suggests, to go forward. This would mean a partial pooling of national reserves so that the Germans would share some responsibility for French or Italian deficits. And it would mean that each of the member countries would accept common rules governing monetary policy and the creation of credit. A European central bank would hold an increasing proportion of each country's reserves of foreign exchange and gold and would issue ECUs to national central banks. A central bank's holding of ECUs would constitute what the economists call the monetary base. As in a pyramid, the size of the base determines the amount of credit that can be built up upon it. Thus all the member countries would be locked into a common trend in policy which could be reflationary.

It sounds easy. But though there would be all sorts of technical problems to be sorted out – for instance over the question of exchange controls with the world outside the Community – the basic obstacles are all political. It does involve some loss of national autonomy in the management of the national economy. Yet the opportunities it would open up to the Europeans for economic diplomacy – and not only with the United States – would be tremendous.

Taking the next policy step would undoubtedly speed up the private use of ECUs. ECU bonds and ECU Treasury bills would draw funds away from dollar bonds and US Treasury Bills. If the dollar weakened while the ECU stayed more or less stable, the flow would accelerate. This would give the European Community a powerful tool with which to negotiate with third parties. The Saudi Arabians could be invited to invoice oil destined for Europe in ECUs, or to invest some of their reserves in ECUs instead of dollars. An ECU-backed export credit scheme could be devised for Latin America. Negotiations could be opened with the Japanese. In no time, if past experience is anything to go by, the United States would recognize a challenge to the dollar. Their first (negative) reaction might to be threaten, as they have done before, to take US troops out of Europe. This is why opening up some negotiation on the NATO front is so important. But without a strong nudge from Europe, no-one could be confident that some recent shifts in US policy towards more help for LDC debtors or more intervention to restore order in unruly foreign exchange markets were anything more than short-lived exercises in public relations. In September 1985 the United States agreed in the Group of Five to collective intervention to bring the dollar down and to keep major exchange rates within 'target zones'. In the same month, there was the Baker Plan to provide larger and longer-term finance for developing countries. So far so good – but for how long?

Are there no alternatives?

There are only two possible alternatives to radical reforms of the kind suggested here. One is to carry on trying to muddle through. The other is to try to turn the clock back.

This second option is conceivable, but only, I believe, after an economic or financial catastrophe of terrifying proportions. What is involved in turning the clock back is no less than a retreat to national responsibility for national financial systems and national capital markets insulated from each other by government controls of many kinds. Some distinguished economists have gone as far as to advocate what they call with disarming obliqueness, 'controlled disintegration', that is, splitting up again. The first to do so was the late Fred Hirsch who wrote in 1977: 'A degree of controlled dis-integration in the world economy is a legitimate objective for the 1980s and may be the most realistic one for a moderate international economic order (Hirsch 1977, p.55). As mentioned earlier (see p. 152), the idea was quoted with approval by one of the IMF's most distinguished officials, Jacques Polak. Writing for the Group of Thirty, an unofficial brains trust of economists and ex-central bankers in New York, Polak concluded that it was futile and misleading to pin too much hope on the capacity of national governments so to coordinate their domestic economic management that foreign exchange markets would be stabilized, interest rates stay steady at a reasonable level and economic growth be maintained: 'Once it is realised that international decision-making is indeed very difficult, one can hardly argue that any economic policies that have significant international effects should be brought for harmonisation. On the contrary one would look for a very large role to be played by decentralised decision-making (Polak 1981, p. 19).

As a practical policy-maker with long experience of the international financial system, Polak is understandably more sceptical than an academic economist like Professor Ronald McKinnon, who has been the prime advocate of trilateral policy coordination among the major countries. McKinnon's schemes are technically feasible but politically naive. They would only work if the Germans and Japanese were always prepared to follow every twist and turn of American monetary policy – and this, as a matter of simple historical fact, they have never been willing to do.

'Controlled dis-integration' is, though, just a euphemistic way of describing a return to the 1950s. Either it means that the Euromarkets would have to be closed down altogether – which would be very difficult to do since they can now operate by computer and satellite communications systems almost without a territorial base, so that even if Singapore and the Bahamas and Macao were all to cooperate, it still might not work. Or else it means that US banks would be forced to close down their foreign branches – unless they were willing to disconnect them, so to speak, from the parent bank so that they functioned as independent banks. For national financial systems to function autonomously, any transfer of funds into dollars out of the national currency or out of the national currency into dollars would have to be stopped. Large international businesses would have to run accounts with different banks in each of the countries in which they operated. There would understandably be tremendous opposition from industry and commercial as well as banking interests. These powerful interests would point out – and with every justification – that 'controlled dis-integration' would leave the structure of international credit and finance much reduced in size and capacity. It could hardly be done by stages. But to do it suddenly would be such a shock to the world economy that the check to confidence and enterprise would be a very high price to pay for reducing the risk and the instability of the present system.

But what if we carry on trying to muddle through?

The answer, in a nutshell, is that though the consequences might just be economically bearable, they would be politically unacceptable to a free society.

Opinions on detail may differ. But the broad outline of what to expect is fairly clear. We have an increasing risk of quiet default on LDC debts. They will not confront the creditors with a refusal to pay. They will swear that they mean to pay in full, one day. There will be a good deal of sympathy with the debtors – and not much with the creditors – because many people feel that the banks have made large profits and have done very well out of high interest rates. They have even been able to earn extra money with management fees and consulting fees out of rescheduling debt. But the consequence will be that the banks will not recover their confidence in lending to developing countries for a long time to come. If official aid, whether bilateral or from the big international organizations, is slow to make up more than fraction of the difference, the debtor countries will remain short of purchasing power. A weaker dollar will mean that their ability to earn foreign exchange by exporting – raw materials invoiced in dollars included – will actually be diminished. And if the dollar weakens, the prospects of lower interest rates will recede because the United States will have to try and make it attractive to stay in dollars if it is not to be in trouble financing its large budget deficit.

The more the United States sells assets to (i.e. borrows from) foreigners, the bigger the temptation sooner or later to depreciate its debts by inflation. American farmers and American industrial workers could reasonably argue that for them that course is preferable to the low farm prices and high unemployment which result from an unduly strong dollar.

Continuing uncertainty about the future is not, however, conducive to long-term productive investment. The economic cycle would be back again in the stagflation of the mid-1970s. The political wheel would turn again and the time would come when another Ronald Reagan and another Paul Volcker would slam on the monetary brakes and bring about another dip in the economic roller-coaster, landing us all once more in a still deeper recession.

At this time, the need to hedge against uncertainty will become ever more insistent. Big operators in every sector will do it as a matter of course, passing the cost on to consumers. Small operators will still find their fortunes as little within their own control as if they had put their capital on a roulette wheel. Only the brokers and the speculators will grow fat and rich. Every aspiring school-leaver and undergraduate will want to be a financial dealer of some sort. Except for a few fast-growing high-technology sectors, industry will remain in a depressed state because the risks of long-term investment will be too great for all except the state enterprises (whose losses can go on the taxpayer's bill) and the large corporations which will increasingly be their look-alike.

Because of the information problem (discussed in chapter 5) and the ignorance among the controllers and regulators of what the bankers and speculators are up to, it must be expected that we have not seen the last financial scandal or the biggest banking collapse. Another Continental Illinois crisis cannot be ruled out. And the outcome will be the same, that the US government has to take over the liabilities and debts because the consequences for the economy at large of doing otherwise would be too great. The nationalization of banking will be taken a step further.

But it is the political repercussions of this depressing economic scenario which are far more serious. When a whole generation becomes disillusioned with the economic system and can see no escape from the roller-coaster alternation of deflation and stagflation, there are bound to be political reactions. European experience of the 1930s suggests that there are two common responses. One is a total revulsion against politics of all kinds – a mental switching-off process which probably reached its peak in the Fourth Republic in France. The other is to follow some political mountebank, a demagogue like Adolf Hitler, who will wrap a hodge-podge of social prejudices in a package of phoney history and phoney science that arouses strong and violent nationalist emotions. Government in the first instance becomes weak and unstable. In the second it becomes brutal, corrupt, repressive, and often aggressive.

These political consequences must sooner or later spill over into international relations. Weakness in some countries and strong government in others invites aggression. Holding together an alliance of liberal democracies with common values becomes more and more difficult. The lack of vision of what the future might hold undermines morale in the present. For a while the United States will probably be able to enjoy, as it does now, the privileged immunities of its dominant position, military, political and economic. It will be able to use its bargaining power as military protector, or as interventionist meddler, or as major trading partner to get its own way and to make others undergo the painful adjustments. But in the end it cannot prosper or maintain an alliance that way. Muddling through simply will not work.

By New Year's Eve on December 31, 1999, we shall have reached the end of a century. If, by then, we have still not succumbed to a nuclear holocaust, that will be one thing to celebrate. But unless positive, practical steps are taken soon to cool and control the financial casino, there will not be much else. For most people, the social consequences of playing Snakes and Ladders with people's lives will have been made only too plain. Only those financial gamblers that still survive in the great office blocks towering over the city centres of the capitalist world will be raising their glasses. For the rest, the American Century will be coming to a mournful and miserable close.

Notes

1   I call it so only for convenience. Properly speaking, it should be called the credit problem, for it is the drying up of credit which caused the anxiety about the ability of debtor to repay. Good debtors do not need to repay. The richer they get, the happier their creditors are to hold on to their IOUs. Japan is the classic example of a country which only 80 years ago was deeply in debt.

2   In his 1985 Ditchley Lecture. The gist of it was summarized in the *Economist* of 24 August 1985, p. 56.

Bibliography

Aglietta, M., 1983, *La Violence de la Monnaie*, Paris, PUF.

Althusser, L., 1971, *Lenin and Philosophy*, London, New Left Books.

Amin, S., 1980, *Class and Nation: historically and in the current crisis*, New York, Monthly Review Press.

Anderson, P., 1976, *Considerations on Western Marxism*, London, New Left Books.

Archer, C., 1983, *International Organisations*, London, Allen & Unwin.

Attali, J., 1977, *La Parole et l'Outil*, Paris.

Bagehot, W., 1873, *Lombard Street: a description of the money market*, London.

Berle, A. and Meaus, 1933, *The Modern Corporation and Private Property*, New York.

Blair, J., 1977, *The Control of Oil*, London, Macmillan.

Block, F., 1977, *The Origins of International Economic Disorder*, Berkeley and London, University of California Press.

Brandt Commission, 1980, *North–South: a programme for survival?*, London and Sydney, Pan.

Brandt Commission, 1983, *Common Crisis: North–South cooperation for world recovery*, London and Sydney, Pan.

Brett, E. A., 1983, *International Money and the Capitalist Crisis*, London, Gower.

Brunhoff, S. de, 1976, *La Crise de l'Etat*, Paris, Maspero.

Brunhoff, S. de, 1978, *State, Capital and Economic Policy*, London, Pluto.

Calleo, D., 1982, *The Imperious Economy*, Cambridge, Mass. and New York, Harvard University Press.

Camps, M. and Diebold Jr., W., 1983, 'The New Multilateralism: can the world trading system be saved?', New York, Council on Foreign Relations.

Cardoso, F. H. and Faletto, E., 1979, *Dependency and Development in Latin America*, Berkeley, University of California Press.

Cecco, M. de, 1982, 'Credit creation in the Eurocurrency markets', European University Institute, Working Paper No. 23.

Cline, W., 1983, *International Debt and the Stability of the World Economy*, Washington DC, Institute for International Economics.

Cline, W., ed., 1983, *Trade Policy in the 1980s*, Washington.

Cline, W., 1984, *International Debt: systemic risk and policy response*, Washington, Institute for International Economics, April.

Commonwealth Group of Experts, 1984, *Debt Crisis and the World Economy*, London, Commonwealth Secretariat.

Commonwealth Secretariat, 1985, 'Development Prospects, Policy Options and Negotiations', London.

Collier, D., ed., 1979, *The New Authoritarianism in Latin America*, Princeton University Press.

Coombs, C., 1976, *The Arena of International Finance*, New York.

Corden, W., 1984, *The Revival of Protectionism*, New York, Group of Thirty Occasional Paper No. 14.

Cornwell, R., 1983, *God's Banker: An account of the life and death of Roberto Calvi*, London, Gollancz.

Dale, R., 1982, *Bank Supervision Around the World*, New York, Group of Thirty.

Dale, R. and Mattione, R., 1984, *Managing Global Debt*, Washington, Brookings Institution.

Dale, R., 1985, *The Regulation of International Banking*, Cambridge, Woodhead–Faulkner.

Davis, S., 1984, 'Markets, States and Transnational Corporations: power in the world grain trading system', University of London PhD Thesis.

Davis, J. S., 1975, *The World Between the Wars, 1919–39*, Baltimore, Johns Hopkins University Press.

Delamaide, D., 1984, *Debt Shock*, London, Weidenfeld.

Desai, M., 1981, *Testing Monetarism*, London, Frances Pinter.

Duchene, F., 1984, *Industrial Adjustment Policies of Western Europe*, London, Macmillan.

Dufey, G. and Giddy, I. H., 1979, *The International Money Market*.

Duijn, J. J. van, 1983, *The Long Wave in Economic Life*, London, Allen & Unwin.

Emery, H. C., 1896, *Commodity Exchanges*, New York.

Emmanuel, A., 1969, *The Economics of Unequal Exchange: a study of the imperialism of trade*, Paris, Maspero; 1971, London, New York, Monthly Review Press; 1974, published as *Le Profit et les Crises*, Paris, Maspero.

Fabra, P., 1978, *Les flux monétaires dans un monde écartelé entre l'inflation et la deflation*, Madrid European Cultural Foundation.

Fitoussi, J. P., 1982, 'Politique monétaire passive ou politique economique?', in *Observatoire Francais des Conjuntures Economiques*, Paris, June.

Frankel, S. H., 1977, *Money: Two Philosophies: the conflict of trust and authority*, Oxford, Blackwell.

Freeman, C., Clark, J. and Soete, L., 1982, *Unemployment and Technical Innovation*, Westport, Connecticut, Greenward Press.

Freeman, C., 1984, *Long Waves in the World Economy*, London, Frances Pinter.

Friedman, M. and Schwarz, A., 1963, *A Monetary History of the United States 1866–1945*, Princeton University Press.

Friedman, M., 1977, 'Inflation and Unemployment: the new dimension of politics', Nobel Lecture, London, Institute of Fiscal Affairs.

Galtung, J., 1975, *Social Imperialism and Subimperialism*, Oslo, University of Oslo.

Gilbert, M. (with posthumous editing by Peter Oppenheimer and Michael Dealtry), 1980, *The Quest for World Monetary Order: the gold–dollar system and its aftermath*, New York, Chichester, Wiley.

Gilpin, R., 1968, *France in the Age of the Scientific State*, Princeton University Press.

Gilpin, R., 1975, *US Power and the Multinational Corporation*, New York, Basic Books.

Gilpin, R., 1975, *The US and the Multinational Corporation*, New York, Basic Books.

Griffith-Jones, S. and Lipton, M., 1984, 'International Lenders of Last Resort: and changes required?', London Midland Bank.

Group of Thirty, 1985, *The Foreign Exchange Market on the 1980s*, New York, Group of Thirty.

Grubel, H., 1979, *A Proposal for the Establishment of an International Deposit Insurance Corporation*, Princeton Essay in International Finance No. 133.

Gunder Frank, A., 1966, *The Development of Under-development*, Boston, Free Press.

Guttenberg, J. and Herring, R., 1983, 'The lender of last resort function in an international context', Princeton Essay in International Finance No. 151.

Hirsch, F. and Doyle, M., 1977, *Alternatives to Monetary Disorder*, Council on Foreign Relations.

Hirschmann, A. O., 1983, *Rival Interpretations of Market Society: civilizing, destructive or feeble?*, Journal of Economic Literature, December.

Hopkins, T. and Puchala, D., 1979, *The Global Political Economy of Food*, Madison, University Press of Wisconsin.

Hopkins, T. and Wallerstein, I., eds, 1982, *World Systems Analysis*, Beverly Hills, California, Sage.

Hu, Y. S., 1984, *Industrial Banking and Special Credit Institutions: a comparative study*, London, Policy Studies Institute.

Kaletsky, A., 1985, *The Costs of Default*, New York Priority Press for 20th Centry Fund.

Kaufman, H., 1985, 'Dangers in the rapid growth of debt', address to National Press Club, Washington DC, January 16.

Keohane, R. and Nye, J., 1977, *Power and Interdependence*, Boston, Little, Brown.

Keohane, R., 1984, *After Hegemony*, Cambridge, Mass., Harvard University Press.

Keynes, J. M., 1971, *Collected Writings*, 15 vols., London, Macmillan.

Kindleberger, C., ed., *The International Corporation*.

Kindleberger, C., 1973, *The World in Depression, 1929–1933*, Berkeley, University of California Press; London, Allen Lane.

Knight, F., 1921, *Risk, Uncertainty and Profit*, Ithaca, Cornell University Press; 1933, reprinted in LSE reprint series, London.

Knorr, K., 1975, *The Power of Nations: the political economy of international relations*, New York, Basic Books.

Krasner, S., 1978, *Defending the National Interest*, Princeton University Press.

Krasner, S., ed., 1983, *International Regimes*, Ithaca, NY, Cornell University Press.

Kuhn, T. S., 1962, *The Structure of Scientific Revolutions*, Chicago, Chicago University Press.

Lever, H. and Huhne, C., 1985, *Debt and Danger: the world financial crisis*, London, Penguin.

Lewis, W. A., 1949, *Economic Survey 1919–39*, London, Allen & Unwin, reprinted 1970.

Llewellyn, D., 1982, 'Avoiding an International Banking Crisis', in National Westminster Bank *Quarterly Review*, August.

Lomax, D., 1982, 'The Oil-Finance Cycle Revisited', in National Westminster Bank *Quarterly Review*, November.

Lombra, R. and Witte, W., eds, 1982, *The Political Economy of Domestic and International Monetary Relations*, University of Iowa Press.

Maddison, A., 1982, *Phases of Capitalist Development*, Oxford, Oxford University Press.

Magdoff, H., and Sweezy, P., 1969, *The Deepening Crisis of US Capitalism*, New York, Monthly Review Press.

Mandel, E., 1977, *The Second Slump*, London, New Left Books.

Mangoldt, H. von, 1855, *Die Lehre vom Unternehmergewinn*, Leipzig.

Matthews, R. C. O., ed., 1982, *Slower Growth in the Western World*, London, Heinemann.

Mayer, M., 1980, *The Fate of the Dollar*, New York, Times Books.

Mayer, M., 1982, 'The settlements revolution', *Institutional Investor*, April.

McKinnon, R., 1974, 'A New Tripartite Monetary Standard or a Limping Dollar Standard?', Princeton Essay in International Finance No. 106.

McKinnon, R., 1982, 'Inflationary and deflationary world money', *American Economic Review*, June.

McKinnon, R., 1984, 'An International Standard for Monetary Stabilization', International Economics No. 8, Institute for International Economics, Washington.

Mendelsohn, S., 1980, *Money on the Move*, New York, McGraw Hill.

Mendelsohn, S., 1984, *The Debt of Nations*, New York, Priority Press.

Mikdashi, Z., 'Oil-exporting countries and oil-importing countries: what kind of interdependence', *Millennium*, Vol. 9, No. 1.

Mikdashi, Z., 1976, *The International Politics of Natural Resources*, Ithaca, Cornell University Press.

Mikdashi, Z., 1986, *World Oil: corporate and government challenges*, London, Frances Pinter.

Minsky, H., 1979, *The Financial Instability Hypothesis: capitalist processes and the behaviour of the economy*, paper for a colloquium on financial cases and the lender of last resort, Bad Homburg, published Rome, Confederazione Generale dell'industria Italiana.

Minsky, H., 1982, *Can it Happen Again? essays on instability and finance*, Armonk, NY, M. E. Sharpe.

Moffitt, M., 1984, *The World's Money: international banking from Bretton Woods to the brink of insolvency*, London, Michael Joseph.

Morgan, D., 1979, *Merchants of Grain*, New York, Viking; 1980, London, Penguin.

Nader, R., 1976, *The Taming of the Giant Corporation*, New York, Norton.

Naisbitt, R., 1984, *Megatrends*, London, Futura.

Nau, H., 1984, *International Reagonomics: a domestic approach to the world economy*, Washington, Georgetown University, monograph, December.

Nicholas, D., 1985, *Commodities Futures Trading*, London, Mansell.

O'Donnell, G., 1973, *Modernization and Bureaucratic Authoritarianism in Southern American Politics*, Berkeley, University of California Press.

Olson, M., 1975, *The Logic of Collective Goods*, Harvard University Press.

Olson, M., 1982, *The Rise and Decline of Nations: economic growth, stagflation and social rigidities*, Cambridge, Mass., Harvard University Press.

Parboni, R., 1980, *The Dollar and its Rivals: recession, inflation and international finance*, Milan, Etais Libri.

Penrose, E., 1971, *Growth of Firms, Middle East Oil and Other Essays*, London, Cass.

Polak, J., 1981, 'Coordination of National Economic Policies', Group of Thirty Occasional Paper No. 7, New York.

Poulantzas, N., 1973, *Political Power and Social Classes*, London, New Left Books.

Rohatyn, F., 1982, 'The state of the banks', *New York Review of Books*, November.

Rostow, W., 1976, *The World Economy: history and prospect*, Austin, Texas, University of Texas Press.

Rostow, W., 1978, *Getting from Here to There*, New York, McGraw Hill.

Rostow, W., 1980, *Why the Poor Get Richer and the Rich Slow Down*, London, Macmillan.

Rowthorn, R., 1980, *Capitalism, Conflict and Inflation*, London, Lawrence and Wishart.

Ruckdeschel, F., 1975, 'Risk in foreign and domestic lending of US banks', *Columbia Journal of World Business*, Winter.

Rueff, J., 1971, *La Pêche Monétaire de l'Occident*, Paris, Plon.

Rustow, D., 1983, *Oil and Turmoil*, New York, Norton.

Rustow, D. and Mugno, J., 1977, *OPEC – Success and Prospects*, Oxford, Martin Robertson.

Sampson, A., 1981, *The Money Lenders*, London, Hodder & Stoughton.

Schumpeter, J., 1939, *Business Cycles*, 2 vols., New York and London, McGraw Hill.

Scitovsky, T., 1977, *The Joyless Economy*, London, Galaxy.

Shonfield, A., ed., 1976, *International Economic Relations in the Western World 1957–71*, Introduction to Vol. 1, Oxford University Press.

Simmel, G., 1907, *Die Philosophie des Geldes*, Leipzig; 1978, translated as *The Philosophy of Money*, by T. Bottomore and D. Frisby.

Spero, J., 1980, *The Fall of the Franklin National Bank*, New York, Columbia University Press.

Stewart, E., 1985, 'Banks, governments and risk medium-term syndicated international capital market loans to Nigeria, 1977–83', unpublished London University PhD thesis.

Stewart, F., ed., 1982, *International Financial Cooperation*, London, Frances Pinter.

Stoffaes, C., 1979, *La grande menace industrielle*, Paris, Calmann-Levy.

Strange, S., 1971, *Sterling and British Policy*, London, Oxford University Press.

Strange, S., 1976, *International Monetary Relations*, Vol. 2 of A. Shonfield, ed., *International Economic Relations of the Western World 1959–71*, Oxford University Press.

Strange, S., 1981, 'Reactions to Brandt', *International Studies Quarterly*, 25, 2.

Strange, S. and Tooze, R., eds, 1982, *The International Management of Surplus Capacity*, London, Allen & Unwin.

Strange, S., 1983, 'The Credit Crisis', *SAIS Review*, Washington, Summer.

Swoboda, A., 1980, *Credit Creation in the Euromarket: alternative theories and implications for control*, New York, Group of Thirty Occasional Paper No. 2.

Tobin, J., 1984, 'Unemployment in the 1980s: macroeconomic diagnosis and prescription', in A. Pierre, ed., *Unemployment and Growth in the Western Economies*, New York, Council on Foreign Relations.

Triffin, R., 1964, *The Evolution of the International Monetary System*, Princeton Studies in International Finance, Princeton University Press.

Triffin, R., 1966, *The World Money Maze*, New Haven, Yale University Press.

Triffin, R., 1969, *Gold and the Dollar Crisis*, New York, Yale University Press; first appeared in Banca Nazionale del Lavoro, *Quarterly Review*, June 1959.

Tsoukalis, L., ed., 1985, *The Politics of International Monetary Relations: towards a new international economic order*, London, Sage.

Tumlir, J., 1983, 'The World Economy Today: crisis or new beginning?', National Westminster Bank *Quarterly Review*, August, pp. 26–44.

Vaubel, R., 1978, *Strategies for Currency Unification*, Tübingen, Mohr.

Vernon, R., 1971, *Sovereignty at Bay*, New York, Basic Books.

Versluysen, E., 1981, *The Political Economy of International Finance*, Farnborough, Gower.

Wallerstein, I., 1974, *The Modern World System*, London, Academic Press.

Wallerstein, I., 1979, *The Capitalist World Economy*, Cambridge and London, Cambridge University Press.

Whitman, M. von N., 1984, 'Persistent Unemployment: economic policy perspectives in US and Europe', in A. Pierre, *Unemployment and Growth in the Western Economies*, New York, Council on Foreign Relations.

Williamson, J., 1977, *The Failure of International Monetary Reform, 1971–4*, New York, Von Nostrand Reinhold.

Wohlers Scharf, T., 1984, *Arab Banking*, OECD Development Centre.

Index

aid 33, 154, 191
Amin, Samir 88–9, 96
Anderson, Perry 85
Argentina 51
Asiatic mode of production 105
Atlantic Alliance 5, 152
  deterioration of relations within
    174
authority–market relationship 25

Bagehot, Walter 110
Baker, James 182
Bank of England 130
  as supervisor of UK financial
    institutions 130–1
Bank for International Settlements (BIS) 45, 83, 123,
  137–41, 159, 160
banking system 4
  instability of 5–6, 174
  insurance for 160
  lack of information on inter-
    bank lending 141, 143
  limits of central bank super-
    vision 158–9

Basle Concordat (1975) 45–6, 159,
  178, 181
Belgium 8
Blair, John 72
Brandt Report 32, 80, 153–5
Brazil 33, 51
Bretton Woods System 6, 147
  breakdown of 67
Britain 8, 14, 55, 78
  system of financial control in
    129–31
Brunhoff, Suzanne de 91–2
Bruno, Michael 78
Burns, Arthur 39

Callaghan, James 79
Calleo, David 90
Canada 8, 141
capital accumulation
  as problem in world economy
    90–1
Capitalist World Economy, The
  (Wallerstein) 87
Cecco, Marcello de 125, 141
Class and Nation (Amin) 88

Colchester, Nicholas 118
commodity markets 53, 112–13,
    117
  reopening of London markets
    37–8
  use by US farmers for hedging
    113
commodity prices 64–5
Common Agricultural Policy
    (CAP) 113
Conference on International
    Economic Cooperation
    (CIEC) 45
Connally, John 38, 41, 42
Considerations on Western Marxism
    (Anderson) 85
Control of Oil, The (Blair) 72
Coombs, Charles 39–40
coordination of national financial
    policies 149–53
  McKinnon proposals for 150–1
currency speculation 11

debt problem
  see international debt
Desai, Meghnad 79
determinist explanations for world
    economic depression 62–70,
    98–9
  political determinism 62–6
  technical determinism 66–70
developing countries 13–14, 80,
    142, 180–5
  and capping of interest rates
    162, 183
  effect on of shrunken credit
    structure 169
  and foreign direct investment
    164
  oil importing developing
    countries (NOPECs) 43, 45

and world economic depression
    80
Dobb, Maurice 92
dollar
  devaluation 5, 7
  preference for in international
    market place 165, 176

Emery, H. C. 112
Emmanuel, Arghiri 87
Emminger, Otmar 46–7
Eurocurrency markets 6–7, 38,
    106, 109, 112, 142
  as creator of credit 122–5
  impact of on Interest Equaliza-
    tion Tax 47–8
  and shift of risk 48–9
European Community 151, 186–9
  linking security and financial
    management 167, 185–6
European currency snake 8
European currency unit (ECU)
    187–8
European Monetary System
    (EMS) 151, 187–8
exchange rates 4, 175, 187–8
  floating 5, 8, 14
  fluctuations 39–40
export credits 33–6

Federal Deposit Insurance
    Corporation (FDIC) 160
Federal Reserve Bank of New
    York 39, 51, 56, 176
financial futures 113–15
financial systems, control of 128
France 8, 157, 187
Frankel, S. H. 135–6
free trade 146–7
Friedman, Milton 79, 98, 112

Galbraith, J. K. 36
Galtung, Johann 87
General Agreement on Tariffs and
    Trade (GATT) 74
General Arrangements to Borrow
    (GAB) 7
General Theory (Keynes) 134
Gilbert, Milton 55, 83, 96
Gilpin, Robert 68–9
Glyn, Andrew 90–1
gold exchange system 67–8
Gold Pool 7
government spending
    and economic disorder 81, 98
Griffith-Jones, Stephanie 159
Group of Ten 42, 46, 83
Group of Thirty 46, 189
growth 63
    slowing of 4 and
    technological innovation 63–4
Grubel, Herbert 160

Hayek, Friedrich A. 79, 133, 135
hegemonic stability 22, 67–9, 147
Hirsch, Fred 153, 189
Hungary 33

inflation 4, 8, 75, 83
    and Eurocurrency transactions
    122–5
    marxist analysis of 89–91
    and the 'oil shock' 71–2
interest rates 3, 4, 7, 10, 12
    'rate-capping' for LDCs 161,
    183
    volatility of 14–17
International Bank for
    Reconstruction and
    Development (IBRD)
    see World Bank
international debt 4, 163, 181–5

BIS statistics on 137–8
handling bad debt 32–3
as political weapon 33
and proposed creation of SDRs
    156–7
resolution of problem through
    international support system
    159–62
international division of labour 88
International Energy Agency
    (IEA) 44
international financial system 4,
    147
controlled disintegration of
    167, 189–90
crises and chronic problems in
    173
ignorance and control of
    system 136–7
implications of current trends
    in 168–9, 191
and need for wise US
    hegemony 171–3
problems of monitoring activity
    in the system 137–44
respective risks of domestic
    and foreign lending 127–8
and short-term credit 163–4
unworkability of Brandt
    proposals 154–5
international lender of last resort
    159–60
International Monetary Fund
    (IMF) 42, 43, 74, 124, 157,
    162, 168, 182–3
Committee of Twenty and
    international monetary
    reform 41–2
Oil Facility 45
1968 Stockholm agreement on
    SDRs 7, 186

international organizations 153,
  170–1
  reluctance of states to transfer
    power to 154–5, 165, 170–1
  role in Brandt Report prescrip-
    tions 154
international politics
  and explaining economic
    disorder 65–6
  and limits on financial policy
    coordination 148, 150–1
international trade
  as explanation of world
    economic depression 61–2
Italy 8, 141

Japan 8, 55, 78, 142, 149, 162,
  180

Kalecki, Michael 92
Kaufman, Henry 57
Keohane, Robert 29, 67–9
Keynes, J. M. 134–6
Keynesianism 77–80, 97–8,
  134–6, 157
  marxist critique of 77–8
  moral objection to 135–6
  view of economic disorder
    77–8
Kindleberger, Charles 36, 68–9
Kissinger, Henry 44
Knight, Frank 107–9, 116–17,
  119
Kondratiev, Nikolai 63
  see also long waves
Kuhn, Thomas 64

Labour Party 80
Lambert, Richard 115
Late Capitalism (Mandel) 92
Lennep, Emile van 46

less developed countries (LDCs)
  see developing countries
Lewis, Arthur 80
Lipton, Michael 159
Logic of Collective Action, The
  (Olson) 69
Lombard Street (Bagehot) 110
London International Financial
    Futures Exchange (LIFFE)
    114
long waves 63–5, 146

Magdoff, Harry 90
Mandel, Ernest 92–5
Marx, Karl 104
  weakness of *Das Kapital* 95–6
marxist analysis of economic
    depression 84–96
  critique of Keynesian approach
    91–3
Matthews, R. C. 71
Mayer, Martin 126
McKinnon, Ronald 82, 150–1, 190
Mexico 33, 46, 51, 162, 173
Mikdashi, Zuhayr 44, 72
Minsky, Hyman 77–8
*Modern Corporation and Private
    Property, The* (Berle and
    Means) 36
monetarism 55–8, 75–6, 79–80
  and global approach to
    depression 82
  and US budget deficit 56
monetary policy
  proposed US, West German
    and Japanese coordination of
    82–3
money
  increased velocity of 125–7
  social and political issues
    behind 103–9

trust in as neutral medium
105–6
Money: Two Philosophies
(Frankel) 135
Morse, Jeremy 46
multinational corporations
see transnational corporations

neo-mercantilism
reaction to world depression
81–2
Netherlands, The 8, 65
newly industrializing countries
(NICs) 66
Niebuhr, Reinhold 74
North Atlantic Treaty
Organization (NATO)
burden sharing and US deficit
31, 186, 189
Nye, Joseph 29

oil prices 4, 5, 17–20, 89
and disruption of economic
system 71–2
Olson, Mancur 69–70
Organization for Economic
Cooperation and
Development (OECD) 74,
138
Organization of Petroleum
Exporting Countries (OPEC)
43–4, 72, 164

Parboni, Riccardo 95
Penrose, Edith 44
Polak, Jacques 152–3, 167,
189–90
Poland 33, 128
political risk analysis 117
political system
erosion of confidence in 2–3

Portugal 65
protectionism 61–2, 74–5, 147

regime change 29
revolution
as response to economic crisis
90, 92, 93, 95–6, 146
Rise and Decline of Nations, The
(Olson) 70
Risk, Certainty and Profit
(Knight) 107
Rohatyn, Felix 161–2
Rostow, Walt 64
Rowthorn, Robert 93–4, 96
Ruckdeschel, F. 127
Rueff, Jacques 6, 89

Schultz, George 42
Schumpeter, Joseph 63
Schweizer, Pierre Paul 42, 96
Second Slump, The (Mandel) 92
Simmel, Georg 104–5, 135
*Slower Growth in the Western
World* (Matthews) 71
Smith, Adam 108, 110
Smithsonian Agreement (1971) 7,
38–40
special drawing rights (SDRs) 41
proposed creation to overcome
illiquidity 156–8
Special United Nations Fund for
Economic Development
implications of failure to agree
on 32
speculation 109
and erosion of trust in global
financial system 119
and price volatility 116
role in adding to instability 118
and uncertainty 110–11
Spero, Joan 141

State, Capital and Economic Policy
  (de Brunhoff) 91–2
state intervention in markets
  74–6, 133
Stoffaes, Christian 81
Structure of Scientific Revolutions,
  The (Kuhn) 64
Sweezy, Paul 90
Switzerland 8, 128–9, 141, 161
Swoboda, A. 123–4

technology
  in banking and finance 54
  and cyclical swings 63–4
  impact on money markets 26–7
  and information supply 117
  and increased speculative
    trading 115–16
  and increased velocity of
    money 125–6
  and power of states in world
    economy 70
  role in undermining US
    financial regulation 132
Tobin, James 152
transnational corporations (TNCs)
  12–13, 88, 139, 164
  UN Code of Conduct for 26
Triffin, Robert 6, 41, 73–4, 186

uncertainty 106–19
  attempts to manage by big
    companies 118–19
  and demand for information
    109, 111–12, 117
  difficulty of calculating in
    business 107–9
  importance for speculative
    markets 111
Union of Soviet Socialist
  Republics (USSR) 85

United Kingdom
  see Britain
United Nations
  Code of Conduct for Trans-
    national Corporations 26
  Conference on the Law of the
    Sea (UNCLOS) 26, 28
United States
  balance of payments deficit 6,
    67–8, 83
  Depository Institutions
    Deregulation and Monetary
    Control Act (1980) 126
  Federal Reserve System 166,
    176, 180
  impact of domestic policy on
    world economy 22–3, 27–8,
    47–58
  International Banking Act
    (1980) 50
  as key national authority in
    international financial
    system 165–7, 171, 175
  role as hegemonic power 21–2,
    66–7, 147
  role of Office of the
    Comptroller of the Currency
    (OCC) 51–3, 176
  system of financial regulation
    131–3
  tax on foreign lending 7, 47–8

Vernon, Raymond 36
Volker, Paul 84, 176

Wallich, Henry 46, 127
West Germany 7, 8, 149–50, 161
wheat markets 27–8
Whitman, Marina 152
Williamson, John 42, 156
Wilson, Harold 37–8

Witteveen, Johannes 45, 46, 83, 96

World Bank 43, 139, 182

World Economy: History and Prospect, The (Rostow) 64

World System, The (Wallerstein) 87